# CLEMENTINA

## A. E. W. MASON

1st WORLD
LIBRARY
Literary Society

# Clementina

A. E. W. Mason

© 1st World Library, 2007
PO Box 2211
Fairfield, IA 52556
www.1stworldlibrary.com
First Edition

LCCN: 2007934070

Softcover ISBN: 978-1-4218-9601-4
Hardcover ISBN: 978-1-4218-9701-1
eBook ISBN: 978-1-4218-9501-7

Purchase *"Clementina"*
as a traditional bound book at:
www.1stWorldLibrary.com/purchase.asp?ISBN=978-1-4218-9601-4

1st World Library is a literary, educational organization
dedicated to:

- Creating a free internet library of downloadable ebooks

- Hosting writing competitions and offering book publishing
scholarships.

Interested in more 1st World Library books? contact:
literacy@1stworldlibrary.com
Check us out at: www.1stworldlibrary.com

# 1ˢᵗ World Library Literary Society

## Giving Back to the World

"If you want to work on the core problem, it's early school literacy."

**- James Barksdale, former CEO of Netscape**

"No skill is more crucial to the future of a child, or to a democratic and prosperous society, than literacy."

**- Los Angeles Times**

"Literacy... means far more than learning how to read and write... The aim is to transmit... knowledge and promote social participation."

**- UNESCO**

"Literacy is not a luxury, it is a right and a responsibility. If our world is to meet the challenges of the twenty-first century we must harness the energy and creativity of all our citizens."

**- President Bill Clinton**

"Parents should be encouraged to read to their children, and teachers should be equipped with all available techniques for teaching literacy, so the varying needs and capacities of individual kids can be taken into account."

**- Hugh Mackay**

**THIS BOOK IS DEDICATED TO ANDREW LANG,**

**ESQ. AS A TOKEN OF MUCH FRIENDSHIP**

# CONTENTS

I. A CHANCE MEETING ........................................................9

II. BAD NEWS ...................................................................17

III. WOGAN MAKES A PROPOSAL .......................................24

IV. SHOWS THAT THERE ARE BETTER
   HIDING-PLACES THAN A WINDOW-CURTAIN........36

V. SHOWS THAT A DISHONEST LANDLORD
   SHOULD AVOID WHITE PAINT ...............................56

VI. WOGAN CONTINUES HIS JOURNEY ........................72

VII. WOGAN IS MISTAKEN FOR A MORE
   NOTABLE MAN.........................................................93

VIII. AT SCHLESTADT ..................................................... 105

IX. GAYDON MINDS HIS OWN BUSINESS ................... 123

X. A MONTH OF WAITING............................................ 140

XI. THE PRINCE OF BADEN VISITS CLEMENTINA .... 147

XII. THE NIGHT OF THE 27TH. IN THE STREETS
   OF INNSPRUCK...................................................... 156

XIII. THE NIGHT OF THE 27TH. IN
   CLEMENTINA'S APARTMENTS ............................ 167

XIV. THE ESCAPE............................................................ 184

XV. THE FLIGHT TO ITALY:
   WOGAN'S CITY OF DREAMS ................................ 193

XVI. THE FLIGHT TO ITALY: THE POTENT
   EFFECTS OF A WATER-JUG ................................. 213

XVII. THE FLIGHT TO ITALY: A GROWING CLOUD .. 222

XVIII. WOGAN AND CLEMENTINA CONTINUE
   THEIR JOURNEY ALONE ................................. 233

XIX. THE ATTACK AT PERI...............................................253

XX. THE GOD OF THE MACHINE
    DOES NOT APPEAR.....................................................261

XXI. COMPLICATIONS AT BOLOGNA ..........................277

XXII. CLEMENTINA TAKES MR. WOGAN TO
    VISIT THE CAPRARA PALACE .............................289

XXIII. WOGAN LEARNS THAT HE HAS MEDDLED....299

XXIV. MARIA VITTORIA REAPPEARS.........................313

XXV. THE LAST .................................................................329

THE EPILOGUE .................................................................337

# CHAPTER I

## A CHANCE MEETING

The landlord, the lady, and Mr. Charles Wogan were all three, it seemed, in luck's way that September morning of the year 1719. Wogan was not surprised, his luck for the moment was altogether in, so that even when his horse stumbled and went lame at a desolate part of the road from Florence to Bologna, he had no doubt but that somehow fortune would serve him. His horse stepped gingerly on for a few yards, stopped, and looked round at his master. Wogan and his horse were on the best of terms. "Is it so bad as that?" said he, and dismounting he gently felt the strained leg. Then he took the bridle in his hand and walked forward, whistling as he walked.

Yet the place and the hour were most unlikely to give him succour. It was early morning, and he walked across an empty basin of the hills. The sun was not visible, though the upper air was golden and the green peaks of the hills rosy. The basin itself was filled with a broad uncoloured light, and lay naked to it and extraordinarily still. There were as yet no shadows; the road rose and dipped across low ridges of turf, a ribbon of dead and unillumined white; and the grass at any distance from the road had the darkness of peat. He led his horse forward for perhaps a mile, and then turning a corner by a knot of trees came unexpectedly upon a wayside inn. In front of the inn stood a travelling carriage with its team of horses. The backs of the horses smoked, and the candles of the lamps were still burning in the broad daylight. Mr. Wogan quickened his pace. He would beg a seat on the box to the next posting stage. Fortune had served him. As he came near he heard from the interior of the inn a woman's voice, not unmusical so much as shrill with impatience, which perpetually ordered and protested. As he came nearer he heard a man's voice obsequiously answering the protests, and as the sound of his footsteps rang in front of the inn both voices immediately stopped. The door was flung hastily open, and the landlord and the lady ran out onto the road.

"Sir," said the lady in Italian, "I need a postillion."

To Wogan's thinking she needed much more than a postillion. She needed certainly a retinue of servants. He was not quite sure that she did not need a nurse, for she was a creature of an exquisite fragility, with the pouting face of a child, and the childishness was exaggerated by a great muslin bow she wore at her throat. Her pale hair, where it showed beneath her hood, was fine as silk and as glossy; her eyes had the colour of an Italian sky at noon, and her cheeks the delicate tinge of a carnation. The many laces and ribbons, knotted about her dress in a manner most mysterious to Wogan, added to her gossamer appearance; and, in a word, she seemed to him something too flowerlike for the world's rough usage.

"I must have a postillion," she continued.

"Presently, madam," said the landlord, smiling with all a Tuscan peasant's desire to please. "In a minute. In less than a minute."

A. E. W. Mason

He looked complacently about him as though at any moment now a crop of postillions might be expected to flower by the roadside. The lady turned from him with a stamp of the foot and saw that Wogan was curiously regarding her carriage. A boy stood at the horses' heads, but his dress and sleepy face showed that he had not been half an hour out of bed, and there was no one else. Wogan was wondering how in the world she had travelled as far as this inn. The lady explained.

"The postillion who drove me from Florence was drunk—oh, but drunk! He rolled off his horse just here, opposite the door. See, I beat him," and she raised the beribboned handle of a toy-like cane. "But it was no use. I broke my cane over his back, but he would not get up. He crawled into the passage where he lies."

Wogan had some ado not to smile. Neither the cane nor the hand which wielded it would be likely to interfere even with a sober man's slumbers.

"And I must reach Bologna to-day," she cried in an extreme agitation. "It is of the last importance."

"Fortune is kind to us both, madam," said Wogan, with a bow. "My horse is lamed, as you see. I will be your charioteer, for I too am in a desperate hurry to reach Bologna."

Immediately the lady drew back.

"Oh!" she said with a start, looking at Wogan.

Wogan looked at her.

"Ah!" said he, thoughtfully.

They eyed each other for a moment, each silently speculating what the other was doing alone at this hour and in such a haste to reach Bologna.

"You are English?" she said with a great deal of unconcern, and she asked in English. That *she* was English, Wogan already knew from her accent. His Italian, however, was more than passable, and he was a wary man by nature as well as by some ten years' training in a service where wariness was the first need, though it was seldom acquired. He could have answered "No" quite truthfully, being Irish. He preferred to answer her in Italian as though he had not understood.

"I beg your pardon. Yes, I will drive you to Bologna if the landlord will swear to look after my horse." And he was very precise in his directions.

The landlord swore very readily. His anxiety to be rid of his vociferous guest and to get back to bed was extreme. Wogan climbed into the postillion's saddle, describing the while such remedies as he desired to be applied to the sprained leg.

"The horse is a favourite?" asked the lady.

"Madam," said Wogan, with a laugh, "I would not lose that horse for all the world, for the woman I shall marry will ride on it into my city of dreams."

The lady stared, as she well might. She hesitated with her foot upon the step.

"Is he sober?" she asked of the landlord.

"Madam," said the landlord, unabashed, "in this district he is nicknamed the water drinker."

A. E. W. Mason

"You know him, then? He is Italian?"

"He is more. He is of Tuscany."

The landlord had never seen Wogan in his life before, but the lady seemed to wish some assurance on the point, so he gave it. He shut the carriage door, and Wogan cracked his whip.

The postillion's desires were of a piece with the lady's. They raced across the valley, and as they climbed the slope beyond, the sun came over the crests. One moment the dew upon the grass was like raindrops, the next it shone like polished jewels. The postillion shouted a welcome to the sun, and the lady proceeded to breakfast in her carriage. Wogan had to snatch a meal as best he could while the horses were changed at the posting stage. The lady would not wait, and Wogan for his part was used to a light fare. He drove into Bologna that afternoon.

The lady put her head from the window and called out the name of a street. Her postillion, however, paid no heed: he seemed suddenly to have grown deaf; he whipped up his horses, shouted encouragements to them and warnings to the pedestrians on the roads. The carriage rocked round corners and bounced over the uneven stones. Wogan had clean forgotten the fragility of the traveller within. He saw men going busily about, talking in groups and standing alone, and all with consternation upon their faces. The quiet streets were alive with them. Something had happened that day in Bologna,—some catastrophe. Or news had come that day,— bad news. Wogan did not stop to inquire. He drove at a gallop straight to a long white house which fronted the street. The green latticed shutters were closed against the sun, but there were servants about the doorway, and in their aspect, too, there was something of disorder. Wogan called to one of them, jumped down from his saddle, and ran through the open doorway into a great hall with frescoed walls all ruined by neglect. At the back of the hall a marble staircase, guarded by a pair of marble lions, ran up to a landing and divided. Wogan set foot on the staircase and heard an exclamation of surprise. He looked up. A burly, good-humoured man in the gay embroideries of a courtier was descending towards him.

"You?" cried the courtier. "Already?" and then laughed. He was the only man whom Wogan had seen laugh since he drove into Bologna, and he drew a great breath of hope.

"Then nothing has happened, Whittington? There is no bad news?"

"There is news so bad, my friend, that you might have jogged here on a mule and still have lost no time. Your hurry is clean wasted," answered Whittington.

Wogan ran past him up the stairs, and so left the hall and the open doorway clear. Whittington looked now straight through the doorway, and saw the carriage and the lady on the point of stepping down onto the kerb. His face assumed a look of extreme surprise. Then he glanced up the staircase after Wogan and laughed as though the conjunction of the lady and Mr. Wogan was a rare piece of amusement. Mr. Wogan did not hear the laugh, but the lady did. She raised her head, and at the same moment the courtier came across the hall to meet her. As soon as he had come close, "Harry," said she, and gave him her hand.

He bent over it and kissed it, and there was more than courtesy in the warmth of the kiss.

"But I'm glad you've come. I did not look for you for another week," he said in a low voice. He did not, however, offer to help her to alight.

"This is your lodging?" she asked.

"No," said he, "the King's;" and the woman shrank suddenly back amongst her cushions. In a moment, however, her face was again at the door.

"Then who was he,—my postillion?"

"Your postillion?" asked Whittington, glancing at the servant who held the horses.

"Yes, the tall man who looked as if he should have been a scholar and had twisted himself all awry into a soldier. You must have passed him in the hall."

Whittington stared at her. Then he burst again into a laugh.

"Your postillion, was he? That's the oddest thing," and he lowered his voice. "Your postillion was Mr. Charles Wogan, who comes from Rome post-haste with the Pope's procuration for the marriage. You have helped him on his way, it seems. Here's a good beginning, to be sure."

The lady uttered a little cry of anger, and her face hardened out of all its softness. She clenched her fists viciously, and her blue eyes grew cold and dangerous as steel. At this moment she hardly looked the delicate flower she had appeared to Wogan's fancy.

"But you need not blame yourself," said Whittington, and he lowered his head to a level with hers. "All the procurations in Christendom will not marry James Stuart to Clementina Sobieski."

"She has not come, then?"

"No, nor will she come. There is news to-day. Lean back from the window, and I will tell you. She has been arrested at Innspruck."

The lady could not repress a crow of delight.

"Hush," said Whittington. Then he withdrew his head and resumed in his ordinary voice, "I have hired a house for your Ladyship, which I trust will be found convenient. My servant will drive you thither."

He summoned his servant from the group of footmen about the entrance, gave him his orders, bowed to the ground, and twisting his cane sauntered idly down the street.

A. E. W. Mason

## CHAPTER II

## BAD NEWS

Wogan mounted the stairs, not daring to speculate upon the nature of the bad news. But his face was pale beneath its sunburn, and his hand trembled on the balustrade; for he knew—in his heart he knew. There could be only one piece of news which would make his haste or tardiness matters of no account.

Both branches of the stairs ran up to a common landing, and in the wall facing him, midway between the two stairheads, was a great door of tulip wood. An usher stood by the door, and at Wogan's approach opened it. Wogan, however, signed to him to be silent. He wished to hear, not to speak, and so he slipped into the room unannounced. The door was closed silently behind him, and at once he was surprised by the remarkable silence, almost a cessation of life it seemed, in a room which was quite full. Wherever the broad bars of sunshine fell, as they slanted dusty with motes through the open lattices of the shutters, they striped a woman's dress or a man's velvet coat. Yet if anyone shuffled a foot or allowed a petticoat to rustle, that person glanced on each side guiltily. A group of people were gathered in front of the doorway. Their backs were towards Wogan, and they were looking towards the centre of the room. Wogan raised himself on his toes and looked that way too. Having looked he sank down again, aware at once that he had travelled of late a long way in a little time, and that he was intolerably tired. For that one glance was enough to deprive him of his last possibility of doubt. He had seen the Chevalier de St. George, his King, sitting apart in a little open space, and over against him a short squarish man, dusty as Wogan himself, who stood and sullenly waited. It was Sir John Hay, the man who had been sent to fetch the Princess Clementina privately to Bologna, and here he now was back at Bologna and alone.

Wogan had counted much upon this marriage, more indeed than any of his comrades. It was to be the first step of the pedestal in the building up of a throne. It was to establish in Europe a party for James Stuart as strong as the party of Hanover. But so much was known to everyone in that room; to Wogan the marriage meant more. For even while he found himself muttering over and over with dry lips, as white and exhausted he leaned against the door, Clementina's qualifications,—"Daughter of the King of Poland, cousin to the Emperor and to the King of Portugal, niece to the Electors of Treves, Bavaria, and Palatine,"—the image of the girl herself rose up before his eyes and struck her titles from his thoughts. She was the chosen woman, chosen by him out of all Europe—and lost by John Hay!

He remembered very clearly at that moment his first meeting with her. He had travelled from court to court in search of the fitting wife, and had come at last to the palace at Ohlau in Silesia. It was in the dusk of the evening, and as he was ushered into the great stone hall, hung about and carpeted with barbaric skins, he had seen standing by the blazing wood fire in the huge chimney a girl in a riding dress. She raised her head, and the firelight struck upwards on her face, adding a warmth to its bright colours and a dancing light to the depths of her dark eyes. Her hair was drawn backwards

A. E. W. Mason

from her forehead, and the frank, sweet face revealed to him from the broad forehead to the rounded chin told him that here was one who joined to a royal dignity the simple nature of a peasant girl who works in the fields and knows more of animals than of mankind. Wogan was back again in that stone hall when the voice of the Chevalier with its strong French accent broke in upon his vision.

"Well, we will hear the story. Well, you left Ohlau with the Princess and her mother and a mile-long train of servants in spite of my commands of secrecy."

There was more anger and less despondency than was often heard in his voice. Wogan raised himself again on tiptoes and noticed that the Chevalier's face was flushed and his eyes bright with wrath.

"Sir," pleaded Hay, "the Princess's mother would not abate a man."

"Well, you reached Ratisbon. And there?"

"There the English minister came forward from the town to flout us with an address of welcome in which he used not our incognitos but our true names."

"From Ratisbon then no doubt you hurried? Since you were discovered, you shed your retinue and hurried?"

"Sir, we hurried—to Augsburg," faltered Hay. He stopped, and then in a burst of desperation he said, "At Augsburg we stayed eight days."

"Eight days?"

There was a stir throughout the room; a murmur began and

ceased. Wogan wiped his forehead and crushed his handkerchief into a hard ball in his palm. It seemed to him that here in this room he could see the Princess Clementina's face flushed with the humiliation of that loitering.

"And why eight days in Augsburg?"

"The Princess's mother would have her jewels reset. Augsburg is famous for its jewellers," stammered Hay.

The murmur rose again; it became almost a cry of stupefaction. The Chevalier sprang from his chair. "Her jewels reset!" he said. He repeated the words in bewilderment. "Her jewels reset!" Then he dropped again into his seat.

"I lose a wife, gentlemen, and very likely a kingdom too, so that a lady may have her jewels reset at Augsburg, where, to be sure, there are famous jewellers."

His glance, wandering in a dazed way about the room, settled again on Hay. He stamped his foot on the ground in a feverish irritation.

"And those eight days gave just the time for a courier from the Emperor at Vienna to pass you on the road and not press his horse. One should be glad of that. It would have been a pity had the courier killed his horse. Oh, I can fashion the rest of the story for myself. You trailed on to Innspruck, where the Governor marched out with a troop and herded you in. They let *you* go, however. No doubt they bade you hurry back to me."

"Sir, I did hurry," said Hay, who was now in a pitiable confusion. "I travelled hither without rest."

The anger waned in the Chevalier's eyes as he heard the plea,

A. E. W. Mason

and a great dejection crept over his face.

"Yes, you would do that," said he. "That would be the time for you to hurry with a pigeon's swiftness so that your King might taste his bitter news not a minute later than need be. And what said she upon her arrest?"

"The Princess's mother?" asked Hay, barely aware of what he said.

"No. Her Highness, the Princess Clementina. What said she?"

"Sir, she covered her face with her hands for perhaps the space of a minute. Then she leaned forward to the Governor, who stood by her carriage, and cried, 'Shut four walls about me quick! I could sink into the earth for shame.'"

Wogan in those words heard her voice as clearly as he saw her face and the dry lips between which the voice passed. He had it in his heart to cry aloud, to send the words ringing through that hushed room, "She would have tramped here barefoot had she had one guide with a spirit to match hers." For a moment he almost fancied that he had spoken them, and that he heard the echo of his voice vibrating down to silence. But he had not, and as he realised that he had not, a new thought occurred to him. No one had remarked his entrance into the room. The group in front still stood with their backs towards him. Since his entrance no one had remarked his presence. At once he turned and opened the door so gently that there was not so much as a click of the latch. He opened it just wide enough for himself to slip through, and he closed it behind him with the same caution. On the landing there was only the usher. Wogan looked over the balustrade; there was no one in the hall below.

"You can keep a silent tongue," he said to the usher. "There's profit in it;" and Wogan put his hand into his pocket. "You have not seen me if any ask."

"Sir," said the man, "any bright object disturbs my vision."

"You can see a crown, though," said Wogan.

"Through a breeches pocket. But if I held it in my hand—"

"It would dazzle you."

"So much that I should be blind to the giver."

The crown was offered and taken.

Wogan went quietly down the stairs into the hall. There were a few lackeys at the door, but they would not concern themselves at all because Mr. Wogan had returned to Bologna. He looked carefully out into the street, chose a moment when it was empty, and hurried across it. He dived into the first dark alley that he came to, and following the wynds and byways of the town made his way quickly to his lodging. He had the key to his door in his pocket, and he now kept it ready in his hand. From the shelter of a corner he watched again till the road was clear; he even examined the windows of the neighbouring houses lest somewhere a pair of eyes might happen to be alert. Then he made a run for his door, opened it without noise, and crept secretly as a thief up the stairs to his rooms, where he had the good fortune to find his servant. Wogan had no need to sign to him to be silent. The man was a veteran corporal of French Guards who after many seasons of campaigning in Spain and the Low Countries had now for five years served Mr. Wogan. He looked at his master and without a word went off to make his bed.

A. E. W. Mason

Wogan sat down and went carefully over in his mind every minute of the time since he had entered Bologna. No one had noticed him when he rode in as the lady's postillion,—no one. He was sure of that. The lady herself did not know him from Adam, and fancied him an Italian into the bargain—of that, too, he had no doubt. The handful of lackeys at the door of the King's house need not be taken into account. They might gossip among themselves, but Wogan's appearances and disappearances were so ordinary a matter, even that was unlikely. The usher's silence he had already secured. There was only one acquaintance who had met and spoken with him, and that by the best of good fortune was Harry Whittington,—the idler who took his banishment and his King's misfortunes with an equally light heart, and gave never a thought at all to anything weightier than a gamecock.

Wogan's spirits revived. He had not yet come to the end of his luck. He sat down and wrote a short letter and sealed it up.

"Marnier," he called out in a low voice, and his servant came from the adjoining room, "take this to Mr. Edgar, the King's secretary, as soon as it grows dusk. Have a care that no one sees you deliver it. Lock the parlour door when you go, and take the key. I am not yet back from Rome." With that Wogan remembered that he had not slept for forty-eight hours. Within two minutes he was between the sheets; within five he was asleep.

# CHAPTER III

## WOGAN MAKES A PROPOSAL

Wogan waked up in the dark and was seized with a fear that he had slept too long. He jumped out of bed and pushed open the door of his parlour. There was a lighted lamp in the room, and Marnier was quietly laying his master's supper.

"At what hour?" asked Wogan.

"Ten o'clock, monsieur, at the little postern in the garden wall."

"And the time now?"

"Nine."

Wogan dressed with some ceremony, supped, and at eight minutes to ten slipped down the stairs and out of doors. He had crushed his hat down upon his forehead and he carried his handkerchief at his face. But the streets were dark and few people were abroad. At a little distance to his left he saw above the housetops a glow of light in the air which marked the Opera-House. Wogan avoided it; he kept again to the alleys and emerged before the Chevalier's lodging. This he passed, but a hundred yards farther on he turned down a side

A. E. W. Mason

street and doubled back upon his steps along a little byway between small houses. The line of houses, however, at one point was broken by a garden wall. Under this wall Wogan waited until a clock struck ten, and while the clock was still striking he heard on the other side of the wall the brushing of footsteps amongst leaves and grass. Wogan tapped gently on a little door in the wall. It was opened no less gently, and Edgar the secretary admitted him, led him across the garden and up a narrow flight of stairs into a small lighted cabinet. Two men were waiting in that room. One of them wore the scarlet robe, an old man with white hair and a broad bucolic face, whom Wogan knew for the Pope's Legate, Cardinal Origo. The slender figure of the other, clad all in black but for the blue ribbon of the Garter across his breast, brought Wogan to his knee.

Wogan held out the Pope's procuration to the Chevalier, who took it and devoutly kissed the signature. Then he gave his hand to Wogan with a smile of friendliness.

"You have outsped your time by two days, Mr. Wogan. That is unwise, since it may lead us to expect again the impossible of you. But here, alas, your speed for once brings us no profit. You have heard, no doubt. Her Highness the Princess Clementina is held at Innspruck in prison."

Wogan rose to his feet.

"Prisons, sir," he said quietly, "have been broken before to-day. I myself was once put to that necessity." The words took the Chevalier completely by surprise. He leaned back in his chair and stared at Wogan.

"An army could not rescue her," he said.

"No, but one man might."

"You?" he exclaimed. He pressed down the shade of the lamp to throw the light fully upon Wogan's face. "It is impossible!"

"Then I beg your Majesty to expect the impossible again."

The Chevalier drew his hand across his eyes and stared afresh at Wogan. The audacity of the exploit and the imperturbable manner of its proposal caught his breath away. He rose from his chair and took a turn or two across the room.

Wogan watched his every gesture. It would be difficult he knew to wring the permission he needed from his dejected master, and his unruffled demeanour was a calculated means of persuasion. An air of confidence was the first requisite. In reality, however, Wogan was not troubled at this moment by any thought of failure. It was not that he had any plan in his head; but he was fired with a conviction that somehow this chosen woman was not to be wasted, that some day, released by some means in spite of all the pressure English Ministers could bring upon the Emperor, she would come riding into Bologna.

The Chevalier paused in his walk and looked towards the Cardinal.

"What does your Eminence say?"

"That to the old the impulsiveness of youth is eternally charming," said the Cardinal, with a foppish delicacy of speaking in an odd contrast to his person.

Mr. Wogan understood that he had a second antagonist.

"I am not a youth, your Eminence," he exclaimed with all the indignation of twenty-seven years. "I am a man."

"But an Irishman, and that spells youth. You write poetry too, I believe, Mr. Wogan. It is a heady practice."

Wogan made no answer, though the words stung. An argument with the Cardinal would be sure to ruin his chance of obtaining the Chevalier's consent. He merely bowed to the Cardinal and waited for the Chevalier to speak.

"Look you, Mr. Wogan; while the Emperor's at war with Spain, while England's fleet could strip him of Sicily, he's England's henchman. He dare not let the Princess go. We know it. General Heister, the Governor of Innspruck, is under pain of death to hold her safe."

"But, sir, would the world stop if General Heister died?"

"A German scaffold if you fail."

"In the matter of scaffolds I have no leaning towards any one nationality."

The Cardinal smiled. He liked a man of spirit, though he might think him absurd. The Chevalier resumed his restless pacing to and fro.

"It is impossible."

But he seemed to utter the phrase with less decision this second time. Wogan pressed his advantage at the expense of his modesty.

"Sir, will you allow me to tell you a story,—a story of an impossible escape from Newgate in the heart of London by a man in fetters? There were nine grenadiers with loaded muskets standing over him. There were two courtyards to cross, two walls to climb, and beyond the walls the unfriendly streets. The man hoodwinked his sentries, climbed his two walls, crossed the unfriendly streets, and took refuge in a cellar, where he was discovered. From the cellar in broad daylight he fought his way to the roofs, and on the roofs he played such a game of hide-and-seek among the chimney-tops—" Wogan broke off from his story with a clear thrill of laughter; it was a laugh of enjoyment at a pleasing recollection. Then he suddenly flung himself down on his knee at the feet of his sovereign. "Give me leave, your Majesty," he cried passionately. "Let me go upon this errand. If I fail, if the scaffold's dressed for me, why where's the harm? Your Majesty loses one servant out of his many. Whereas, if I win—" and he drew a long breath. "Aye, and I shall win! There's the Princess, too, a prisoner. Sir, she has ventured much. I beg you give me leave."

The Chevalier laid his hand gently upon Wogan's shoulder, but he did not assent. He looked again doubtfully to the Cardinal, who said with his pleasant smile, "I will wager Mr. Wogan a box at the Opera on the first night that he returns, that he will return empty-handed."

Wogan rose to his feet and replied good-humouredly, "It's a wager I take the more readily in that your Eminence cannot win, though you may lose. For if I return empty-handed, upon my honour I'll not return at all."

The Cardinal condescended to laugh. Mr. Wogan laughed too. He had good reason, for here was his Eminence in a kindly temper and the Chevalier warming out of his melancholy. And, indeed, while he was still laughing the Chevalier caught him by the arm as a friend might do, and in an outburst of confidence, very rare with him, he said, "I would that I could laugh so. You and Whittington, I do envy

A. E. W. Mason

you. An honest laugh, there's the purge for melancholy. But I cannot compass it," and he turned away.

"Sure, sir, you'll put us all to shame when I bring her Royal Highness out of Innspruck."

"Oh, that!" said the Chevalier, as though for the moment he had forgotten. "It is impossible," and the phrase was spoken now in an accent of hesitation. Moreover, he sat down at a table, and drawing a sheet of paper written over with memoranda, he began to read aloud with a glance towards Wogan at the end of each sentence.

"The house stands in the *faubourgs* of Innspruck. There is an avenue of trees in front of the house; on the opposite side of the avenue there is a tavern with the sign of 'The White Chamois.'"

Wogan committed the words to memory.

"The Princess and her mother," continued the Chevalier, "are imprisoned in the east side of the house."

"And how guarded, sir?" asked Wogan.

The Chevalier read again from his paper.

"A sentry at each door, a third beneath the prisoners' windows. They keep watch night and day. Besides, twice a day the magistrate visits the house."

"At what hours?"

"At ten in the morning. The same hour at night."

"And on each visit the magistrate sees the Princess?"

"Yes, though she lies abed."

Wogan stroked his chin. The Cardinal regarded him quizzically.

"I trust, Mr. Wogan, that we shall hear Farini. There is talk of his coming to Bologna."

Wogan did not answer. He was silent; he saw the three sentinels standing watchfully about the house; he heard them calling "All's well" each to the other. Then he asked, "Has the Princess her own servants to attend her?"

"Only M. Chateaudoux, her chamberlain."

"Ah!"

Wogan leaned forward with a question on his tongue he hardly dared to ask. So much hung upon the answer.

"And M. Chateaudoux is allowed to come and go?"

"In the daylight."

Wogan turned to the Cardinal. "The box will be the best box in the house," Wogan suggested.

"Oh, sir," replied the Cardinal, "on the first tier, to be sure."

Wogan turned back to the Chevalier.

"All that I need now is a letter from your Majesty to the King of Poland and a few rascally guineas. I can leave Bologna before a soul's astir in the morning. No one but Whittington saw me to-day, and a word will keep him silent. There will be secrecy—" but the Chevalier suddenly cut him short.

"No," said he, bringing the palm of his hand down upon the table. "Here's a blow that we must bend to! It's a dream, this plan of yours."

"But a dream I'll dream so hard, sir, that I'll dream it true," cried Wogan, in despair.

"No, no," said the Chevalier. "We'll talk no more of it. There's God's will evident in this arrest, and we must bend to it;" and at once Wogan remembered his one crowning argument. It was so familiar to his thoughts, it had lain so close at his heart, that he had left it unspoken, taking it as it were for granted that others were as familiar with it as he.

"Sir," said he, eagerly, "I have never told you, but the Princess Clementina when a child amongst her playmates had a favourite game. They called it kings and queens. And in that game the Princess was always chosen Queen of England."

The Chevalier started.

"Is that so?" and he gazed into Wogan's eyes, making sure that he spoke the truth.

"In very truth it is," and the two men stood looking each at the other and quite silent.

It was the truth, a mere coincidence if you will, but to both these men omens and auguries were the gravest matters.

"There indeed is God's finger pointing," cried Wogan. "Sir, give me leave to follow it."

The Chevalier still stood looking at him in silence. Then he said suddenly, "Go, then, and God speed you! You are a gallant gentleman."

He sat down thereupon and wrote a letter to the King of Poland, asking him to entrust the rescue of his daughter into Wogan's hands. This letter Wogan took and money for his journey.

"You will have preparations to make," said the Chevalier. "I will not keep you. You have horses?"

Mr. Wogan had two in a stable at Bologna. "But," he added, "there is a horse I left this morning six miles this side of Fiesole, a black horse, and I would not lose it."

"Nor shall you," said the Chevalier.

Wogan crept back to his lodging as cautiously as he had left it. There was no light in any window but in his own, where his servant, Marnier, awaited him. Wogan opened the door softly and found the porter asleep in his chair. He stole upstairs and made his preparations. These, however, were of the simplest kind, and consisted of half-a-dozen orders to Marnier and the getting into bed. In the morning he woke before daybreak and found Marnier already up. They went silently out of the house as the dawn was breaking. Marnier had the key to the stables, and they saddled the two horses and rode through the blind and silent streets with their faces muffled in their cloaks.

They met no one, however, until they were come to the outskirts of the town. But then as they passed the mouth of an alley a man came suddenly out and as suddenly drew back. The morning was chill, and the man was closely wrapped.

Wogan could not distinguish his face or person, and looking

A. E. W. Mason

down the alley he saw at the end of it only a garden wall, and over the top of the wall a thicket of trees and the chimney-tops of a low house embosomed amongst them. He rode on, secure in the secrecy of his desperate adventure. But that same morning Mr. Whittington paid a visit to Wogan's lodging and asked to be admitted. He was told that Mr. Wogan had not yet returned to Bologna.

"So, indeed, I thought," said he; and he sauntered carelessly along, not to his own house, but to one smaller, situated at the bottom of a *cul-de-sac* and secluded amongst trees. At the door he asked whether her Ladyship was yet visible, and was at once shown into a room with long windows which stood open to the garden. Her Ladyship lay upon a sofa sipping her coffee and teasing a spaniel with the toe of her slipper.

"You are early," she said with some surprise.

"And yet no earlier than your Ladyship," said Whittington.

"I have to make my obeisance to my King," said she, stifling a yawn. "Could one, I ask you, sleep on so important a day?"

Mr. Whittington laughed genially. Then he opened the door and glanced along the passage. When he turned back into the room her Ladyship had kicked the spaniel from the sofa and was sitting bolt upright with all her languor gone.

"Well?" she asked quickly.

Whittington took a seat on the sofa by her side.

"Charles Wogan left Bologna at daybreak. Moreover, I have had a message from the Chevalier bidding me not to mention that I saw him in Bologna yesterday. One could hazard a guess at the goal of so secret a journey."

"Ohlau!" exclaimed the lady, in a whisper. Then she nestled back upon the sofa and bit the fragment of lace she called her handkerchief.

"So there's an end of Mr. Wogan," she said pleasantly.

Whittington made no answer.

"For there's no chance that he'll succeed," she continued with a touch of anxiety in her voice.

Whittington neither agreed nor contradicted. He asked a question instead.

"What is the sharpest spur a man can know? What is it that gives a man audacity to attempt and wit to accomplish the impossible?"

The lady smiled.

"The poets tell us love," said she, demurely.

Whittington nodded his head.

"Wogan speaks very warmly of the Princess Clementina."

Her Ladyship's red lips lost their curve. Her eyes became thoughtful, apprehensive.

"I wonder," she said slowly.

"Yes, I too wonder," said Whittington.

A. E. W. Mason

Outside the branches of the trees rustled in the wind and flung shadows, swift as ripples, across the sunlit grass. But within the little room there was a long silence.

# CHAPTER IV

## SHOWS THAT THERE ARE BETTER HIDING-PLACES THAN A WINDOW-CURTAIN

M. Chateaudoux, the chamberlain, was a little portly person with a round, red face like a cherub's. He was a creature of the house, one that walked with delicate steps, a conductor of ceremonies, an expert in the subtleties of etiquette; and once he held his wand of office in his hand, there was nowhere to be found a being so precise and consequential. But out of doors he had the timidity of a cat. He lived, however, by rule and rote, and since it had always been his habit to take the air between three and four of the afternoon, he was to be seen between those hours at Innspruck on any fine day mincing along the avenue of trees before the villa in which his mistress was held prisoner.

On one afternoon during the month of October he passed a hawker, who, tired with his day's tramp, was resting on a bench in the avenue, and who carried upon his arm a half-empty basket of cheap wares. The man was ragged; his toes were thrusting through his shoes; it was evident that he wore no linen, and a week's growth of beard dirtily stubbled his chin,—in a word, he was a man from whom M. Chateaudoux's prim soul positively shrank. M. Chateaudoux went quickly by, fearing to be pestered for alms. The

A. E. W. Mason

hawker, however, remained seated upon the bench, drawing idle patterns upon the gravel with a hazel stick stolen from a hedgerow.

The next afternoon the hawker was in the avenue again, only this time on a bench at the opposite end; and again he paid no heed to M. Chateaudoux, but sat moodily scraping the gravel with his stick.

On the third afternoon M. Chateaudoux found the hawker seated in the middle of the avenue and over against the door of the guarded villa. M. Chateaudoux, when his timidity slept, was capable of good nature. There was a soldier with a loaded musket in full view. The hawker, besides, had not pestered him. He determined to buy some small thing,—a mirror, perhaps, which was always useful,—and he approached the hawker, who for his part wearily flicked the gravel with his stick and drew a curve here and a line there until, as M. Chateaudoux stopped before the bench, there lay sketched at his feet the rude semblance of a crown. The stick swept over it the next instant and left the gravel smooth.

But M. Chateaudoux had seen, and his heart fluttered and sank. For here were plots, possibly dangers, most certainly trepidations. He turned his back as though he had seen nothing, and constraining himself to a slow pace walked towards the door of the villa. But the hawker was now at his side, whining in execrable German and a strong French accent the remarkable value of his wares. There were samplers most exquisitely worked, jewels for the most noble gentleman's honoured sweetheart, and purses which emperors would give a deal to buy. Chateaudoux was urged to take notice that emperors would give sums to lay a hand on the hawker's purses.

M. Chateaudoux pretended not to hear.

"I want nothing," he said, "nothing in the world;" and he repeated the statement in order to drown the other's voice.

"A purse, good gentleman," persisted the hawker, and he dangled one before Chateaudoux's eyes. Not for anything would Chateaudoux take that purse.

"Go away," he cried; "I have a sufficiency of purses, and I will not be plagued by you."

They were now at the steps of the villa, and the sentry, lifting the butt of his musket, roughly thrust the hawker back.

"What have you there? Bring your basket here," said he; and to Chateaudoux's consternation the hawker immediately offered the purse to the sentinel.

"It is only the poor who have kind hearts," he said; "here's the proper purse for a soldier. It is so hard to get the money out that a man is saved an ocean of drink."

The hawker's readiness destroyed any suspicions the sentinel may have felt.

"Go away," he said, "quick!"

"You will buy the purse?"

The sentinel raised his musket again.

"Then the kind gentleman will," said the hawker, and he thrust the purse into M. Chateaudoux's reluctant hand. Chateaudoux could feel within the purse a folded paper. He was committed now without a doubt, and in an extreme alarm he flung a coin into the roadway and got him into the house. The sentinel carelessly dropped the butt of his musket on the coin.

"Go," said he, and with a sudden kick he lifted the hawker half across the road. The hawker happened to be Charles Wogan, who took a little matter like that with the necessary philosophy. He picked himself up and limped off.

Now the next day a remarkable thing happened. M. Chateaudoux swerved from the regularity of his habits. He walked along the avenue, it is true; but at the end of it he tripped down a street and turned out of that into another which brought him to the arcades. He did not appear to enjoy his walk; indeed, any hurrying footsteps behind startled him exceedingly and made his face turn white and red, and his body hot and cold. However, he proceeded along the arcades to the cathedral, which he entered; and just as the clock struck half-past three, in a dark corner opposite to the third of the great statues he drew his handkerchief from his pocket.

The handkerchief flipped out a letter which fell onto the ground. In the gloom it was barely visible; and M. Chateaudoux walked on, apparently unconscious of his loss. But a comfortable citizen in a snuff-coloured suit picked it up and walked straight out of the cathedral to the Golden Fleece Inn in the Hochstrasse, where he lodged. He went up into his room and examined the letter. It was superscribed "To M. Chateaudoux," and the seal was broken. Nevertheless, the finder did not scruple to read it. It was a love-letter to the little gentleman from one Friederika.

"I am heart-broken," wrote Friederika, "but my fidelity to my Chateaudoux has not faltered, nor will not, whatever I may be called upon to endure. I cannot, however, be so undutiful as to accept my Chateaudoux's addresses without my father's consent; and my mother, who is of the same mind with me, insists that even with that consent a runaway marriage is not to be thought of unless my Chateaudoux can provide me with a suitable woman for an attendant."

These conditions fulfilled, Friederika was willing to follow her Chateaudoux to the world's end. The comfortable citizen in the snuff-coloured suit sat for some while over that letter with a strange light upon his face and a smile of great happiness. The comfortable citizen was Charles Wogan, and he could dissociate the obstructions of the mother from the willingness of the girl.

The October evening wove its veils from the mountain crests across the valleys; the sun and the daylight had gone from the room before Wogan tore that letter up and wrote another to the Chevalier at Bologna, telling him that the Princess Clementina would venture herself gladly if he could secure the consent of Prince Sobieski, her father. And the next morning he drove out in a carriage towards Ohlau in Silesia.

It was as the Chevalier Warner that he had first journeyed thither to solicit for his King the Princess Clementina's hand. Consequently he used the name again. Winter came upon him as he went; the snow gathered thick upon the hills and crept down into the valleys, encumbering his path. The cold nipped his bones; he drove beneath great clouds and through a stinging air, but of these discomforts he was not sensible. For the mission he was set upon filled his thoughts and ran like a fever in his blood. He lay awake at nights inventing schemes of evasion, and each morning showed a flaw, and the schemes crumbled. Not that his faith faltered. At some one moment he felt sure the perfect plan, swift and secret, would be revealed to him, and he lived to seize the moment. The people with whom he spoke became as shadows; the inns where he rested were confused into a common semblance. He was like a man in a trance, seeing ever before

A. E. W. Mason

his eyes the guarded villa at Innspruck, and behind the walls, patient and watchful, the face of the chosen woman; so that it was almost with surprise that he looked down one afternoon from the brim of a pass in the hills and saw beneath him, hooded with snow, the roofs and towers of Ohlau.

At Ohlau Wogan came to the end of his luck. From the moment when he presented his letter he was aware of it. The Prince was broken by his humiliation and the sufferings of his wife and daughter. He was even inclined to resent them at the expense of the Chevalier, for in his welcome to Wogan there was a measure of embarrassment. His shoulders, which had before been erect, now stooped, his eyes were veiled, the fire had burnt out in him; he was an old man visibly ageing to his grave. He read the letter and re-read it.

"No," said he, impatiently; "I must now think of my daughter. Her dignity and her birth forbid that she should run like a criminal in fear of capture, and at the peril very likely of her life, to a king who, after all, is as yet without a crown." And then seeing Wogan flush at the words, he softened them. "I frankly say to you, Mr. Warner, that I know no one to whom I would sooner entrust my daughter than yourself, were I persuaded to this project. But it is doomed to fail. It would make us the laughing-stock of Europe, and I ask you to forget it. Do you fancy the Emperor guards my daughter so ill that you, single-handed, can take her from beneath his hand?"

"Your Highness, I shall choose some tried friends to help me."

"There is no single chance of success. I ask you to forget it and to pass your Christmas here as my very good friend. The sight is longer in age, Mr. Warner, than in youth, and I see far enough now to know that the days of Don Quixote are dead. Here is a matter where all Europe is ranged and alert on one side or the other. You cannot practise secrecy. At Ohlau your face is known, your incognito too. Mr. Warner came to Ohlau once before, and the business on which he came is common knowledge. The motive of your visit now, which I tell you openly is very grateful to me, will surely be suspected."

Wogan had reason that night to acknowledge the justice of the Prince's argument. He accepted his hospitality, thinking that with time he would persuade him to allow the attempt; and after supper, while making riddles in verse to amuse some of the ladies of the court, one of them, the Countess of Berg, came forward from a corner where she had been busy with pencil and paper and said, "It is our turn now. Here, Mr. Warner, is an acrostic which I ask you to solve for me." And with a smile which held a spice of malice she handed him the paper. Upon it there were ten rhymed couplets. Wogan solved the first four, and found that the initial letters of the words were C, L, E, M. The answer to the acrostic was "Clementina." Wogan gave the paper back.

"I can make neither head nor tail of it," said he. "The attempt is beyond my powers."

"Ah," said she, drily, "you own as much? I would never have believed you would have owned it."

"But what is the answer?" asked a voice at which Wogan started.

"The answer," replied the Countess, "is Mary, Queen of Scots, who was most unjustly imprisoned in Fotheringay," and she tore the paper into tiny pieces.

Wogan turned towards the voice which had so startled him

and saw the gossamer lady whom he had befriended on the road from Florence. At once he rose and bowed to her.

"I should have presented you before to my friend, Lady Featherstone," said the Countess, "but it seems you are already acquainted."

"Indeed, Mr. Warner did me a great service at a pinch," said Lady Featherstone. "He was my postillion, though I never paid him, as I do now in thanks."

"Your postillion!" cried one or two of the ladies, and they gathered about the great stove as Lady Featherstone told the story of Wogan's charioting.

"I bade him hurry," said she, "and he outsped my bidding. Never was there a postillion so considerately inconsiderate. I was tossed like a tennis ball, I was one black bruise, I bounced from cushion to cushion; and then he drew up with a jerk, sprang off his horse, vanished into a house and left me, panting and dishevelled, a twist of torn ribbons and lace, alone in my carriage in the streets of Bologna."

"Bologna. Ah!" said the Countess, with a smile of significance at Wogan.

Wogan was looking at Lady Featherstone. His curiosity, thrust into the back of his mind by the more important matter of his mission now revived. What had been this lady's business who travelled alone to Bologna and in such desperate haste?

"Your Ladyship, I remember," he said, "gave me to understand that you were sorely put to it to reach Bologna."

Her Ladyship turned her blue eyes frankly upon Wogan.

Then she lowered them.

"My brother," she explained, "lay at death's door in Venice. I had just landed at Leghorn, where I left my maid to recover from the sea, and hurrying across Italy as I did, I still feared that I should not see him alive."

The explanation was made readily in a low voice natural to one remembering a great distress, but without any affectation of gesture or so much as a glance sideways to note whether Wogan received it trustfully or not. Wogan, indeed, was reassured in a great measure. True, the Countess of Berg was now his declared enemy, but he need not join all her friends in that hostility.

"I was able, most happily," continued Lady Featherstone, "to send my brother homewards in a ship a fortnight back, and so to stay with my friend here on my way to Vienna, for we English are all bitten with the madness of travel. Mr. Warner will bear me out?"

"To be sure I will," said Wogan, stoutly. "For here am I in the depths of winter journeying to the carnival in Italy."

The Countess smiled, all disbelief and amusement, and Lady Featherstone turned quickly towards him.

"For my frankness I claim a like frankness in return," said she, with a pretty imperiousness.

Wogan was a little startled. He suddenly remembered that he had pretended to know no English on the road to Bologna, nor had he given any reason for his haste. But it was upon neither of these matters that she desired to question him.

"You spoke in parables," said she, "which are detestable

things. You said you would not lose your black horse for the world because the lady you were to marry would ride upon it into your city of dreams. There's a saying that has a provoking prettiness. I claim a frank answer."

Wogan was silent, and his face took on the look of a dreamer.

"Come," said one. It was the Princess Charlotte, the second daughter of the Prince Sobieski, who spoke. "We shall not let you off," said she.

Wogan knew that she would not. She was a girl who was never checked by any inconvenience her speech might cause. Her tongue was a watchman's rattle, and she never spoke but she laughed to point the speech.

"Be frank," said the Countess; "it is a matter of the heart, and so proper food for women."

"True," answered Wogan, lightly, "it is a matter of the heart, and in such matters can one be frank—even to oneself?"

Wogan was immediately puzzled by the curious look Lady Featherstone gave him. The words were a mere excuse, yet she seemed to take them very seriously. Her eyes sounded him.

"Yes," she said slowly; "are you frank, even to yourself?" and she spoke as though a knowledge of the answer would make a task easier to her.

Wogan's speculations, however, were interrupted by the entrance of Princess Casimira, Sobieski's eldest daughter. Wogan welcomed her coming for the first time in all his life, for she was a kill-joy, a person of an extraordinary decorum.

According to Wogan, she was "that black care upon the horseman's back which the poets write about." Her first question if she was spoken to was whether the speaker was from top to toe fitly attired; her second, whether the words spoken were well-bred. At this moment, however, her mere presence put an end to the demands for an explanation of Wogan's saying about his horse, and in a grateful mood to her he slipped from the room.

This evening was but one of many during that Christmastide. Wogan must wear an easy countenance, though his heart grew heavy as lead. The Countess of Berg was the Prince Constantine's favourite; and Wogan was not slow to discover that her smiling face and quiet eyes hid the most masterful woman at that court. He made himself her assiduous servant, whether in hunting amid the snow or in the entertainments at the palace, but a quizzical deliberate word would now and again show him that she was still his enemy. With the Princess Casimira he was a profound critic of observances: he invented a new cravat and was most careful that there should never be a wrinkle in his stockings; with the Princess Charlotte he laughed till his head sang. He played all manner of parts; the palace might have been the stage of a pantomime and himself the harlequin. But for all his efforts it did not seem that he advanced his cause; and if he made headway one evening with the Prince, the next morning he had lost it, and so Christmas came and passed.

But two days after Christmas a courier brought a letter to the castle. He came in the evening, and the letter was carried to Wogan while he was at table. He noticed at once that it was in his King's hand, and he slipped it quickly into his pocket. It may have been something precipitate in his manner, or it may have been merely that all were on the alert to mark his actions, but at once curiosity was aroused. No plain words were said; but here and there heads nodded together and whispered, and while some eyed Wogan suspiciously, a few women whose hearts were tuned to a sympathy with the Princess in her imprisonment, or touched with the notion of a romantic attachment, smiled upon him their encouragement. The Countess of Berg for once was unobservant, however.

Wogan made his escape from the company as soon as he could, and going up to his apartments read the letter. The moon was at its full, and what with the clear, frosty air, and the snow stretched over the world like a white counterpane, he was able to read the letter by the window without the light of a candle. It was written in the Chevalier's own cipher and hand; it asked anxiously for news and gave some. Wogan had had occasion before to learn that cipher by heart. He stood by the window and spelled the meaning. Then he turned to go down; but at the door his foot slipped upon the polished boards, and he stumbled onto his knee. He picked himself up, and thinking no more of the matter rejoined the company in a room where the Countess of Berg was playing upon a harp.

"The King," said Wogan, drawing the Prince apart, "leaves Bologna for Rome."

"So the letter came from him?" asked the Prince, with an eagerness which could not but seem hopeful to his companion.

"And in his own hand," replied Wogan.

The Prince shuffled and hesitated as though he was curious to hear particulars. Wogan thought it wise to provoke his curiosity by disregarding it. It seemed that there was wisdom in his reticence, for a little later the Prince took him aside while the Countess of Berg was still playing upon her harp, and said,—

"Single-handed you could do nothing. You would need friends."

Wogan took a slip of paper from his pocket and gave it to the Prince.

"On that slip," said he, "I wrote down the names of all the friends whom I could trust, and by the side of the names the places where I could lay my hands upon them. One after the other I erased the names until only three remained."

The Prince nodded and read out the names.

"Gaydon, Misset, O'Toole. They are good men?"

"The flower of Ireland. Those three names have been my comfort these last three weeks."

"And all the three at Schlestadt. How comes that about?"

"Your Highness, they are all three officers in Dillon's Irish regiment, and so have that further advantage."

"Advantage?"

"Your Highness," said Wogan, "Schlestadt is near to Strasbourg, which again is not far from Innspruck, and being in French territory would be the most convenient place to set off from."

There was a sound of a door shutting; the Prince started, looked at Wogan, and laughed. He had been upon the verge of yielding; but for that door Wogan felt sure he would have yielded. Now, however, he merely walked away to the Countess of Berg, and sitting beside her asked her to play a particular tune. But he still held the slip of paper in his hand

A. E. W. Mason

and paid but a scanty heed to the music, now and then looking doubtfully towards Wogan, now and then scanning that long list of names. His lips, too, moved as though he was framing the three selected names, Gaydon, Misset, O'Toole, and "Schlestadt" as a bracket uniting them. Then he suddenly rose up and crossed the room to Wogan.

"My daughter wrote that a woman must attend her. It is a necessary provision."

"Your Highness, Misset has a wife, and the wife matches him."

"They are warned to be ready?"

"At your Highness's first word that slip of paper travels to Schlestadt. It is unsigned, it imperils no one, it betrays nothing. But it will tell its story none the less surely to those three men, for Gaydon knows my hand."

The Prince smiled in approval.

"You have prudence, Mr. Warner, as well as audacity," said he. He gave the paper back, listened for a little to the Countess, who was bending over her harp-strings, and then remarked, "The Prince's letter was in his own hand too?"

"But in cipher."

"Ah!"

The Prince was silent for a while. He balanced himself first on one foot, then on the other.

"Ciphers," said he, "are curious things, compelling to the imagination and a provocation to the intellect."

Mr. Wogan kept a grave face and he replied with unconcern, though his heart beat quick; for if the Prince had so much desire to see the Chevalier's letter, he must be well upon his way to consenting to Wogan's plan.

"If your Highness will do me the honour to look at this cipher. It has baffled the most expert."

His Highness condescended to be pleased with Wogan's suggestion. Wogan crossed the room towards the door; but before he reached it, the Countess of Berg suddenly took her fingers from her harp-strings with a gesture of annoyance.

"Mr. Warner," she said, "will you do me the favour to screw this wire tighter?" And once or twice she struck it with her fingers.

"May I claim that privilege?" said the Prince.

"Your Highness does me too much honour," said the Countess, but the Prince was already at her side. At once she pointed out to him the particular string. Wogan went from the room and up the great staircase. He was lodged in a wing of the palace. From the head of the staircase he proceeded down a long passage. Towards the end of this passage another short passage branched off at a right angle on the left-hand side. At the corner of the two passages stood a table with a lamp and some candlesticks. This time Wogan took a candle, and lighting it at the lamp turned into the short passage. It was dark but for the light of Wogan's candle, and at the end of it facing him were two doors side by side. Both doors were closed, and of these the one on the left gave onto his room.

Wogan had walked perhaps halfway from the corner to his door before he stopped. He stopped suddenly and held his

A. E. W. Mason

breath. Then he shaded his candle with the palm of his hand and looked forward. Immediately he turned, and walking on tiptoe came silently back into the big passage. Even this was not well lighted; it stretched away upon his right and left, full of shadows. But it was silent. The only sounds which reached Wogan as he stood there and listened were the sounds of people moving and speaking at a great distance. He blew out his candle, cautiously replaced it on the table, and crept down again towards his room. There was no window in this small passage, there was no light there at all except a gleam of silver in front of him and close to the ground. That gleam of silver was the moonlight shining between the bottom of one of the doors and the boards of the passage. And that door was not the door of Wogan's room, but the room beside it. Where his door stood, there might have been no door at all.

Yet the moon which shone through the windows of one room must needs also shine into the other, unless, indeed, the curtains were drawn. But earlier in the evening Wogan had read a letter by the moonlight at his window; the curtains were not drawn. There was, therefore, a rug, an obstruction of some sort against the bottom of the door. But earlier in the evening Wogan's foot had slipped upon the polished boards; there had been no mat or skin at all. It had been pushed there since. Wogan could not doubt for what reason. It was to conceal the light of a lamp or candle within the room. Someone, in a word, was prying in Wogan's room, and Wogan began to consider who. It was not the Countess, who was engaged upon her harp, but the Countess had tried to detain him. Wogan was startled as he understood the reason of her harp becoming so suddenly untuned. She had spoken to him with so natural a spontaneity, she had accepted the Prince's aid with so complete an absence of embarrassment; but none the less Wogan was sure that she knew. Moreover, a door had shut—yes, while he was speaking to the Prince a door had shut.

So far Wogan's speculations had travelled when the moonlight streamed out beneath his door too. It made now a silver line across the passage broken at the middle by the wall between the rooms. The mat had been removed, the candle put out, the prying was at an end; in another moment the door would surely open. Now Wogan, however anxious to discover who it was that spied, was yet more anxious that the spy should not discover that the spying was detected. He himself knew, and so was armed; he did not wish to arm his enemies with a like knowledge. There was no corner in the passage to conceal him; there was no other door behind which he could slip. When the spy came out, Wogan would inevitably be discovered. He made up his mind on the instant. He crept back quickly and silently out of the mouth of the passage, then he made a noise with his feet, turned again into the passage, and walked loudly towards his door. Even so he was only just in time. Had he waited a moment longer, he would have been detected. For even as he turned the corner there was already a vertical line of silver on the passage wall; the door had been already opened. But as his footsteps sounded on the boards, that line disappeared.

He walked slowly, giving his spy time to replace the letter, time to hide. He purposely carried no candle, he reached his door and opened it. The room to all seeming was empty. Wogan crossed to a table, looking neither to the right nor the left, above all not looking towards the bed hangings. He found the letter upon the table just as he had left it. It could convey no knowledge of his mission, he was sure. It had not even the appearance of a letter in cipher; it might have been a mere expression of Christmas good wishes from one friend to another. But to make his certainty more sure, and at the same time to show that he had no suspicion anyone was hiding in the room, he carried the letter over to the window, and at once he was aware of the spy's hiding-place. It was not the bed hangings, but close at his side the heavy window curtain bulged. The spy was at his very elbow; he had but to lift his arm—and of a sudden the letter slipped from his hand to the floor. He did not drop it on purpose, he was fairly surprised; for looking down to read the letter he had seen protruding from the curtain a jewelled shoe buckle, and the foot which the buckle adorned seemed too small and slender for a man's.

Wogan had an opportunity to make certain. He knelt down and picked up the letter; the foot was a woman's. As he rose up again, the curtain ever so slightly stirred. Wogan pretended to have remarked nothing; he stood easily by the window with his eyes upon his letter and his mind busy with guessing what woman his spy might be. And he remained on purpose for some while in this attitude, designing it as a punishment. So long as he stood by the window that unknown woman cheek by jowl with him must hold her breath, must never stir, must silently endure an agony of fear at each movement that he made.

At last he moved, and as he turned away he saw something so unexpected that it startled him. Indeed, for the moment it did more than startle him, it chilled him. He understood that slight stirring of the curtain. The woman now held a dagger in her hand, and the point of the blade stuck out and shone in the moonlight like a flame.

Wogan became angry. It was all very well for the woman to come spying into his room; but to take a dagger to him, to think a dagger in a woman's hand could cope with him,—that was too preposterous. Wogan felt very much inclined to sweep that curtain aside and tell his visitor how he had escaped from Newgate and played hide-and-seek amongst the chimney-pots. And although he restrained himself from that, he allowed his anger to get the better of his prudence. Under the impulse of his anger he acted. It was a whimsical thing that he did, and though he suffered for it he could never afterwards bring himself to regret it. He deliberately knelt down and kissed the instep of the foot which protruded from the curtain. He felt the muscles of the foot tighten, but the foot was not withdrawn. The curtain shivered and shook, but no cry came from behind it, and again the curtain hung motionless. Wogan went out of the room and carried the letter to the Prince. The Countess of Berg was still playing upon her harp, and she gave no sign that she remarked his entrance. She did not so much as shoot one glance of curiosity towards him. The Prince carried the letter off to his cabinet, while Wogan sat down beside the Countess and looked about the room.

"I have not seen Lady Featherstone this evening," said he.

"Have you not?" asked the Countess, easily.

"Not so much as her foot," replied Wogan.

The conviction came upon him suddenly. Her hurried journey to Bologna and her presence at Ohlau were explained to him now by her absence from the room. His own arrival at Bologna had not remained so secret as he had imagined. The fragile and gossamer lady, too flowerlike for the world's rough usage, was the woman who had spied in his room and who had possessed the courage to stand silent and motionless behind the curtain after her presence there had been discovered. Wogan had a picture before his eyes of the dagger she had held. It was plain that she would stop at nothing to hinder this marriage, to prevent the success of his design; and somehow the contrast between her appearance and her actions had something uncanny about it. Wogan was inclined to shiver as he sat chatting with the Countess. He

A. E. W. Mason

was not reassured when Lady Featherstone boldly entered the room; she meant to face him out. He remarked, however, with a trifle of satisfaction that for the first time she wore rouge upon her cheeks.

# CHAPTER V

## SHOWS THAT A DISHONEST LANDLORD SHOULD AVOID WHITE PAINT

Wogan, however, was not immediately benefited by his discovery. He knew that if a single whisper of it reached the Prince's ear there would be at once an end to his small chances. The old man would take alarm; he might punish the offender, but he would none the less surely refuse his consent to Wogan's project. Wogan must keep his lips quite closed and let his antagonists do boldly what they would.

And that they were active he found a way to discover. The Countess from this time plied him with kindness. He must play cards with her and Prince Constantine in the evening; he must take his coffee in her private apartments in the morning. So upon one of these occasions he spoke of his departure from Ohlau.

"I shall go by way of Prague;" and he stopped in confusion and corrected himself quickly. "At least, I am not sure. There are other ways into Italy."

The Countess showed no more concern than she had shown over her harp-string. She talked indifferently of other matters

A. E. W. Mason

as though she had barely heard his remark; but she fell into the trap. Wogan was aware that the Governor of Prague was her kinsman; and that afternoon he left the castle alone, and taking the road to Vienna, turned as soon as he was out of sight and hurried round the town until he came out upon the road to Prague. He hid himself behind a hedge a mile from Ohlau, and had not waited half an hour before a man came riding by in hot haste. The man wore the Countess's livery of green and scarlet; Wogan decided not to travel by way of Prague, and returned to the castle content with his afternoon's work. He had indeed more reason to be content with it than he knew, for he happened to have remarked the servant's face as well as his livery, and so at a later time was able to recognise it again. He had no longer any doubt that a servant in the same livery was well upon his way to Vienna. The roads were bad, it was true, and the journey long; but Wogan had not the Prince's consent, and could not tell when he would obtain it. The servant might return with the Emperor's order for his arrest before he had obtained it. Wogan was powerless. He sent his list of names to Gaydon in Schlestadt, but that was the only precaution he could take. The days passed; Wogan spent them in unavailing persuasions, and New Year's Day came and found him still at Ohlau and in a great agitation and distress.

Upon that morning, however, while he was dressing, there came a rap upon his door, and when he opened it he saw the Prince's treasurer, a foppish gentleman, very dainty in his words.

"Mr. Warner," said the treasurer, "his Highness has hinted to me his desires; he has moulded them into the shape of a prayer or a request."

"In a word, he has bidden you," said Wogan.

"Fie, sir! There's a barbarous and improper word, an ill-sounding word; upon my honour, a word without dignity or merit and banishable from polite speech. His Highness did most prettily entreat me with a fine gentleness of condescension befitting a Sunday or a New Year's Day to bring and present and communicate from hand to hand a gift,—a most incomparable proper gift, the mirror and image of his most incomparable proper friendship."

Wogan bowed, and requested the treasurer to enter and be seated the while he recovered his breath.

"Nay, Mr. Warner, I must be concise, puritanical, and unadorned in my language as any raw-head or bloody-bones. The cruel, irrevocable moments pass. I could consume an hour, sir, before I touched as I may say the hem of the reason of my coming."

"Sir, I do not doubt it," said Wogan.

"But I will not hinder you from forthwith immediately and at once incorporating with your most particular and inestimable treasures this jewel, this turquoise of heaven's own charming blue, encased and decorated with gold."

The treasurer drew the turquoise from his pocket. It was of the size of an egg. He placed it in Wogan's hand, who gently returned it.

"I cannot take it," said he.

"Gemini!" cried the treasurer. "But it is more than a turquoise, Mr. Warner. Jewellers have delved in it. It has become subservient to man's necessities. It is a snuff-box."

"I cannot take it."

A. E. W. Mason

"King John of Poland, he whom the vulgar call Glorious John, did rescue and enlarge it from its slavery to the Grand Vizier of Turkey at the great battle of Vienna. There is no other in the world—"

Wogan cut the treasurer short.

"You will take it again to his Highness. You will express to him my gratitude for his kindness, and you will say furthermore these words: 'Mr. Warner cannot carry back into Italy a present for himself and a refusal for his Prince.'"

Wogan spoke with so much dignity that the treasurer had no words to answer him. He stood utterly bewildered; he stared at the jewel.

"Here is a quandary!" he exclaimed. "I do declare every circumstance of me trembles," and shaking his head he went away. But in a little he came again.

"His Highness distinguishes you, Mr. Warner, with imperishable honours. His Highness solicits your company to a solitary dinner. You shall dine with him alone. His presence and unfettered conversation shall season your soup and be the condiments of your meat."

Wogan's heart jumped. There could be only one reason for so unusual an invitation on such a day, and he was not mistaken; for as soon as the Prince was served in a little room, he dismissed the lackeys and presented again the turquoise snuff-box with his own hands.

"See, Mr. Wogan, your persuasions and your conduct have gained me over," said he. "Your refusal of this bagatelle assures me of your honour. I trust myself entirely to your discretion; I confide my beloved daughter to your care. Take from my hands the gift you refused this morning, and be assured that no prince ever gave to any man such full powers as I will give to you to-night."

Wogan's gratitude wellnigh overcame him. The thing that he had worked for and almost despaired of had come to pass. For a while he could not speak; he flung himself upon his knees and kissed the Prince's hand. That very night he received the letter giving him full powers, and the next morning he drove off in a carriage of his Highness drawn by six Polish horses towards the town of Strahlen on the road to Prague. At Strahlen he stayed a day, feigning a malady, and sent the carriage back. The following day, however, he took horse, and riding along by-roads and lanes avoided Prague and hurried towards Schlestadt.

He rode watchfully, avoiding towns, and with an eye alert for every passer-by. That he was ahead of any courier from the Emperor at Vienna he did not doubt, but, on the other hand, the Countess of Berg and Lady Featherstone had the advantage of him by some four days. There would be no lack of money to hinder him; there would be no scruple as to the means. Wogan remembered the moment in his bedroom when he had seen the dagger bright in the moon's rays. If he could not be arrested, there were other ways to stop him. Accidents may happen to any man.

However, he rode unhindered with the Prince's commission safe against his breast. He felt the paper a hundred times a day to make sure that it was not stolen nor lost, nor reduced to powder by a miracle. Day by day his fears diminished, since day by day he drew a day's journey nearer to Schlestadt. The paper became a talisman in his thoughts,—a thing endowed with magic properties to make him invisible like the cloak or cap of the fairy tales. Those few lines in writing not a week back had seemed an unattainable prize,

A. E. W. Mason

yet he had them; and so now they promised him that other unattainable thing, the enlargement of the Princess. It was in his nature, too, to grow buoyant in proportion to the difficulties of his task. He rode forward, therefore, with a good heart, and one sombre evening of rain came to a village some miles beyond Augsburg.

The village was a straggling half-mile of low cottages, lost as it were on the level of a wide plain. Across this plain, bare but for a few lines of poplars and stunted willow-trees, Wogan had ridden all the afternoon; and so little did the thatched cottages break the monotony of the plain's appearance, that though he had had the village within his vision all that while, he came upon it unawares. The dusk was gathering, and already through the tiny windows the meagre lights gleamed upon the road and gave to the falling raindrops the look of steel beads. Four days would now bring Wogan to Schlestadt. The road was bad and full of holes. He determined to go no farther that night if he could find a lodging in the village, and coming upon a man who stood in his path he stopped his horse.

"Is there an inn where a traveller may sleep?" he asked.

"Assuredly," replied the man, "and find forage for his horse. The last house—but I will myself show your Honour the way."

"There is no need, my friend, that you should take a colic," said Wogan.

"I shall earn enough drink to correct the colic," said the man. He had a sack over his head and shoulders to protect him from the rain, and stepped out in front of Wogan's horse. They came to the end of the street and passed on into the open darkness. About twenty yards farther a house stood by itself at the roadside, but there were only lights in one or two of the upper windows, and it held out no promise of hospitality. In front of it, however, the man stopped; he opened the door and halloaed into the passage. Wogan stopped too, and above his head something creaked and groaned like a gibbet in the wind. He looked up and saw a sign-board glimmering in the dusk with a new coat of white paint. He had undoubtedly come to the inn, and he dismounted.

The landlord advanced at that moment to the door.

"My man," said he, "will take your horse to the stable;" and the fellow who had guided Wogan led the horse off.

"Oh, is he your man?" said Wogan. "Ah!" And he followed the landlord into the house.

It was not only the sign-board which had been newly painted, for in the narrow passage the landlord stopped Wogan.

"Have a care, sir," said he; "the walls are wet. It will be best if you stand still while I go forward and bring a light."

He went forward in the dark and opened a door at the end of the passage. A glow of ruddy light came through the doorway, and Wogan caught a glimpse of a brick-floored kitchen and a great open chimney and one or two men on a bench before the fire. Then the door was again closed. The closing of the door seemed to Wogan a churlish act.

"The hospitality," said he to himself, "which plants a man in the road so that a traveller on a rainy night may not miss his bed should at least leave the kitchen door open. Why should I stay here in the dark?"

Wogan went forward, and from the careful way in which he walked,—a way so careful and stealthy indeed that his footsteps made no sound,—it might have been inferred that he believed the floor to be newly painted too. He had, at all events, no such scruples about the kitchen door, for he seized the handle and flung it open quickly. He was met at once by a cold draught of wind. A door opposite and giving onto a yard at the back had been opened at precisely the same moment; and as Wogan stepped quickly in at his door a man stepped quickly out by the door opposite and was lost in the darkness.

"What! Are you going?" the landlord cried after him as he turned from the fire at which he was lighting a candle.

"Wilhelm has a wife and needs must," at once said a woman who was reaching down some plates from a dresser.

The landlord turned towards the passage and saw Wogan in the doorway.

"You found your way, sir," said he, looking at Wogan anxiously.

"Nor are your walls any poorer of paint on that account," said Wogan as he took his wet cloak and flung it over a chair.

The landlord blew out his candle and busied himself about laying the table. A great iron pot swung over the fire by a chain, and the lid danced on the top and allowed a savoury odour to escape. Wogan sat himself down before the fire and his clothes began to steam.

"You laugh at my paint, sir," said the landlord. He was a fat, good-humoured-looking man, communicative in his manner as a Boniface should be, and his wife was his very complement. "You laugh at my paint, but it is, after all, a very important thing. What is a great lady without her rouge-pot, when you come to think of it? It is the same with an inn. It must wear paint if it is to attract attention and make a profit."

"There is philosophy in the comparison," said Wogan.

"Sir, an innkeeper cannot fail of philosophy if he has his eyes and a spark of intelligence. The man who took refuge in a tub because the follies of his fellows so angered him was the greatest fool of them all. He should have kept an inn on the road to Athens, for then the follies would have put money into his pocket and made him laugh instead of growl."

His wife came over to the fireplace and lifted the lid of the pot.

"The supper is ready," said she.

"And perhaps, sir, while you are eating it you can think of a name for my inn."

"Why, it has a sign-board already," said Wogan, "and a name, too, I suppose."

"It has a sign-board, but without a device," said the landlord, and while Wogan drew a chair to the table he explained his predicament.

"There is another inn five miles along the road, and travellers prefer to make their halt there. They will not stop here. My father, sir, set it all down to paint. It was his dream, sir, to paint the house from floor to ceiling; his last words bade me pinch and save until I could paint. Well, here is the house

A. E. W. Mason

painted, and I am anxious for a new device and name which shall obliterate the memory of the other. 'The Black Eagle' is its old name. Ask any traveller familiar with the road between Augsburg and Schlestadt, and he will counsel you to avoid 'The Black Eagle.' You are travelling to Schlestadt, perhaps."

Wogan had started ever so slightly.

"To Strasbourg," he said, and thereafter ate his supper in silence, taking count with himself. "My friend," so his thoughts ran, "the sooner you reach Schlestadt the better. Here are you bleating like a sheep at a mere chance mention of your destination. You have lived too close with this fine scheme of yours. You need your friends."

Wogan began to be conscious of an unfamiliar sense of loneliness. It grew upon him that evening while he sat at the table; it accompanied him up the stairs to bed. Other men of his age were now seated comfortably by their own hearths, while he was hurrying about Europe, a vagabond adventurer, risking his life for—and at once the reason why he was risking his life rose up to convict him a grumbler.

The landlord led him into a room in the front of the house which held a great canopied bed and little other furniture. There was not even a curtain to the window. Wogan raised his candle and surveyed the dingy walls.

"You have not spent much of your new paint on your guest-room, my friend."

"Sir, you have not marked the door," said his host, reproachfully.

"True," said Wogan, with a yawn; "the door is admirably white."

"The frame of the door does not suffer in a comparison." The landlord raised and lowered his candle that Wogan might see.

"I do not wish to be unjust to the frame of the door," said Wogan, and he drew off his boots. The landlord bade his guest good-night and descended the stairs.

Wogan, being a campaigner, was methodical even though lost in reflection. He was reflecting now why in the world he should lately have become sensible of loneliness; but at the same time he put the Prince's letter beneath his pillow and a sheathed hunting-knife beside the letter. He had always been lonely, and the fact had never troubled him; he placed a chair on the left of the bed and his candle on the chair. Besides, he was not really lonely, having a host of friends whom he had merely to seek out; he took the charges from his pistol lest they should be damp, and renewed them and placed the pistols by the candle. He had even begun to pity himself for his loneliness, and pity of that sort, he recognised, was a discreditable quality; the matter was altogether very disquieting. He propped his sword against the chair and undressed. Wogan cast back in his memories for the first sensations of loneliness. They were recent, since he had left Ohlau, indeed. He opened the window; the rain splashed in on the sill, pattered in the street puddles below, and fell across the country with a continuous roar as though the level plain was a stretched drum. No; he had only felt lonely since he had come near to Schlestadt, since, in a word, he had deemed himself to have outstripped pursuit. He got into his bed and blew out the candle.

For a moment the room was black as pitch, then on his left side the darkness thinned at one point and a barred square of grey became visible; the square of grey was the window. Wogan understood that his loneliness came upon him with

A. E. W. Mason

the respite from his difficulties, and concluded that, after all, it was as well that he had not a comfortable fireside whereby to sun himself. He turned over on his right side and saw the white door and its white frame. The rain made a dreary sound outside the window, but in three days he would be at Schlestadt. Besides he fell asleep.

And in a little he dreamed. He dreamed that he was swinging on a gibbet before the whole populace of Innspruck, that he died to his bewilderment without any pain whatever, but that pain came to him after he was quite dead,—not bodily pain at all, but an anguish of mind because the chains by which he was hanged would groan and creak, and the populace, mistaking that groaning for his cries, scoffed at him and ridiculed his King for sending to rescue the Princess Clementina a marrowless thing that could not die like a man. Wogan stirred in his sleep and waked up. The rain had ceased, and a light wind blew across the country. Outside the sign-board creaked and groaned upon its stanchion. Once he became aware of that sound he could no longer sleep for listening to it; and at last he sprang out of bed, and leaning out of the window lifted the sign-board off the stanchion and into his bedroom.

It was a plain white board without any device on it. "True," thought Wogan, "the man wants a new name for his inn." He propped the board against the left side of his bed, since that was nearest to the window, got between the sheets, and began to think over names. He turned on his right side and fell asleep again.

He was not to sleep restfully that night. He waked again, but very slowly, and without any movement of his body. He lay with his face towards the door, dreamily considering that the landlord, for all his pride in his new paint, had employed a bad workman who had left a black strip of the door unpainted,—a fairly wide strip, too, which his host should never have overlooked.

Wogan was lazily determining to speak to the landlord about it when his half-awakened mind was diverted by a curious phenomenon, a delusion of the eyes such as he had known to have befallen him before when he had stared for a long while on any particular object: the strip of black widened and widened. Wogan waited for it to contract, as it would be sure to do. But it did not contract, and—so Wogan waked up completely.

He waked up with a shock of the heart, with all his senses startled and strained. But he had been gradually waking before, and so by neither movement nor cry did he betray that he was awake. He had not locked the door of his room; that widening strip of black ran vertically down from the lintel to the ground and between the white door and the white door frame. The door was being cautiously pushed open; the strip of black was the darkness of the passage coming through.

Wogan slid his hand beneath his pillow, and drew the knife from its sheath as silently as the door opened. The strip of black ceased to widen, there was a slight scuffling sound upon the floor which Wogan was at no loss to understand. It was the sound of a man crawling into the room upon his hands and knees.

Wogan lay on his side and felt grateful to his host,—an admirable man,—for he had painted his door white, and now he crawled through it on his hands and knees. No doubt he would crawl to the side of the bed; he did. To feel, no doubt, for Mr. Wogan's coat and breeches and any little letter which might be hiding in the pockets. But here Wogan was wrong. For he saw a dark thing suddenly on the counterpane at the

A. E. W. Mason

edge of the bed. The dark thing travelled upwards very softly; it had four fingers and a thumb. It was, no doubt, travelling towards the pillow, and as soon as it got there— but Wogan watching that hand beneath his dosed eyelids had again to admit that he was wrong. It did not travel towards the pillow; to his astonishment it stole across towards him, it touched his chest very gently, and then he understood. The hand was creeping upwards towards his throat.

Meanwhile Wogan had seen no face, though the face must be just below the level of the bed. He only saw the hand and the arm behind it. He moved as if in his sleep, and the hand disappeared. As if in his sleep, he flung out his left arm and felt for the sign-board standing beside his bed. The bed was soft. Wogan wanted something hard, and it had occurred to him that the sign-board would very well serve his turn. An idea, too, which seemed to him diverting, had presented itself to his mind.

With a loud sigh and a noisy movement such as a man halfway between wakefulness and sleep may make he flung himself over onto his left side. At the same moment he lifted the white sign-board onto the bed. It seemed that he could not rest on his left side, for he flung over again to his right and pulled the bedclothes over as he turned. The sign-board now lay flat upon the bed, but on the right side between himself and the man upon the floor. His mouth uttered a little murmur of contentment, he drew down the hand beneath the pillow, and in a second was breathing regularly and peacefully.

The hand crept onto the bed again and upwards, and suddenly lay spread out upon the board and quite still. Just for a second the owner of that hand had been surprised and paralysed by the unexpected. It was only that second which Wogan needed. He sat up, and with his right arm he drove his hunting knife down into the back of the hand and pinned it fast to the board; with his left he felt for, found, and gripped a mouth already open to cry out. He dropped his hunting knife, caught the intruder round the waist, lifted him onto the bed, and setting a knee upon his chest gagged him with an end of the sheet. The man fought wildly with his free hand, beating the air. Wogan knelt upon that arm with his other knee.

Wogan needed a rope, but since he had none he used the sheets and bound his prisoner to the bed. Then he got up and went to the door. The house was quite silent, quite dark. Wogan shut the door gently—there was no key in the lock— and bending over the bed looked into the face of his assailant. The face was twisted with pain, the whites of the eyes glared horribly, but Wogan could see that the man was his landlord.

He stood up and thought. There was another man who had met him in the village and had guided him to the inn; there was still a third who had gone out of the kitchen as Wogan had entered it; there was the wife, too, who might be awake.

Wogan crossed to the window and looked out. The window was perhaps twenty feet from the ground, but the stanchion was three feet below the window. He quickly put on his clothes, slipped the letter from under his pillow into a pocket, strapped his saddle-bag and lowered it from the window by a blanket. He had already one leg on the sill when a convulsive movement of the man on the bed made him stop. He climbed back into the room, drew the knife out of the board and out of the hand pinned to the board, and making a bandage wrapped the wound up.

"You must lie there till morning, my friend," Wogan whispered in his ear, "but here's a thing to console you. I

A. E. W. Mason

have found a name for your inn; I have painted the device upon your sign-board. The 'Inn of the Five Red Fingers.' There's never a passer-by but will stop to inquire the reason of so conspicuous a sign;" and Wogan climbed out of the window, lowered himself till he hung at the full length of his arms from the stanchion, and dropped on the ground. He picked up his saddle-bag and crept round the house to the stable. The door needed only a push to open it. In the hay-loft above he heard a man snoring. Mr. Wogan did not think it worth while to disturb him. He saddled his horse, walked it out into the yard, mounted, and rode quietly away.

He had escaped, but without much credit to himself.

"There was no key in the door," he thought. "I should have noticed it. Misset, the man of resources, would have tilted a chair backwards against that door with its top bar wedged beneath the door handle." Certainly Wogan needed Misset if he was to succeed in his endeavour. He was sunk in humiliation; his very promise to rescue the Princess shrank from its grandeur and became a mere piece of impertinence. But he still had his letter in his pocket, and in time that served to enhearten him. Only two more days, he thought. On the third night he would sleep in Schlestadt.

# CHAPTER VI

## WOGAN CONTINUES HIS JOURNEY

The next afternoon Wogan came to the town of Ulm.

"Gaydon," he said to himself as he watched its towers and the smoke curling upwards from its chimneys, "would go no further to-day with this letter in his pocket. Gaydon—the cautious Gaydon—would sleep in this town and in its most populous quarter. Gaydon would put up at the busiest inn. Charles Wogan will follow Gaydon's example."

Wogan rode slowly through the narrow streets of gabled houses until he came to the market square. The square was frequented; its great fountain was playing; citizens were taking the air with their wives and children; the chief highway of the town ran through it; on one side stood the frescoed Rathhaus, and opposite to it there was a spacious inn. Wogan drew up at the doorway and saw that the hall was encumbered with baggage. "Gaydon would stop here," said he, and he dismounted. The porter came forward and took his horse.

"I need a room," said Wogan, and he entered the house. There were people going up and down the stairs. While he was unstrapping his valise in his bedroom, a servant with an

A. E. W. Mason

apron about his waist knocked at the door and inquired whether he could help him.

"No," said Wogan; and he thought with more confidence than ever, "here, to be sure, is where Gaydon would sleep."

He supped at the ordinary in the company of linen merchants and travellers, and quite recovered his spirits. He smoked a pipe of tobacco on a bench under the trees of the square, and giving an order that he should be called at five went up to his bedroom.

There was a key in the lock of the door, which Wogan turned; he also tilted a chair and wedged the handle. He opened the window and looked out. His room was on the first floor and not very high from the ground. A man might possibly climb through the window. Gaydon would assuredly close the shutters and the window, so that no one could force an entrance without noise. Wogan accordingly did what Gaydon would assuredly have done, and when he blew out his candle found himself in consequence in utter darkness. No glimmer of light was anywhere visible. He had his habits like another, and one of them was to sleep without blinds or curtains drawn. His present deflection from this habit made him restless; he was tired, he wished above all things to sleep, but sleep would not come. He turned from one side to the other, he punched his pillows, he tried to sleep with his head low, and when that failed with his head high.

He resigned himself in the end to a sleepless night, and lying in his bed drew some comfort from the sound of voices and the tread of feet in the passages and the rooms about him. These, at all events, were companionable, and they assured him of safety. But in a while they ceased, and he was left in a silence as absolute as the darkness. He endured this silence for perhaps half an hour, and then all manner of infinitesimal sounds began to stir about him. The lightest of footsteps moved about his bed, faint sighs breathed from very close at hand, even his name was softly whispered. He sat suddenly up in his bed, and at once all these sounds became explained to him. They came from the street and the square outside the window. So long as he sat up they were remote, but the moment he lay down again they peopled the room.

"Sure," said Wogan, "here is a lesson for architects. Build no shutters to a house when the man that has to live in it has a spark of imagination, else will he go stark raving mad before the mortar's dry. Window shutters are window shutters, but they are the doors of Bedlam as well. Now Gaydon should have slept in this room. Gaydon's a great man. Gaydon has a great deal of observation and common sense, and was never plagued with a flim-flam of fancies. To be sure, I need Gaydon, but since I have not Gaydon, I'll light a candle."

With that Wogan got out of bed. He had made himself so secure with his key and his tilted chair and his shutters that he had not thought of placing his candle by his bedside. It stood by his looking-glass on the table. Now the room was so pitch dark that Wogan could do no more than guess at the position even of the window. The table, he remembered, was not far from the door, and the door was at some distance from his bed, and in the wall on his right. He moved forward in the darkness with his hands in front of him, groping for the table. The room was large; in a little his hands touched something, and that something was a pillar of the bed. He had missed his way in his bedroom. Wogan laughed to himself and started off again; and the next thing which his outstretched hands touched was a doorknob. The table should now be a little way to his left. He was just turning away in that direction, when it occurred to him that he ought to have felt the rim of the top bar of his tilted chair underneath the door-handle. He stooped down and felt for

A. E. W. Mason

the chair; there was no chair, and he stood very still.

The fears bred of imagination had now left him; he was restored by the shock of an actual danger. He leaned forward quietly and felt if the key was still in the lock. But there was no lock to this door. Wogan felt the surface of the door; it was of paper. It was plainly the door of a cupboard in the wall, papered after the same pattern as the wall, which by the flickering light of his single candle he had overlooked.

He opened the door and stretched out his arms into the cupboard. He touched something that moved beneath his hand, a stiff, short crop of hair, the hair of a man's head. He drew his arm away as though an adder had stung it; he did not utter a cry or make a movement. He stood for a moment paralysed, and during that moment a strong hand caught him by the throat.

Wogan was borne backwards, his assailant sprang at him from the cupboard, he staggered under the unexpected vigour of the attack, he clutched his enemy, and the two men came to the ground with a crash. Even as he fell Wogan thought, "Gaydon would never have overlooked that cupboard."

It was the only reflection, however, for which he could afford time. He was undermost, and the hand at his throat had the grip of a steel glove. He fought with blows from his fists and his bent knees; he twisted his legs about the legs of his enemy; he writhed his body if so he might dislodge him; he grappled wildly for his throat. But all the time his strength grew less; he felt that his temples were swelling, and it seemed to him that his eyes must burst. The darkness of the room was spotted with sparks of fire; the air was filled with a continuous roar like a million chariots in a street. He saw the face of his chosen woman, most reproachful and yet kind, gazing at him from behind the bars which now would never be broken, and then there came a loud banging at the door. The summons surprised them both, so hotly had they been engaged, so unaware were they of the noise which their fall had made.

Wogan felt his assailant's hand relax and heard him say in a low muffled voice, "It is nothing. Go to bed! I fell over a chair in the dark."

That momentary relaxation was, he knew, his last chance. He gathered his strength in a supreme effort, lurched over onto his left side, and getting his right arm free swung it with all his strength in the direction of the voice. His clenched fist caught his opponent full under the point of the chin, and the hand at Wogan's throat clutched once and fell away limp as an empty glove. Wogan sat up on the floor and drew his breath. That, after all, was more than his antagonist was doing. The knocking at the door continued; Wogan could not answer it, he had not the strength. His limbs were shaking, the sweat clotted his hair and dripped from his face. But his opponent was quieter still. At last he managed to gather his legs beneath him, to kneel up, to stand shakily upon his feet. He could no longer mistake the position of the door; he tottered across to it, removed the chair, and opened it.

The landlord with a couple of servants stepped back as Wogan showed himself to the light of their candles. Wogan heard their exclamations, though he did not clearly understand them, for his ears still buzzed. He saw their startled faces, but only dimly, for he was dazzled by the light. He came back into the room, and pointing to his assailant,—a sturdy, broad man, who now sat up opening and shutting his eyes in a dazed way,—"Who is that?" he asked, gasping rather than speaking the words.

"Who is that?" repeated the landlord, staring at Wogan.

　　　　　　A. E. W. Mason

"Who is that?" said Wogan, leaning against the bed-post.

"Why, sir, your servant. Who should he be?"

Wogan was silent for a little, considering as well as his rambling wits allowed this new development.

"Ah!" said Wogan, "he came here with me?" "Yes, since he is your servant."

The landlord was evidently mystified; he was no less evidently speaking with sincerity. Wogan reflected that to proffer a charge against the assailant would involve his own detention in Ulm.

"To be sure," said he, "I know. This is my servant. That is precisely what I mean." His wits were at work to find a way out of his difficulty. "This is my servant? What then?" he asked fiercely.

"But I don't understand," said the landlord.

"You don't understand!" cried Wogan. "Was there ever such a landlord? He does not understand. This is my servant, I tell you."

"Yes, sir, but—but—"

"Well?"

"We were roused—there was a noise—a noise of men fighting."

"There would have been no noise," said Wogan, trium-phantly, "if you had prepared a bed for my servant. He would not have crept into my cupboard to sleep off his drunkenness."

"But, sir, there was a bed."

"You should have seen that he was carried to it. As it is, here have I been driven to beat him and to lose my night's rest in consequence. It is not fitting. I do not think that your inn is well managed."

Wogan expressed his indignation with so majestic an air that the landlord was soon apologising for having disturbed a gentleman in the proper exercise of belabouring his valet.

"We will carry the fellow away," said he.

"You will do nothing of the kind," said Wogan. "He shall get back into his cupboard and there he shall remain till daybreak. Come, get up!"

Wogan's self-appointed valet got to his feet. There was no possibility of an escape for him since there were three men between him and the door. On the other hand, obedience to Wogan might save him from a charge of attempted theft.

"In with you," said Wogan, and the man obeyed. His head no doubt was still spinning from the blow, and he had the stupid look of one dazed.

"There is no lock to the door," said the landlord.

"There is no need of a lock," said Wogan, "so long as one has a chair. The fellow will do very well till the morning. But I will take your three candles, for it is not likely that I shall sleep."

Wogan smoked his pipe all the rest of the night, reclining on a couple of chairs in front of the cupboard. In the morning he made his valet walk three miles by his horse's side. The man

A. E. W. Mason

dared not disobey, and when Wogan finally let him go he was so far from the town that, had he confederates there, he could do no harm.

Wogan continued his journey. Towns, it was proved, were no safer to him than villages. He began to wonder how it was that no traps had been laid for him on the earlier stages of his journey, and he suddenly hit upon the explanation. "It was that night," said he to himself, "when the Prince sat by the Countess with the list of my friends in his hands. The names were all erased but three, and against those three was that other name of Schlestadt. No doubt the Countess while she bent over her harp-strings took a look at that list. I must run the gauntlet into Schlestadt."

Towards evening he came to Stuttgart and rode through the Schloss Platz and along the Koenigstrasse. Wogan would not sleep there, since there the Duke of Wuertemberg held his court, and in that court the Countess of Berg was very likely to have friends. He rode onwards through the valley along the banks of the Nesen brook until he came to its junction with the Neckar.

A mile farther a wooden mill stood upon the river-bank, beyond the mill was a tavern, and beyond the tavern stood a few cottages. At some distance from the cottages along the road, Wogan could see a high brick wall, and over the top the chimneys and the slate roof of a large house. Wogan stopped at the tavern. It promised no particular comfort, it was a small dilapidated house; but it had the advantage that it was free from new paint. It seemed to Wogan, however, wellnigh useless to take precautions in the choice of a lodging; danger leaped at him from every quarter. For this last night he must trust to his luck; and besides there was the splash of the water falling over the mill-dam. It was always something to Wogan to fall asleep with that sound in his ears. He dismounted accordingly, and having ordered his supper asked for a room.

"You will sleep here?" exclaimed his host.

"I will at all events lie in bed," returned Wogan.

The innkeeper took a lamp and led the way up a narrow winding stair.

"Have a care, sir," said he; "the stairs are steep."

"I prefer them steep."

"I am afraid that I keep the light from you, but there is no room for two to walk abreast."

"It is an advantage. I do not like to be jostled on the stairs."

The landlord threw open a door at the top of the stairs.

"The room is a garret," he said in apology.

"So long as it has no cupboards it will serve my turn."

"Ah! you do not like cupboards."

"They fill a poor man with envy of those who have clothes to hang in them."

Wogan ascertained that there were no cupboards. There was a key, too, in the lock, and a chest of drawers which could be moved very suitably in front of the door.

"It is a good garret," said Wogan, laying down his bag upon a chair.

A. E. W. Mason

"The window is small," continued the landlord.

"One will be less likely to fall out," said Wogan. One would also, he thought, be less likely to climb in. He looked out of the window. It was a good height from the ground; there was no stanchion or projection in the wall, and it seemed impossible that a man could get his shoulders through the opening. Wogan opened the window to try it, and the sound of someone running came to his ears.

"Oho!" said he, but he said it to himself, "here's a man in a mighty hurry."

A mist was rising from the ground; the evening, too, was dark. Wogan could see no one in the road below, but he heard the footsteps diminishing into a faint patter. Then they ceased altogether. The man who ran was running in the direction of Stuttgart.

"Yes, your garret will do," said Wogan, in quite a different voice. He had begun to think that this night he would sleep, and he realised now that he must not. The man might be running on his own business, but this was the last night before Wogan would reach his friends. Stuttgart was only three miles away. He could take no risks, and so he must stay awake with his sword upon his knees. Had his horse been able to carry him farther, he would have ridden on, but the horse was even more weary than its master. Besides, the narrow staircase made his room an excellent place to defend.

"Get my supper," said he, "for I am very tired."

"Will your Excellency sup here?" asked the landlord.

"By no manner of means," returned Wogan, who had it in his mind to spy out the land. "I detest nothing so much as my own company."

He went downstairs into the common room and supped off a smoked ham and a bottle of execrable wine. While he ate a man came in and sat him down by the fire. The man had a hot, flushed face, and when he saluted Wogan he could hardly speak.

"You have been running," said Wogan, politely.

"Sir, running is a poor man's overcoat for a chilly evening; besides it helps me to pay with patience the price of wine for vinegar;" and the fellow called the landlord.

Presently two other men entered, and taking a seat by the fire chatted together as though much absorbed in their private business. These two men wore swords.

"You have a good trade," said Wogan to the landlord.

"The mill brings me custom."

The door opened as the landlord spoke, and a big loud-voiced man cheerily wished the company good evening. The two companions at the fire paid no heed to the civility; the third, who had now quite recovered his breath, replied to it. Wogan pushed his plate away and called for a pipe. He thought it might perhaps prove well worth his while to study his landlord's clients before he retired up those narrow stairs. The four men gave no sign of any common agreement, nor were they at all curious as to Wogan. If they spoke at all, they spoke as strangers speak. But while Wogan was smoking his first pipe a fifth man entered, and he just gave one quick glance at Wogan. Wogan behind a cloud of tobacco-smoke saw the movement of the head and detected the look. It might signify nothing but curiosity, of course, but

Wogan felt glad that the stairs were narrow. He finished his pipe and was knocking out the ashes when it occurred to him that he had seen that fifth man before; and Wogan looked at him more carefully, and though the fellow was disguised by the growth of a beard he recognised him. It was the servant whom Wogan had seen one day in the Countess of Berg's livery of green and red galloping along the road to Prague.

"I know enough now," thought Wogan. "I can go to bed. The staircase is a pretty place with which we shall all be more familiar in an hour or two." He laughed quietly to himself with a little thrill of enjoyment. His fatigue had vanished. He was on the point of getting up from the table when the two men by the fire looked round towards the last comer and made room for him upon their settle. But he said, "I find the room hot, and will stay by the door."

Wogan changed his mind at the words; he did not get up. On the contrary, he filled his pipe a second time very thoughtfully. He had stayed too long in the room, it seemed; the little staircase was, after all, likely to prove of no service. He did not betray himself by any start or exclamation, he did not even look up, but bending his head over his pipe he thought over the disposition of the room. The fireplace was on his right; the door was opposite to him; the window in the wall at his left. The window was high from the ground and at some distance. On the other hand, he had certain advantages. He was in a corner, he had the five men in front of him, and between them and himself stood a solid table. A loaded pistol was in his belt, his sword hung at his side, and his hunting knife at his waist. Still the aspect of affairs was changed.

"Five men," thought he, "upon a narrow staircase are merely one man who has to be killed five times, but five men in a room are five simultaneous assailants. I need O'Toole here, I need O'Toole's six feet four and the length of his arm and the weight of him—these things I need—but are there five or only four?" And he was at once aware that the two men at the fire had ceased to talk of their business. No one, indeed, was speaking at all, and no one so much as shuffled a foot. Wogan raised his head and proceeded to light his pipe; and he saw that all the five men were silently watching him, and it seemed to him that those five pairs of eyes were unnaturally bright.

However, he appeared to be entirely concerned with his pipe, which, however hard he puffed at it, would not draw. No doubt the tobacco was packed too tight in the bowl. He loosened it, and when he had loosened it the pipe had gone out. He fumbled in his pocket and discovered in the breast of his coat a letter. This letter he glanced through to make sure that it was of no importance, and having informed himself upon the point he folded it into a long spill and walked over to the hearth.

The five pairs of eyes followed his movements. He, however, had no attention to spare. He bent down, lit his spill in the flame, and deliberately lighted his pipe. The tobacco rose above the rim of the bowl like a head of ale in a tankard. Wogan, still holding the burning spill in his right hand, pressed down the tobacco with the little finger of his left, and lighted the pipe again. By this time his spill had burned down to his fingers. He dropped the end into the fire and walked back to his seat. The five pairs of eyes again turned as he turned. He stumbled at a crack in the floor, fell against the table with a clatter of his sword, and rolled noisily into his seat. When he sat down a careful observer might have noticed that his pistol was now at full cock.

He had barely seated himself when the polite man, who had come first hot and short of breath into the room, crossed the

A. E. W. Mason

floor and leaning over the table said with a smile and the gentlest voice, "I think, sir, you ought to know that we are all very poor men."

"I, too," replied Wogan, "am an Irishman."

The polite man leaned farther across the table; his voice became wheedling in its suavity. "I think you ought to know that we are all very poor men."

"The repetition of the remark," said Wogan, "argues certainly a poverty of ideas."

"We wish to become less poor."

"It is an aspiration which has pushed many men to creditable feats."

"You can help us."

"My prayers are at your disposal," said Wogan.

"By more than your prayers;" and he added in a tone of apology, "there are five of us."

"Then I have a guinea apiece for you," and Wogan thrust the table a little away from him to search his pockets. It also gave him more play.

"We do not want your money. You have a letter which we can coin."

Wogan smiled.

"There, sir, you are wrong."

The polite man waved the statement aside. "A letter from Prince Sobieski," said he.

"I had such a letter a minute ago, but I lit my pipe with it under your nose."

The polite man stepped back; his four companions started to their feet.

The servant from Ohlau cried out with an oath, "It's a lie."

Wogan shrugged his shoulders and crossed his legs.

"Here's a fine world," said he. "A damned rag of a lackey gives a gentleman the lie."

"You will give me the letter," said the polite man, coming round the table. He held his right hand behind his back.

"You can sweep up the ashes from the hearth," said Wogan, who made no movement of any kind. The polite man came close to his side; Wogan let him come. The polite man stretched out his left hand towards Wogan's pocket. Wogan knocked the hand away, and the man's right arm swung upwards from behind his back with a gleaming pistol in the hand. Wogan was prepared for him; he had crossed his legs to be prepared, and as the arm came round he kicked upwards from the knee. The toe of his heavy boot caught the man upon the point of the elbow. His arm was flung up; the pistol exploded and then dropped onto the floor. That assailant was for the time out of action, but at the same moment the lackey came running across the floor, his shoulders thrust forward, a knife in his hand.

Wogan had just time to notice that the lackey's coat was open at his breast. He stood up, leaned over the table, caught the

A. E. W. Mason

lapels one in each hand as the fellow rushed at him, and lifting the coat up off his shoulders violently jammed it backwards down his arms as though he would strip him of it. The lackey stood with his arms pinioned at his elbows for a second. During that second Wogan drew his hunting knife from his belt and drove it with a terrible strength into the man's chest.

"There's a New Year's gift for your mistress, the Countess of Berg," cried Wogan; and the lackey swung round with the force of the blow and then hopped twice in a horrible fashion with his feet together across the room as though returning to his place, and fell upon the floor, where he lay twisting.

The polite man was nursing his elbow in a corner; there were three others left,—the man with the cheery voice, who had no weapon but a knobbed stick, and the companions on the settle. These two had swords and had drawn them. They leaped over the lackey's body and rushed at Wogan one a little in advance of the other. Wogan tilted the heavy table and flung it over to make a barricade in front of him. It fell with a crash, and the lower rim struck upon the instep of the leader and pinned his foot. His companion drew back; he himself uttered a cry and wrenched at his foot. Wogan with his left hand drew his sword from the scabbard, and with the same movement passed it through his opponent's body. The man stood swaying, pinned there by his foot and held erect. Then he made one desperate lunge, fell forward across the barricade, and hung there. Wogan parried the lunge; the sword fell from the man's hand and clattered onto the floor within the barricade. Wogan stamped upon it with his heel and snapped the blade. He had still two opponents; and as they advanced again he suddenly sprung onto the edge of the table, gave one sweeping cut in a circle with his sword, and darted across the room. The two men gave ground; Wogan passed between them. Before they could strike at his back he was facing them again. He had no longer his barricade, but on the other hand his shoulders were against the door.

The swordsman crossed blades with him, and at the first pass Wogan realised with dismay that his enemy was a swordsman in knowledge as well as in the possession of the weapon. He had a fencer's suppleness of wrist and balance of body; he pressed Wogan hard and without flurry. The blade of his sword made glittering rings about Wogan's, and the point struck at his breast like an adder.

Wogan was engaged with his equal if not with his better. He was fighting for his life with one man, and he would have to fight for it with two, nay, with three. For over his opponent's shoulder he saw his first polite antagonist cross to the table and pick up from the ground the broken sword. One small consolation Wogan had; the fellow picked it up with his left hand, his right elbow was still useless. But even that consolation lasted him for no long time, for out of the tail of his eye he could see the big fellow creeping up with his stick raised along the wall at his right.

Wogan suddenly pressed upon his opponent, delivering thrust upon thrust, and forced him to give ground. As the swordsman drew back, Wogan swept his weapon round and slashed at the man upon his right. But the stroke was wide of its mark, and the big man struck at the sword with his stick, struck with all his might, so that Wogan's arm tingled from the wrist to the shoulder. That, however, was the least part of the damage the stick did. It broke Wogan's sword short off at the hilt.

Both men gave a cry of delight. Wogan dropped the hilt.

"I have a loaded pistol, my friends; you have forgotten that," he cried, and plucked the pistol from his belt. At the same moment he felt behind him with his left hand for the knob of the door. He fired at the swordsman and his pistol missed, he flung it at the man with the stick, and as he flung it he sprang to the right, threw open the door, darted into the passage, and slammed the door to.

It was the work of a second. The men sprang at him as he opened the door; as he slammed it close a sword-point pierced the thin panel and bit like a searing iron into his shoulder. Wogan uttered a cry; he heard an answering shout in the room, he clung to the handle, setting his foot against the wall, and was then stabbed in the back. For his host was waiting for him in the passage.

Wogan dropped the door-handle and turned. That last blow had thrown him into a violent rage. Possessed by rage, he was no longer conscious of wounds or danger; he was conscious only of superhuman strength. The knife was already lifted to strike again. Wogan seized the wrist which held the knife, grappled with the innkeeper, and caught him about the body. The door of the room, now behind him, was flung violently open. Wogan, who was wrought to a frenzy, lifted up the man he wrestled with, and swinging round hurled him headlong through the doorway. The three men were already on the threshold. The new missile bounded against them, tumbled them one against the other, and knocked them sprawling and struggling on the floor.

Wogan burst into a laugh of exultation; he saw his most dangerous enemy striving to disentangle himself and his sword.

"Aha, my friend," he cried, "you handle a sword very prettily, but I am the better man at cock-shies." And shutting the door to be ran down the passage into the road.

He had seen a house that afternoon with a high garden wall about it a quarter of a mile away. Wogan ran towards it. The mist was still thick, but he now began to feel his strength failing. He was wounded in the shoulder, he was stabbed in the back, and from both wounds the blood was flowing warm. Moreover, he looked backwards once over his shoulder and saw a lantern dancing in the road. He kept doggedly running, though his pace slackened; he heard a shout and an answering shout behind him. He stumbled onto his knees, picked himself up, and staggered on, labouring his breath, dizzy. He stumbled again and fell, but as he fell he struck against the sharp corner of the wall. If he could find an entrance into the garden beyond that wall! He turned off the road to the left and ran across a field, keeping close along the side of the wall. He came to another corner and turned to the right. As he turned he heard voices in the road. The pursuers had stopped and were searching with the lantern for traces of his passage. He ran along the back of the wall, feeling for a projection, a tree, anything which would enable him to climb it. The wall was smooth, and though the branches of trees swung and creaked above his head, their stems grew in the garden upon the other side. He was pouring with sweat, his breath whistled, in his ears he had the sound of innumerable armies marching across the earth, but he stumbled on. And at last, though his right side brushed against the wall, he none the less struck against it also with his chest. He was too dazed for the moment to understand what had happened; all the breath he had left was knocked clean out of his body; he dropped in a huddle on the ground.

In a little he recovered his breath; he listened and could no longer hear any sound of voices; he began to consider. He reached a hand out in front of him and touched the wall; he reached out a hand to the right of him and touched the wall again. The wall projected then abruptly and made a right angle.

A. E. W. Mason

Now Wogan had spent his boyhood at Rathcoffey among cliffs and rocks. This wall, he reflected, could not be more than twelve feet high. Would his strength last out? He came to the conclusion that it must.

He took off his heavy boots and flung them one by one over the wall. Then he pulled off his coat at the cost of some pain and an added weakness, for the coat was stuck to his wounds and had roughly staunched them. He could feel the blood again soaking his shirt. There was all the more need, then, for hurry. He stood up, jammed his back into the angle of the wall, stretched out his arms on each side, pressing with his elbows and hands, and then bending his knees crossed his legs tailor fashion, and set the soles of his stockinged feet firmly against the bricks on each side. He was thus seated as it were upon nothing, but retaining his position by the pressure of his arms and feet and his whole body. Still retaining this position, very slowly, very laboriously, he worked himself up the angle, stopping now and then to regain his breath, now and then slipping back an inch. But he mounted towards the top, and after a while the back of his head no longer touched the bricks. His head was above the coping of the wall.

It was at this moment that he saw the lantern again, just at the corner where he had turned. The lantern advanced slowly; it was now held aloft, now close to the ground. Wogan was very glad he had thrown his boots and coat into the garden. He made a few last desperate struggles; he could now place the palms of his hands behind him upon the coping, and he hoisted himself up and sat on the wall.

The lantern was nearer to him; he lay flat upon his face on the coping, and then lowering himself upon the garden side to the full length of his arms, he let go. He fell into a litter of dead leaves, very soft and comfortable. He would not have exchanged them at that moment for the Emperor's own bed. He lay upon his back and saw the dark branches above his head grow bright and green. His pursuers were flashing their lantern on the other side; there was only the thickness of the wall between him and them. He could even hear them whispering and the brushing of their feet. He lay still as a mouse; and then the earth heaved up and fell away altogether beneath him. Wogan had fainted.

# CHAPTER VII

## WOGAN IS MISTAKEN FOR A MORE
## NOTABLE MAN

It was still night when Wogan opened his eyes, but the night was now clear of mist. There was no moon, however, to give him a guess at the hour. He lay upon his back among the dead leaves, and looking upwards at the stars, caught as it seemed in a lattice-work of branches, floated back into consciousness. He moved, and the movement turned him sick with pain. The knowledge of his wounds came to him and brought with it a clear recollection of the last three nights. The ever-widening black strip in the door on the first night, the clutch at his throat and the leap from the cupboard on the second, the silent watching of those five pairs of eyes on the third, and the lackey with the knife in his breast hopping with both feet horribly across the floor,—the horror of these recollections swept in upon him and changed him from a man into a timorous child. He lay and shuddered until in every creak of the branches he heard the whisper of an enemy, in every flutter of leaves across the lawn a stealthy footstep, and behind every tree-stem he caught the flap of a cloak.

Stiff and sore, he raised himself from the ground, he groped for his boots and coat, and putting them on moved cautiously through the trees, supporting himself from stem to stem. He came to the borders of a wide, smooth lawn, and on the farther side stood the house,—a long, two-storeyed house with level tiers of windows stretching to the right and the left, and a bowed tower in the middle. Through one of the windows in the ground-floor Wogan saw the spark of a lamp, and about that window a fan of yellow light was spread upon the lawn.

Wogan at this moment felt in great need of companionship. He stole across the lawn and looked into the room. An old gentleman with a delicate face, who wore his own white hair, was bending over a book at a desk. The room was warmly furnished, the door of the stove stood open, and Wogan could see the logs blazing merrily. A chill wind swept across the lawn, very drear and ghostly. Wogan crept closer to the window. A great boar-hound rose at the old man's feet and growled; then the old man rose, and crossing to the window pressed his face against the panes with his hands curved about his eyes. Wogan stepped forward and stood within the fan of light, spreading out his arms to show that he came as a supplicant and with no ill intent.

The old man, with a word to his hound, opened the window.

"Who is it?" he asked, and with a thrill not of fear but of expectation in his voice.

"A man wounded and in sore straits for his life, who would gladly sit for a few minutes by your fire before he goes upon his way."

The old man stood aside, and Wogan entered the room. He was spattered from head to foot with mud, his clothes were torn, his eyes sunken, his face was of a ghastly pallor and marked with blood.

A. E. W. Mason

"I am the Chevalier Warner," said Wogan, "a gentleman of Ireland. You will pardon me. But I have gone through so much these last three nights that I can barely stand;" and dropping into a chair he dragged it up to the door of the stove, and crouched there shivering.

The old man closed the window.

"I am Count Otto von Ahlen, and in my house you are safe as you are welcome."

He went to a sideboard, and filling a glass carried it to Wogan. The liquor was brandy. Wogan drank it as though it had been so much water. He was in that condition of fatigue when the most extraordinary events seem altogether commonplace and natural. But as he felt the spirit warming his blood, he became aware of the great difference between his battered appearance and that of the old gentleman with the rich dress and the white linen who stooped so hospitably above him, and he began to wonder at the readiness of the hospitality. Wogan might have been a thief, a murderer, for all Count Otto knew. Yet the Count, with no other protection than his dog, had opened his window, and at that late hour of the night had welcomed him without a word of a question.

"Sir," said Wogan, "my visit is the most unceremonious thing in the world. I plump in upon you in the dark of the morning, as I take it to be, and disturb you at your books without so much as knocking at the door."

"It is as well you did not knock at the door," returned the Count, "for my servants are long since in bed, and your knock would very likely have reached neither their ears nor mine." And he drew up a chair and sat down opposite to Wogan, bending forward with his hands upon his knees. The firelight played upon his pale, indoor face, and it seemed to

Wogan that he regarded his guest with a certain wistfulness. Wogan spoke his thought aloud,—

"Yet I might be any hedgerow rascal with a taste for your plate, and no particular scruples as to a life or two lying in the way of its gratification."

The Count smiled.

"Your visit is not so unexampled as you are inclined to think. Nearly thirty years ago a young man as you are came in just such a plight as you and stood outside this window at two o'clock of a dark morning. Even so early in my life I was at my books," and he smiled rather sadly. "I let him in and he talked to me for an hour of matters strange and dreamlike, and enviable to me. I have never forgotten that hour, nor to tell the truth have I ever ceased to envy the man who talked to me during it, though many years since he suffered a dreadful doom and vanished from among his fellows. I shall be glad, therefore, to hear your story if you have a mind to tell it me. The young man who came upon that other night was Count Philip Christopher von Koenigsmarck."

Wogan started at the mention of this name. It seemed strange that that fitful and brilliant man, whose brief, passionate, guilty life and mysterious end had made so much noise in the world, had crossed that lawn and stood before that window at just such an hour, and maybe had sat shivering in Wogan's very chair.

"I have no such story as Count Philip von Koenigsmarck no doubt had to tell," said Wogan.

"Chevalier," said Count Otto, with a nod of approval, "Koenigsmarck had the like reticence, though he was not always so discreet, I fear. The Princess Sophia Dorothea was at that time on a visit to the Duke of Wuertemberg at the palace in Stuttgart, but Koenigsmarck told me only that he had snatched a breathing space from the wars in the Low Countries and was bound thither again. Rumour told me afterwards of his fatal attachment. He sat where you sit, Chevalier, wounded as you are, a fugitive from pursuit. Even the stains and disorder of his plight could not disguise the singular beauty of the man or make one insensible to the charm of his manner. But I forget my duties," and he rose. "It would be as well, no doubt, if I did not wake my servants?" he suggested.

"Count Otto," returned Wogan, with a smile, "they have their day's work to-morrow."

The old man nodded, and taking a lamp from a table by the door went out of the room.

Wogan remained alone; the dog nuzzled at his hand; but it seemed to Wogan that there was another in the room besides himself and the dog. The sleeplessness and tension of the last few days, the fatigue of his arduous journey, the fever of his wounds, no doubt, had their effect upon him. He felt that Koenigsmarck was at his side; his eyes could almost discern a shadowy and beautiful figure; his ears could almost hear a musical vibrating voice. And the voice warned him,—in some strange unaccountable way the voice warned and menaced him.

"I fought, I climbed that wall, I crossed the lawn, I took refuge here for love of a queen. For love of a queen all my short life I lived. For love of a queen I died most horribly; and the queen lives, though it would have gone better with her had she died as horribly."

Wogan had once seen the lonely castle of Ahlden where that

queen was imprisoned; he had once caught a glimpse of her driving in the dusk across the heath surrounded by her guards with their flashing swords.

He sat chilled with apprehensions and forebodings. They crowded in upon his mind all the more terrible because he could not translate them into definite perils which beyond this and that corner of his life might await him. He was the victim of illusions, he assured himself, at which to-morrow safe in Schlestadt he would laugh. But to-night the illusions were real. Koenigsmarck was with him. Koenigsmarck was by some mysterious alchemy becoming incorporate with him. The voice which spoke and warned and menaced was as much his as Koenigsmarck's.

The old Count opened the door and heard Wogan muttering to himself as he crouched over the fire. The Count carried a basin of water in his hand and a sponge and some linen. He insisted upon washing Wogan's wounds and dressing them in a simple way.

"They are not deep," he said; "a few days' rest and a clever surgeon will restore you." He went from the room again and brought back a tray, on which were the remains of a pie, a loaf of bread, and some fruit.

"While you eat, Chevalier, I will mix you a cordial," said he, and he set about his hospitable work. "You ask me why I so readily opened my window to you. It was because I took you for Koenigsmarck himself come back as mysteriously as he disappeared. I did not think that if he came back now his hair would be as white, his shoulders as bent, as mine. Indeed, one cannot think of Koenigsmarck except as a youth. You had the very look of him as you stood in the light upon the lawn. You have, if I may say so, something of his gallant bearing and something of his grace."

Wogan could have heard no words more distressing to him at this moment.

"Oh, stop, sir. I pray you stop!" he cried out violently, and noting the instant he had spoken the surprise on Count Otto's face. "There, sir, I give you at once by my discourtesy an example of how little I merit a comparison with that courtly nobleman. Let me repair it by telling you, since you are willing to hear, of my night's adventure." And as he ate he told his story, omitting the precise object of his journey, the nature of the letter which he had burned, and any name which might give a clue to the secret of his enterprise.

The Count Otto listened with his eyes as well as his ears; he hung upon the words, shuddering at each danger that sprang upon Wogan, exclaiming in wonder at the shift by which he escaped from it, and at times he looked over towards his books with a glance of veritable dislike.

"To feel the blood run hot in one's veins, to be bedfellows with peril, to go gallantly forward hand in hand with endeavour," he mused and broke off. "See, I own a sword, being a gentleman. But it is a toy, an ornament; it stands over there in the corner from day to day, and my servants clean it from rust as they will. Now you, sir, I suppose—"

"My horse and my sword, Count," said Wogan, "when the pinch comes, they are one's only servants. It would be an ill business if I did not see to their wants."

The old man was silent for a while. Then he said timidly, "It was for a woman, no doubt, that you ran this hazard to-night?"

"For a woman, yes."

The Count folded his hands and leaned forward.

"Sir, a woman is a strange inexplicable thing to me. Their words, their looks, their graceful, delicate shapes, the motives which persuade them, the thoughts which their eyes conceal,—all these qualities make them beings of another world to me. I do envy men at times who can stand beside them, talk with them without fear, be intimate with them, and understand their intricate thoughts."

"Are there such men?" asked Wogan.

"Men who love, such as Count Koenigsmarck and yourself."

Wogan held up his hand with a cry.

"Count, such men, we are told, are the blindest of all. Did not Koenigsmarck prove it? As for myself, not even in that respect can I be ranked with Koenigsmarck. I am a mere man-at-arms, whose love-making is a clash of steel."

"But to-night—this risk you ran; you told me it was for a woman."

"For a woman, yes. For love of a woman, no, no, no!" he exclaimed with surprising violence. Then he rose from his chair.

"But I have stayed my time," said he, "you have never had a more grateful guest. I beg you to believe it."

Count Otto barely heard the words. He was absorbed in the fanciful dreams born of many long solitary evenings, and like most timid and uncommunicative men he made his confidence in a momentary enthusiasm to a stranger.

A. E. W. Mason

"Koenigsmarck spoke for an hour, mentioning no names, so that I who from my youth have lived apart could not make a guess. He spoke with a deal of passion; it seemed that one hour his life was paradise and the next a hell. Even as he spoke he was one instant all faith and the next all despair. One moment he was filled with his unworthiness and wonder that so noble a creature as a woman should bend her heart and lips from her heaven down to his earth. The next he could not conceive any man should be such a witless ass as to stake his happiness on the steadiness of so manifest a weathercock as a woman's favour. It was all very strange talk; it opened to me, just as when a fog lifts and rolls down again, a momentary vision of a world of colours in which I had no share; and to tell the truth it left me with a suspicion which has recurred again and again, that all my solitary years over my books, all the delights which the delicate turning of a phrase, or the chase and capture of an elusive idea, can bring to one may not be worth, after all, one single minute of living passion. Passion, Chevalier! There is a word of which I know the meaning only by hearsay. But I wonder at times, whatever harm it works, whether there can be any great thing without it. But you are anxious to go forward upon your way."

He again took up his lamp, and requesting Wogan to follow him, unlatched the window. Wogan, however, did not move.

"I am wondering," said he, "whether I might be yet deeper in your debt. I left behind me a sword."

Count Otto set his lamp down and took a sword from the corner of the room.

"I called it an ornament, and yet in other hands it might well prove a serviceable weapon. The blade is of Spanish steel. You will honour me by wearing it."

Wogan was in two minds with regard to the Count. On the one hand, he was most grateful; on the other he could not but think that over his books he had fallen into a sickly way of thought. He was quite ready, however, to wear his sword; moreover, when he had hooked the hanger to his belt he looked about the room.

"I had a pistol," he said carelessly, "a very useful thing is a pistol, more useful at times than a sword."

"I keep one in my bedroom," said the Count, setting the lamp down, "if you can wait the few moments it will take me to fetch it."

Mr. Wogan was quite able to wait. He was indeed sufficiently generous to tell Count Otto that he need not hurry. The Count fetched the pistol and took up the lamp again.

"Will you now follow me?"

Wogan looked straight before him into the air and spoke to no one in particular.

"A pistol is, to be sure, more useful than a sword; but there is just one thing more useful on an occasion than a pistol, and that is a hunting knife."

Count Otto shook his head.

"There, Chevalier, I doubt if I can serve you."

"But upon my word," said Wogan, picking up a carving-knife from the tray, "here is the very thing."

"It has no sheath."

A. E. W. Mason

Wogan was almost indignant at the suggestion that he would go so far as to ask even his dearest friend for a sheath. Besides, he had a sheath, and he fitted the knife into it.

"Now," said he, pleasantly, "all that I need is a sound, swift, thoroughbred horse about six or seven years old."

Count Otto for the fourth time took up his lamp.

"Will you follow me?" he said for the fourth time.

Wogan followed the old man across the lawn and round a corner of the house until he came to a long, low building surmounted by a cupola. The building was the stable, and the Count Otto roused one of his grooms.

"Saddle me Flavia," said he. "Flavia is a mare who, I fancy, fulfils your requirements."

Wogan had no complaint to make of her. She had the manners of a courtier. It seemed, too, that she had no complaint to make of Mr. Wogan. Count Otto laid his hand upon the bridle and led the mare with her rider along a lane through a thicket of trees and to a small gate.

"Here, then, we part, Chevalier," said he. "No doubt to-morrow I shall sit down at my table, knowing that I talked a deal of folly ill befitting an old man. No doubt I shall be aware that my books are the true happiness after all. But to-night—well, to-night I would fain be twenty years of age, that I might fling my books over the hedge and ride out with you, my sword at my side, my courage in my hand, into the world's highway. I will beg you to keep the mare as a token and a memory of our meeting. There is no better beast, I believe, in Christendom."

Wogan was touched by the old gentleman's warmth.

"Count," said Wogan, "I will gladly keep your mare in remembrance of your great goodwill to a stranger. But there is one better beast in Christendom."

"Indeed? And which is that?"

"Why, sir, the black horse which the lady I shall marry will ride into my city of dreams." And so he rode off upon his way. The morning was just beginning to gleam pale in the east. Here was a night passed which he had not thought to live through, and he was still alive to help the chosen woman imprisoned in the hollow of the hills at Innspruck. Wogan had reason to be grateful to that old man who stood straining his eyes after him. There was something pathetical in his discontent with his secluded life which touched Wogan to the heart. Wogan was not sure that in the morning the old man would know that the part he had chosen was, after all, the best. Besides, Wogan had between his knees the most friendly and intelligent beast which he had ridden since that morning when he met Lady Featherstone on the road to Bologna. But he had soon other matters to distract his thoughts. However easily Flavia cantered or trotted she could not but sharply remind him of his wounds. He had forty miles to travel before he could reach Schlestadt; and in the villages on the road there was gossip that day of a man with a tormented face who rode rocking in his saddle as though the furies were at his back.

A. E. W. Mason

# CHAPTER VIII

## AT SCHLESTADT

The little town of Schlestadt went to bed betimes. By ten o'clock its burghers were in their night-caps. A belated visitor going home at that hour found his footsteps ring upon the pavement with surprising echoes, and traversed dark street after dark street, seeing in each window, perhaps, a mimic moon, but no other light unless his path chanced to lie through Herzogstrasse. In that street a couple of windows on the first floor showed bright and unabashed, and the curious passer-by could detect upon the blind the shadows of men growing to monstrous giants and dwindling to pigmies according as they approached or retired from the lamp in the room.

There were three men in that room booted as for a journey. Their dress might have misled one into the belief that they were merchants, but their manner of wearing it proclaimed them soldiers. Of the three, one, a short, spare man, sat at the table with his head bent over a slip of paper. His peruke was pushed back from his forehead and showed that the hair about his temples was grey. He had a square face of some strength, and thoughtful eyes.

The second of the three stood by the window. He was, perhaps, a few years younger, thirty-six an observer might have guessed to the other's forty, and his face revealed a character quite different. His features were sharp, his eyes quick; if prudence was the predominating quality of the first, resource took its place in the second. While the first man sat patiently at the table, this one stood impatiently at the window. Now he lifted the blind, now he dropped it again.

The third sat in front of the fire with his face upturned to the ceiling. He was a tall, big man with mighty legs which sprawled one on each side of the hearth. He was the youngest of the three by five years, but his forehead at this moment was so creased, his mouth so pursed up, his cheeks so wrinkled, he had the look of sixty years. He puffed and breathed very heavily; once or twice he sighed, and at each sigh his chair creaked under him. Major O'Toole of Dillon's regiment was thinking.

"Gaydon," said he, suddenly.

The man at the table looked up quickly.

"Misset."

The man at the window turned impatiently.

"I have an idea."

Misset shrugged his shoulders.

Gaydon said, "Let us hear it."

O'Toole drew himself up; his chair no longer creaked, it groaned and cracked.

"It is a lottery," said he, "and we have made our fortunes. We three are the winners, and so our names are not crossed out."

"But I have put no money in a lottery," objected Gaydon.

"Nor I," said Misset.

"And where should I find money either?" said O'Toole. "But Charles Wogan has borrowed it for us and paid it in, and so we're all rich men. What'll I buy with it?"

Misset paced the room.

"The paper came four days ago?" he said.

"Yes, in the morning."

"Five days, then," and he stood listening. Then he ran to the window and opened it. Gaydon followed him and drew up the blind. Both men listened and were puzzled.

"That's the sound of horseshoes," said Gaydon.

"But there's another sound keeping pace with the horseshoes," said Misset.

O'Toole leaned on their shoulders, crushing them both down upon the sill of the window.

"It is very like the sound a gentleman makes when he reels home from a tavern."

Gaydon and Misset raised themselves with a common effort springing from a common thought and shot O'Toole back into the room.

"What if it is?" began Misset.

"He was never drunk in his life," said Gaydon.

"It's possible that he has reformed," said O'Toole; and the three men precipitated themselves down the stairs.

The drunkard was Wogan; he was drunk with fatigue and sleeplessness and pain, but he had retained just enough of his sober nature to spare a tired mare who had that day served him well.

The first intimation he received that his friends were on the watch was O'Toole's voice bawling down the street to him.

"Is it a lottery? Tell me we're all rich men," and he felt himself grasped in O'Toole's arms.

"I'll tell you more wonderful things than that," stammered Wogan, "when you have shown me the way to a stable."

"There's one at the back of the house," said Gaydon. "I'll take the horse."

"No," said Wogan, stubbornly, and would not yield the bridle to Gaydon.

O'Toole nodded approval.

"There are two things," said he, "a man never trusts to his friends. One's his horse; t' other's his wife."

Wogan suddenly stopped and looked at O'Toole. O'Toole answered the look loftily.

"It is a little maxim of philosophy. I have others. They come to me in the night."

Misset laughed. Wogan walked on to the stable. It was a long building, and a light was still burning. Moreover, a groom was awake, for the door was opened before they had come near enough to knock. There were twelve stalls, of which nine were occupied, and three of the nine horses stood ready saddled and bridled.

Wogan sat down upon a corn-bin and waited while his mare was groomed and fed. The mare looked round once or twice in the midst of her meal, twisting her neck as far as her halter allowed.

"I am not gone yet, my lady," said he, "take your time."

Wogan made a ghostly figure in the dim shadowy light. His face was of an extraordinary pallor; his teeth chattered; his eyes burned. Gaydon looked at him with concern and said to the groom, "You can take the saddles off. We shall need no horses to-night."

The four men returned to the house. Wogan went upstairs first. Gaydon held back the other two at the foot of the stairs.

"Not a word, not a question, till he has eaten, or we shall have him in bed for a twelvemonth. Misset, do you run for a doctor. O'Toole, see what you can find in the larder."

Wogan sat before the fire without a word while O'Toole spread the table and set a couple of cold partridges upon it and a bottle of red wine. Wogan ate mechanically for a little and afterwards with some enjoyment. He picked the partridges till the bones were clean, and he finished the bottle of wine. Then he rose to his feet with a sigh of something very like to contentment and felt along the mantel-shelf with his hands. O'Toole, however, had foreseen his wants and handed him a pipe newly filled. While Wogan was lighting the tobacco, Misset came back into the room with word that the doctor was out upon his last rounds, but would come as soon as he had returned home. The four men sat down about the fire, and Wogan reached out his hand and felt O'Toole's arm.

"It is you," he said. "There you are, the three of you, my good friends, and this is Schlestadt. But it is strange," and he laughed a little to himself and looked about the room, assuring himself that this indeed was Gaydon's lodging.

"You received a slip of paper?" said he.

"Four days back," said Gaydon.

"And understood?"

"That we were to be ready."

"Good."

"Then it's not a lottery," murmured O'Toole, "and we've drawn no prizes."

"Ah, but we are going to," cried Wogan. "We are safe here. No one can hear us; no one can burst in. But I am sure of that. Misset knows the trick that will make us safe from interruption, eh?"

Misset looked blankly at Wogan.

"Why, one can turn the key," said he.

"To be sure," said Wogan, with a laugh of admiration for that device of which he had bethought himself, and which he ascribed to Misset, "if there's a key; but if there's no key, why, a chair tilted against the door to catch the handle, eh?"

Misset locked the door, not at all comprehending that device, and returned to his seat.

"We are to draw the greatest prize that ever was drawn," resumed Wogan, and he broke off.

"But is there a cupboard in the room? No matter; I forgot that this is Gaydon's lodging, and Gaydon's not the man to overlook a cupboard."

Gaydon jumped up from his chair.

"But upon my word there is a cupboard," he cried, and crossing to a corner of the room he opened a door and looked in. Wogan laughed again as though Gaydon's examination of the cupboard was a very good joke.

"There will be nobody in it," he cried. "Gaydon will never feel a hand gripping the life out of his throat because he forgot to search a cupboard."

The cupboard was empty, as it happened. But Gaydon had left the door of the street open when he went out to meet Wogan; there had been time and to spare for any man to creep upstairs and hide himself had there been a man in Schlestadt that night minded to hear. Gaydon returned to his chair.

"We are to draw the biggest prize in all Europe," said Wogan.

"There!" cried O'Toole. "Will you be pleased to remember when next I have an idea that I was right?"

"But not for ourselves," added Wogan.

O'Toole's face fell.

"Oh, we are to hand it on to a third party," said he.

"Yes."

"Well, after all, that's quite of a piece with our luck."

"Who is the third party?" asked Misset.

"The King."

Misset started up from his chair and leaned forward, his hands upon the arms.

"The King," said O'Toole; "to be sure, that makes a difference."

Gaydon asked quietly, "And what is the prize?"

"The Princess Clementina," said Wogan. "We are to rescue her from her prison in Innspruck."

Even Gaydon was startled.

"We four!" he exclaimed.

"We four!" repeated Misset, staring at Wogan. His mouth was open; his eyes started from his head; he stammered in his speech. "We four against a nation, against half Europe!"

O'Toole simply crossed to a corner of the room, picked up his sword and buckled it to his waist.

"I am ready," said he.

Wogan turned round in his chair and smiled.

"I know that," said he. "So are we all—all ready; is not that so, my friends? We four are ready." And he looked to Misset and to Gaydon. "Here's an exploit, if we but carry it through, which even antiquity will be at pains to match! It's more than an exploit, for it has the sanctity of a crusade. On the one side there's tyranny, oppression, injustice, the one woman who most deserves a crown robbed of it. And on the other—"

"There's the King," said Gaydon; and the three brief words seemed somehow to quench and sober Wogan.

"Yes," said he; "there's the King, and we four to serve him in his need. We are few, but in that lies our one hope. They will never look for four men, but for many. Four men travelling to the shrine of Loretto with the Pope's passport may well stay at Innspruck and escape a close attention."

"I am ready," O'Toole repeated.

"But we shall not start to-night. There's the passport to be got, a plan to be arranged."

"Oh, there's a plan," said O'Toole. "To be sure, there's always a plan." And he sat down again heavily, as though he put no faith in plans.

Misset and Gaydon drew their chairs closer to Wogan's and instinctively lowered their voices to the tone of a whisper.

"Is her Highness warned of the attempt?" asked Gaydon.

"As soon as I obtained the King's permission," replied

Wogan, "I hurried to Innspruck. There I saw Chateaudoux, the chamberlain of the Princess's mother. Here is a letter he dropped in the cathedral for me to pick up."

He drew the letter from his fob and handed it to Gaydon. Gaydon read it and handed it to Misset. Misset nodded and handed it to O'Toole, who read it four times and handed it back to Gaydon with a flourish of the hand as though the matter was now quite plain to him.

"Chateaudoux has a sweetheart," said he, sententiously. "Very good; I do not think the worse of him."

Gaydon glanced a second time through the letter.

"The Princess says that you must have the Prince Sobieski's written consent."

"I went from Innspruck to Ohlau," said Wogan. "I had some trouble, and the reason of my coming leaked out. The Countess de Berg suspected it from the first. She had a friend, an Englishwoman, Lady Featherstone, who was at Ohlau to outwit me."

"Lady Featherstone!" said Misset. "Who can she be?"

Wogan told them of his first meeting with Lady Featherstone on the Florence road, but he knew no more about her, and not one of the three knew anything at all.

"So the secret's out," said Gaydon. "But you outstripped it."

"Barely," said Wogan. "Forty miles away I had last night to fight for my life."

"But you have the Prince's written consent?" said Misset.

"I had last night, but I made a spill of it to light my pipe. There were six men against me. Had that been found on my dead body, why, there was proof positive of our attempt, and the attempt foiled by sure safeguards. As it is, if we lie still a little while, their fears will cease and the rumour become discredited."

Misset leaned across Gaydon's arm and scanned the letter.

"But her Highness writes most clearly she will not move without that sure token of her father's consent."

Wogan drew from his breast pocket a snuff-box made from a single turquoise.

"Here's a token no less sure. It was Prince Sobieski's New Year's gift to me,—a jewel unique and in an unique setting. This must persuade her. His father, great King John of Poland, took it from the Grand Vizier's tent when the Turks were routed at Vienna."

O'Toole reached out his hand and engulfed the jewel.

"Sure," said he, "it is a pretty sort of toy. It would persuade any woman to anything so long as she was promised it to hang about her neck. You must promise it to the Princess, but not give it to her—no, lest when she has got it she should be content to remain in Innspruck. I know. You must promise it."

Wogan bowed to O'Toole's wisdom and took back the snuff-box. "I will not forget to promise it," said he.

"But here's another point," said Gaydon. "Her Highness, the Princess's mother, insists that a woman shall attend upon her daughter, and where shall we find a woman with the courage and the strength?"

"I have thought of that," said Wogan. "Misset has a wife. By the luckiest stroke in the world Misset took a wife this last spring."

There was at once a complete silence. Gaydon stared into the fire, O'Toole looked with intense interest at the ceiling, Misset buried his face in his hands. Wogan was filled with consternation. Was Misset's wife dead? he asked himself. He had spoken lightly, laughingly, and he went hot and cold as he recollected the raillery of his words. He sat in his chair shocked at the pain which he had caused his friend. Moreover, he had counted surely upon Mrs. Misset.

Then Misset raised his head from his hands and in a trembling voice he said slowly, "My boy would only live to serve his King. Why should he not serve his King before he lives? My wife will say the like."

There was a depth of quiet feeling in his words which Wogan would never have expected from Misset; and the words themselves were words which he felt no man, no king, however much beloved, however generous to his servants, had any right to expect. They took Wogan's breath away, and not Wogan's only, but Gaydon's and O'Toole's, too. A longer silence than before followed upon them. The very simplicity with which they had been uttered was startling, and made those three men doubt at the first whether they had heard aright.

O'Toole was the first to break the silence.

"It is a strange thing that there never was a father since Adam who was not absolutely sure in his heart that his first-born must be a boy. When you come to think philosophically

A. E. W. Mason

about it, you'll see that if fathers had their way the world would be peopled with sons with never a bit of a lass in any corner to marry them."

O'Toole's reflection, if not a reason for laughter, made a pretext for it, at which all—even Misset, who was a trifle ashamed of his display of feeling—eagerly caught. Wogan held his hand out and clasped Misset's.

"That was a great saying," said he, "but so much sacrifice is not to be accepted."

Misset, however, was firm. His wife, he said, though naturally timid, could show a fine spirit on occasion, and would never forgive one of them if she was left behind. He argued until a compromise was reached. Misset should lay the matter openly before his wife, and the four crusaders, to use Wogan's term, would be bound by her decision.

"So you may take it that matter's settled," said Misset. "There will be five of us."

"Six," said Wogan.

"There's another man to join us, then," said Gaydon. "I have it. Your servant, Marnier."

"No, not Marnier, nor any man. Listen. It is necessary that when once her Highness is rescued we must get so much start as will make pursuit vain. We shall be hampered with a coach, and a coach will travel slowly on the passes of Tyrol. The pursuers will ride horses; they must not come up with us. From Innspruck to Italy, if we have never an accident, will take us at the least four days; it will take our pursuers three. We must have one clear day before her Highness's evasion is discovered. Now, the chief magistrate of

Innspruck visits her Highness's apartments twice a day,—at ten in the morning and at ten of the night. The Princess must be rescued at night; and if her escape is discovered in the morning she will never reach Italy, she will be behind the bars again."

"But the Princess's mother will be left," said Gaydon. "She can plead that her daughter is ill."

"The magistrate forces his way into the very bedroom. We must take with us a woman who will lie in her Highness's bed with the curtains drawn about her and a voice so weak with suffering that she cannot raise it above a whisper, with eyes so tired from sleeplessness she cannot bear a light near them. Help me in this. Name me a woman with the fortitude to stay behind."

Gaydon shook his head.

"She will certainly be discovered. The part she plays in the escape must certainly be known. She will remain for the captors to punish as they will. I know no woman."

"Nay," said Wogan; "you exaggerate her danger. Once the escape is brought to an issue, once her Highness is in Bologna safe, the Emperor cannot wreak vengeance on a woman; it would be too paltry." And now he made his appeal to Misset.

"No, my friend," Misset replied. "I know no woman with the fortitude."

"But you do," interrupted O'Toole. "So do I. There's no difficulty whatever in the matter. Mrs. Misset has a maid."

"Oho!" said Gaydon.

A. E. W. Mason

"The maid's name is Jenny."

"Aha!" said Wogan.

"She's a very good friend of mine."

"O'Toole!" cried Misset, indignantly. "My wife's maid—a very good friend of yours?"

"Sure she is, and you didn't know it," said O'Toole, with a chuckle. "I am the cunning man, after all. She would do a great deal for me would Jenny."

"But has she courage?" asked Wogan.

"Faith, her father was a French grenadier and her mother a *vivandiere*. It would be a queer thing if she was frightened by a little matter of lying in bed and pretending to be someone else."

"But can we trust her with the secret?" asked Gaydon.

"No!" exclaimed Misset, and he rose angrily from his chair. "My wife's maid—O'Toole—O'Toole—my wife's maid. Did ever one hear the like?"

"My friend," said O'Toole, quietly, "it seems almost as if you wished to reflect upon Jenny's character, which would not be right."

Misset looked angrily at O'Toole, who was not at all disturbed. Then he said, "Well, at all events, she gossips. We cannot take her. She would tell the whole truth of our journey at the first halt."

"That's true," said O'Toole.

Then for the second time that evening he cried, "I have an idea."

"Well?"

"We'll not tell her the truth at all. I doubt if she would come if we told it her. Jenny very likely has never heard of her Highness the Princess, and I doubt if she cares a button for the King. Besides, she would never believe but that we were telling her a lie. No. We'll make up a probable likely sort of story, and then she'll believe it to be the truth."

"I have it," cried Wogan. "We'll tell her that we are going to abduct an heiress who is dying for love of O'Toole, and whose merciless parents are forcing her into a loveless, despicable marriage with a tottering pantaloon."

O'Toole brought his hand down upon the arm of the chair.

"There's the very story," he cried. "To be sure, you are a great man, Charles. The most probable convincing story that was ever invented! Oh! but you'll hear Jenny sob with pity for the heiress and Lucius O'Toole when she hears it. It will be a bad day, too, for the merciless parents when they discover Jenny in her Highness's bed. She stands six feet in her stockings."

"Six feet!" exclaimed Wogan.

"In her stockings," returned O'Toole. "Her height is her one vanity. Therefore in her shoes she is six feet four."

"Well, she must take her heels off and make herself as short as she can."

"You will have trouble, my friend, to persuade her to that," said O'Toole.

"Hush!" said Gaydon. He rose and unlocked the door. The doctor was knocking for admission below. Gaydon let him in, and he dressed Wogan's wounds with an assurance that they were not deep and that a few days' quiet would restore him.

"I will sleep the night here if I may," said Wogan, as soon as the doctor had gone. "A blanket and a chair will serve my turn."

They took him into Gaydon's bedroom, where three beds were ranged.

"We have slept in the one room and lived together since your message came four days ago," said Gaydon. "Take your choice of the beds, for there's not one of us has so much need of a bed as you."

Wogan drew a long breath of relief.

"Oh! but it's good to be with you," he cried suddenly, and caught at Gaydon's arm. "I shall sleep to-night. How I shall sleep!"

He stretched out his aching limbs between the cool white sheets, and when the lamp was extinguished he called to each of his three friends by name to make sure of their company. O'Toole answered with a grunt on his right, Misset on his left, and Gaydon from the corner of the room.

"But I have wanted you these last three days!" said Wogan. "To-morrow when I tell you the story of them you will know how much I have wanted you."

They got, however, some inkling of Wogan's need before the morrow came. In the middle of the night they were wakened by a wild scream and heard Wogan whispering in an agony for help. They lighted a lamp and saw him lying with his hand upon his throat and his eyes starting from his head with horror.

"Quick," said he, "the hand at my throat! It's not the letter so much, it's my life they want."

"It's your own hand," said Gaydon, and taking the hand he found it lifeless. Wogan's arm in that position had gone to sleep, as the saying is. He had waked suddenly in the dark with the cold pressure at his throat, and in the moment of waking was back again alone in the inn near Augsburg. Wogan indeed needed his friends.

A. E. W. Mason

# CHAPTER IX

## GAYDON MINDS HIS OWN BUSINESS

The next morning Wogan was tossing from side to side in a high fever. The fever itself was of no great importance, but it had consequences of a world-wide influence, for it left Wogan weak and tied to his bed; so that it was Gaydon who travelled to Rome and obtained the Pope's passport. Gaydon consequently saw what otherwise Wogan would have seen; and Gaydon, the cautious, prudent Gaydon, was careful to avoid making an inopportune discovery, whereas Wogan would never have rested until he had made it.

Gaydon stayed in Rome a week, lying snug and close in a lodging only one street removed from that house upon the Tiber where his King lived. Secrets had a way of leaking out, and Gaydon was determined that this one should not through any inattention of his. He therefore never went abroad until dark, and even then kept aloof from the house which overlooked the Tiber. His business he conducted through his servant, sending him to and fro between Edgar, the secretary, and himself. One audience of his King alone he asked, and that was to be granted him on the day of his departure from Rome.

Thus the time hung very heavily upon him. From daybreak to dusk he was cooped within a little insignificant room which looked out upon a little insignificant street. His window, however, though it promised little diversion, was his one resource. Gaydon was a man of observation, and found a pleasure in guessing at this and that person's business from his appearance, his dress, and whether he went fast or slow. So he sat steadily at his window, and after a day or two had passed he began to be puzzled. The moment he was puzzled he became interested. On the second day he drew his chair a little distance back from the window and watched. On the third day he drew his chair close to the window, but at the side and against the wall. In this way he could see everything that happened and everyone who passed, and yet remain himself unobserved.

Almost opposite to his window stood a small mean house fallen into neglect and disrepair. The windows were curtained with dust, many of the panes were broken, the shutters hung upon broken hinges, the paint was peeling from the door. The house had the most melancholy aspect of long disuse. It seemed to belong to no one and to be crumbling pitifully to ruin like an aged man who has no friends. Yet this house had its uses, which Gaydon could not but perceive were of a secret kind. On the very first day that Gaydon sat at his window a man, who seemed from his dress to be of a high consideration, came sauntering along that sordid thoroughfare, where he seemed entirely out of place, like a butterfly on the high seas. To Gaydon's surprise he stopped at the door, gave a cautious look round, and rapped quickly with his stick. At once the door of that uninhabited house was opened. The man entered, the door was closed upon him, and a good hour by Gaydon's watch elapsed before it was opened again to let him out. In the afternoon another man came and was admitted with the same secrecy. Both men had worn their hats drawn down upon their foreheads, and whereas one of them held a muffler to his face, the other had thrust his chin within the folds of his

A. E. W. Mason

cravat. Gaydon had not been able to see the face of either. After nightfall he remarked that such visits became more frequent. Moreover, they were repeated on the next day and the next. Gaydon watched, but never got any nearer to a solution of the mystery. At the end of the sixth day he was more puzzled and interested than ever, for closely as he had watched he had not seen the face of any man who had passed in and out of that door.

But he was to see a face that night.

At nine o'clock a messenger from Edgar, the secretary, brought him a package which contained a letter and the passport for these six days delayed. The letter warned him that Edgar himself would come to fetch him in the morning to his audience with James. The passport gave authority to a Flemish nobleman, the Count of Cernes, to make a pilgrimage to Loretto with his wife and family. The name of Warner had served its turn and could no longer be employed.

As soon as the messenger had gone, Gaydon destroyed Edgar's letter, put the passport safely away in his breast, and since he had not left his room that day, put on his hat. Being a prudent man with a turn for economy, he also extinguished his lamp. He had also a liking for fresh air, so he opened the window, and at the same moment the door of the house opposite was opened. A tall burly man with a lantern in his hand stepped out into the street; he was followed by a slight man of a short stature. Both men were wrapped in their cloaks, but the shorter one tripped on a break in the road and his cloak fell apart. His companion turned at once and held his lantern aloft. Just for a second the light therefore flashed upon a face, and Gaydon at his dark window caught a glimpse of it. The face was the face of his King.

Gaydon was more than ever puzzled. He had only seen the

face for an instant; moreover, he was looking down upon it, so that he might be mistaken. He felt, however, that he was not, and he began to wonder at the business that could take his King to this mysterious house. But there was one thing of which he was sure amidst all his doubts, Rome was not the safest city in the world for a man to walk about at nights. His King would be none the worse off for a second guardian who would follow near enough to give help and far enough for discretion. Gaydon went down his stairs into the street. The lantern twinkled ahead; Gaydon followed it until it stopped before a great house which had lights burning here and there in the windows. The smaller man mounted the steps and was admitted; his big companion with the lantern remained outside.

Gaydon, wishing to make sure of his conjectures one way or the other, walked quickly past him and stole a glance sideways at his face. But the man with the lantern looked at Gaydon at the same moment. Their eyes met, and the lantern was immediately held aloft.

"It is Major Gaydon."

Gaydon had to make the best of the business. He bowed.

"Mr. Whittington, I think."

"Sir," said Whittington, politely, "I am honoured by your memory. For myself, I never forget a face though I see it but for a moment between the light and the dark, but I do not expect the like from my acquaintances. We did meet, I believe, in Paris? You are of Dillon's regiment?"

"And on leave in Rome," said Gaydon, a trifle hastily.

"On leave?" said Whittington, idly. "Well, so far as towns

A. E. W. Mason

go, Rome is as good as another, though, to tell the truth, I find them all quite unendurable. Would I were on leave! but I am pinned here, a watchman with a lantern. I do but lack a rattle, though, to be sure, I could not spring it. We are secret to-night, major. Do you know what house this is?"

"No," replied Gaydon. "But I am waited for and will bid you good-night."

He had a thought that the Chevalier, since he would be secret, had chosen his watchman rather ill. He had no wish to pry, and so was for returning to his lodging; but that careless, imprudent man, Whittington, would not lose a companion so easily. He caught Gaydon by the arm.

"Well, it is the house of Maria Vittoria, Mademoiselle de Caprara, the heiress of Bologna, who has only this evening come to Rome. And so no later than this evening I am playing link-boy, appointed by letters patent, one might say. But what will you? Youth is youth, whether in a ploughboy or a—But my tongue needs a gag. Another word, and I had said too much. Well, since you will be going, good-night. We shall meet, no doubt, in a certain house that overlooks the Tiber."

"Hardly," said Gaydon, "since I leave Rome to-morrow."

"Indeed? You leave Rome to-morrow?" said Whittington. "I would I were as fortunate," and he jerked his thumb dolefully towards the Caprara Palace. Gaydon hesitated for a moment, considering whether or not he should ask Whittington to be silent upon their meeting. But he determined the man was too incautious in his speech. If he begged him not to mention Gaydon's presence in Rome, he would remember it the more surely, and if nothing was said he might forget it. Gaydon wished him good-night and went back to his lodging, walking rather moodily. Whittington looked after him and chuckled.

Meanwhile, in a room of the house two people sat,—one the slight, graceful man who had accompanied Whittington and whom Gaydon had correctly guessed to be his King, the other, Maria Vittoria de Caprara. The Chevalier de St. George was speaking awkwardly with a voice which broke. Maria listened with a face set and drawn. She was a girl both in features and complexion of a remarkable purity. Of colour, but for her red lips, she had none. Her hair was black, her face of a clear pallor which her hair made yet more pale. Her eyes matched her hair, and were so bright and quick a starry spark seemed to glow in the depths of them. She was a poet's simile for night.

The Chevalier ended and sat with his eyes turned away. Maria Vittoria did not change her attitude, nor for a while did she answer, but the tears gathered in her eyes and welled over. They ran down her cheeks; she did not wipe them away, she did not sob, nor did her face alter from its fixity. She did not even close her eyes. Only the tears rained down so silently that the Prince was not aware of them. He had even a thought as he sat with his head averted that she might have shown a trifle more of distress, and it was almost with a reproach upon his lips that he turned to her. Never was a man more glad that he had left a word unspoken. This silent grief of tears cut him to the heart.

"Maria!" he cried, and moved towards her. She made no gesture to repel him, she did not move, but she spoke in a whisper.

"His Holiness the Pope had consented to our marriage. What would I not have done for you?"

The Chevalier stooped over her and took her hand. The hand

A. E. W. Mason

remained inert in his.

"Maria!"

"Would that I were poor! Would that I were powerless! But I am rich—so rich. I could have done so much. I am alone—so much alone. What would I not have done for you?"

"Maria!"

His voice choked upon the word, his lips touched her hair, and she shivered from head to foot. Then her hand tightened fast upon his; she drew him down almost fiercely until he sank upon his knees by her side; she put an arm about his shoulder and held him to her breast.

"But you love me," she said quickly. "Tell me so! Say, 'I love you, I love you, I love you.' Oh that we both could die, you saying it, I hearing it,—die to-night, like this, my arm about you, your face against my heart! My lord, my lord!" and then she flung him from her, holding him at arm's length. "Say it with your eyes on mine! I can see though the tears fall. I shall never hear the words again after to-night. Do not stint me of them; let them flow just as these tears flow. They will leave no more trace than do my tears."

"Maria, I love you," said the Chevalier. "How I do love you!" He took her hands from his shoulders and pressed his forehead upon them. She leaned forward, and in a voice so low it seemed her heart was whispering, not her mouth, she made her prayer.

"Say that you have no room in your thoughts except for me. Say that you have no scrap of love—" He dropped her hands and drew away; she caught him to her. "No, no! Say that you have no scrap of love to toss to the woman there in Innspruck!"

"Maria!" he exclaimed.

"Hush!" said she, with a woful smile. "To-morrow you shall love her; to-morrow I will not ask your eyes to dwell on mine or your hand to quiver as it touches mine. But to-night love no one but me."

For answer he kissed her on the lips. She took his head between her hands and gave the kiss back, gently as though her lips feared to bruise his, slowly as though this one moment must content her for all her life. Then she looked at him for a little, and with a childish movement that was infinitely sad she laid his face side by side with hers so that his cheek touched hers.

"Shall I tell you my thought?" she asked. "Shall I dare to tell you it?"

"Tell it me!"

"God has died to-night. Hush! Do not move! Do not speak! Perhaps the world will slip and crumble if we but stay still." And they remained thus cheek to cheek silent in the room, staring forward with eyes wide open and hopeful. The very air seemed to them a-quiver with expectation. They, too, had an expectant smile upon their lips. But there was no crack of thunder overhead, no roar of a slipping world.

"But we are children," he cried, starting up. "Is it not strange the very pain which tortures us because we are man and woman should sink us into children? We sit hoping that a miracle will split the world in pieces! This is the Caprara Palace; Whittington drowses outside over his lantern; and to-morrow Gaydon rides with his passport northwards to Charles Wogan."

A. E. W. Mason

The name hurt Maria Vittoria like a physical torture. She beat her hands together with a cry, "I hate him! I hate him!"

"Yet I have no better servant!"

"Speak no good word of him in my ears! He robs me of you."

"He risks his life for me."

"I will pray that he may lose it."

"Maria!"

The Chevalier started, thrilled and almost appalled by the violence of her passion.

"I do pray," she cried. "Every fibre in me tingles with the prayer. Oh, I hate him! Why did you give him leave to rescue her?"

"Could I refuse? I did delay him; I did hesitate. Only to-day Gaydon receives the passport, and even so I have delayed too long. Indeed, Maria, I dare not think of the shame, the danger, her Highness has endured for me, lest my presence here, even for this farewell, should too bitterly reproach me."

At that all Maria Vittoria's vehemence left her. She fell to beseechings and entreaties. With her vehemence went also her dignity. She dropped upon her knees and dragged herself across the room to him. To James her humility was more terrible than her passion, for passion had always distinguished her, and he was familiar with it; but pride had always gone hand in hand with it. He stepped forward and would have raised her from the ground, but Maria would have none of his help; she crouched at his feet pleading.

"You told me business would call you to Spain. Go there! Stay there! For a little—oh, not for long! But for a month, say, after your Princess comes triumphing into Bologna. Promise me that! I could not bear that you should meet her as she comes. There would be shouts; I can hear them. No, I will not have it! I can see her proud cursed face a-flush. No! You think too much of what she has suffered. If I could have suffered too! But suffering, shame, humiliation, these fall to women, always have fallen. We have learnt to bear them so that we feel them less than you. My dear lord, believe me! Her suffering is no great thing. If we love we welcome it! Each throb of pain endured for love becomes a thrill of joy. If I could have suffered too!"

It was strange to hear this girl with the streaming eyes and tormented face bewail her fate in that she had not won that great privilege of suffering. She knelt on the ground a splendid image of pain, and longed for pain that she might prove thereby how little a thing she made of it. The Chevalier drew a stool to her side and seating himself upon it clasped her about the waist. She laid her cheek upon his knee just as a dog will do.

"Sweetheart," said he, "I would have no woman suffer a pang for me had I my will of the world. But since that may not be, I do not believe that any woman could be deeper hurt than you are now."

"Not Clementina?"

"No."

Maria uttered a little sigh. Her pain gave her a sort of ownership of the man who caused it. "Nor can she love as deep," she continued quietly. "A Sobieski from the snows! Love was born here in Italy. She robs me of you. I hate her."

Then she raised her face eagerly. "Charles Wogan may fail."

"You do not know him."

"The cleverest have made mistakes and died for them."

"Wogan makes mistakes like another, but somehow gets the better of them in the end. There was a word he said to me when he begged for my permission. I told him his plan was a mere dream. He answered he would dream it true; he will."

"You should have waked him. You were the master, he the servant. You were the King."

"And when can the King do what he wills instead of what he must? Maria, if you and I had met before I sent Charles Wogan to search out a wife for me—"

Maria Vittoria knelt up. She drew herself away.

"He chose her as your wife?"

"If only I had had time to summon him back!"

"He chose her—Charles Wogan. How I hate him!"

"I sent him to make the choice."

"And he might have gone no step beyond Bologna. There was I not a mile distant ready to his hand! But I was too mean, too despicable—"

"Maria, hush!" And the troubled voice in which he spoke rang with so much pain that she was at once contrite with remorse.

"My lord, I hurt you, so you see how I am proven mean. Give me your hand and laugh to me; laugh with your heart and eyes and lips. I am jealous of your pain. I am a woman. I would have it all, gather it all into my bosom, and cherish each sharp stab like a flower my lover gives to me. I am glad of them. They are flowers that will not wither. Add a kiss, sweetheart, the sharpest stab, and so the chief flower, the very rose of flowers. There, that is well," and she rose from her knees and turned away. So she stood for a little, and when she turned again she wore upon her face the smile which she had bidden rise in his.

"Would we were free!" cried the Chevalier.

"But since we are not, let us show brave faces to the world and hide our hearts. I do wish you all happiness. But you will go to Spain. There's a friend's hand in warrant of the wish."

She held out a hand which clasped his firmly without so much as a tremor.

"Good-night, my friend," said she. "Speak those same words to me, and no word more. I am tired with the day's doings. I have need of sleep, oh, great need of it!"

The Chevalier read plainly the overwhelming strain her counterfeit of friendliness put upon her. He dared not prolong it. Even as he looked at her, her lips quivered and her eyes swam.

"Good-night, my friend," said he.

She conducted him along a wide gallery to the great staircase where her lackeys waited. Then he bowed to her and she curtsied low to him, but no word was spoken by either. This little comedy must needs be played in pantomime lest the actors should spoil it with a show of broken hearts.

Maria Vittoria went back to the room. She could have hindered Wogan if she had had the mind. She had the time to betray him; she knew of his purpose. But the thought of betrayal never so much as entered her thoughts.

She hated him, she hated Clementina, but she was loyal to her King. She sat alone in her palace, her chin propped upon her hands, and in a little in her wide unblinking eyes the tears gathered again and rolled down her cheeks and on her hands. She wept silently and without a movement, like a statue weeping.

The Chevalier found Whittington waiting for him, but the candle in his lantern had burned out.

"I have kept you here a wearisome long time," he said with an effort. It was not easy for him to speak upon an indifferent matter.

"I had some talk with Major Gaydon which helped me to beguile it," said Whittington.

"Gaydon!" exclaimed the Chevalier, "are you certain?"

"A man may make mistakes in the darkness," said Whittington.

"To be sure."

"And I never had an eye for faces."

"It was not Gaydon, then?" said the Chevalier.

"It may not have been," said Whittington, "and by the best of good fortune I said nothing to him of any significance whatever."

The Chevalier was satisfied with the reply. He had chosen the right attendant for this nocturnal visit. Had Gaydon met with a more observant man than Whittington outside the Caprara Palace, he might have got a number of foolish suspicions into his head.

Gaydon, however, was at that moment in his bed, saying to himself that there were many matters concerning which it would be an impertinence for him to have one meddlesome thought. By God's blessing he was a soldier and no politician. He fell asleep comforted by that conclusion.

In the morning Edgar, the Chevalier's secretary, came privately to him.

"The King will receive you now," said he. "Let us go."

"It is broad daylight. We shall be seen."

"Not if the street is empty," said Edgar, looking out of the window.

The street, as it chanced, was for the moment empty. Edgar crossed the street and rapped quickly with certain pauses between the raps on the door of that deserted house into which Gaydon had watched men enter. The door was opened. "Follow me," said Edgar. Gaydon followed him into a bare passage unswept and with discoloured walls. A man in a little hutch in the wall opened and closed the door with a string.

Edgar walked forward to the end of the passage with Gaydon at his heels. The two men came to a flight of stone steps, which they descended. The steps led to a dark and dripping cellar with no pavement but the mud, and that depressed into puddles. The air was cold and noisome; the walls to the touch of Gaydon's hand were greasy with slime. He followed Edgar across the cellar into a sort of tunnel. Here Edgar drew an end of candle from his pocket and lighted it. The tunnel was so low that Gaydon, though a shortish man, could barely hold his head erect. He followed Edgar to the end and up a flight of winding steps. The air grew warmer and dryer. They had risen above ground, the spiral wound within the thickness of a wall. The steps ended abruptly; there was no door visible; in face of them and on each side the bare stone walls enclosed them. Edgar stooped down and pressed with his finger on a round insignificant discolouration of the stone. Then he stood up again.

"You will breathe no word of this passage, Major Gaydon," said he. "The house was built a century ago when Rome was more troubled than it is to-day, but the passage was never more useful than now. Men from England, whose names it would astonish you to know, have trodden these steps on a secret visit to the King. Ah!" From the wall before their faces a great slab of the size of a door sank noiselessly down and disclosed a wooden panel. The panel slid aside. Edgar and Gaydon stepped into a little cabinet lighted by a single window. The room was empty. Gaydon took a peep out of the window and saw the Tiber eddying beneath. Edgar went to a corner and touched a spring. The stone slab rose from its grooves; the panel slid back across it; at the same moment the door of the room was opened, and the Chevalier stepped across the threshold.

Gaydon could no longer even pretend to doubt who had walked with Whittington to the Caprara Palace the night before. It was none of his business, however, he assured himself. If his King dwelt with emphasis upon the dangers of the enterprise, it was not his business to remark upon it or to be thereby disheartened. The King said very graciously that he would hold the major and his friends in no less esteem if by any misfortune they came back empty-handed. That was most kind of him, but it was none of Gaydon's business. The King was ill at ease and looked as though he had not slept a wink the livelong night. Well, swollen eyes and a patched pallid face disfigure all men at times, and in any case they were none of Gaydon's business.

He rode out of Rome that afternoon as the light was failing. He rode at a quick trot, and did not notice at the corner of a street a big stalwart man who sauntered along swinging his stick by the tassel with a vacant look of idleness upon the passers-by. He stopped and directed the same vacant look at Gaydon.

But he was thinking curiously, "Will he tell Charles Wogan?"

The stalwart man was Harry Whittington.

Gaydon, however, never breathed a word about the Caprara Palace when he handed the passport to Charles Wogan at Schlestadt. Wogan was sitting propped up with pillows in a chair, and he asked Gaydon many questions of the news at Rome, and how the King bore himself.

"The King was not in the best of spirits," said Gaydon.

"With this," cried Wogan, flourishing the passport, "we'll find a means to hearten him."

Gaydon filled a pipe and lighted it.

"Will you tell me, Wogan," he asked,—"I am by nature

A. E. W. Mason

curious,—was it the King who proposed this enterprise to you, or was it you who proposed it to the King?"

The question had an extraordinary effect. Wogan was startled out of his chair.

"What do you mean?" he exclaimed fiercely. There was something more than fierceness in the words,—an accent of fear, it almost seemed to Gaydon. There was a look almost of fear in his eyes, as though he had let some appalling secret slip. Gaydon stared at him in wonder, and Wogan recovered himself with a laugh. "Faith," said he, "it is a question to perplex a man. I misdoubt but we both had the thought about the same time. 'Wogan,' said he, 'there's the Princess with a chain on her leg, so to speak,' and I answered him, 'A chain's a galling sort of thing to a lady's ankle.' There was little more said if I remember right."

Gaydon nodded as though his curiosity was now satisfied. Wogan's alarm was strange, no doubt, strange and unexpected like the Chevalier's visit to the Caprara Palace. Gaydon had a glimpse of dark and troubled waters, but he turned his face away. They were none of his business.

# CHAPTER X

## A MONTH OF WAITING

In an hour, however, he returned out of breath and with a face white from despair. Wogan was still writing at his table, but at his first glance towards Gaydon he started quickly to his feet, and altogether forgot to cover over his sheet of paper. He carefully shut the door.

"You have bad news," said he.

"There was never worse," answered Gaydon. He had run so fast, he was so discomposed, that he could with difficulty speak. But he gasped his bad news out in the end.

"I went to my brother major to report my return. He was entertaining his friends. He had a letter this morning from Strasbourg and he read it aloud. The letter said a rumour was running through the town that the Chevalier Wogan had already rescued the Princess and was being hotly pursued on the road to Trent."

If Wogan felt any disquietude he was careful to hide it. He sat comfortably down upon the sofa.

"I expected rumour would be busy with us," said he, "but

A. E. W. Mason

never that it would take so favourable a shape."

"Favourable!" exclaimed Gaydon.

"To be sure, for its falsity will be established to-morrow, and ridicule cast upon those who spread and believed it. False alarms are the proper strategy to conceal the real assault. The rumour does us a service. Our secret is very well kept, for here am I in Schlestadt, and people living in Schlestadt believe me on the road to Trent. I will go back with you to the major's and have a laugh at his correspondent. Courage, my friend. We will give our enemies a month. Let them cry wolf as often as they will during that month, we'll get into the fold all the more easily in the end."

Wogan took his hat to accompany Gaydon, but at that moment he heard another man stumbling in a great haste up the stairs. Misset broke into the room with a face as discomposed as Gaydon's had been.

"Here's another who has heard the same rumour," said Wogan.

"It is more than a rumour," said Misset. "It is an order, and most peremptory, from the Court of France, forbidding any officer of Dillon's regiment to be absent for more than twenty-four hours from his duties on pain of being broke. Our secret's out. That's the plain truth of the matter."

He stood by the table drumming with his fingers in a great agitation. Then his fingers stopped. He had been drumming upon Wogan's sheet of paper, and the writing on the sheet had suddenly attracted his notice. It was writing in unusually regular lines. Gaydon, arrested by Misset's change from restlessness to fixity, looked that way for a second, too, but he turned his head aside very quickly. Wogan's handwriting was none of his business.

"We will give them a month," said Wogan, who was conjecturing at the motive of this order from the Court of France. "No doubt we are suspected. I never had a hope that we should not be. The Court of France, you see, can do no less than forbid us, but I should not be surprised if it winks at us on the sly. We will give them a month. Colonel Lally is a friend of mine and a friend of the King. We will get an abatement of that order, so that not one of you shall be cashiered."

"I don't flinch at that," said Misset, "but the secret's out."

"Then we must use the more precautions," said Wogan. He had no doubt whatever that somehow he would bring the Princess safely out of her prison to Bologna. It could not be that she was born to be wasted. Misset, however, was not so confident upon the matter.

"A strange, imperturbable man is Charles Wogan," said he to Gaydon and O'Toole the same evening. "Did you happen by any chance to cast your eye over the paper I had my hand on?"

"I did not," said Gaydon, in a great hurry. "It was a private letter, no doubt."

"It was poetry. There's no need for you to hurry, my friend. It was more than mere poetry, it was in Latin. I read the first line on the page, and it ran, '*Te, dum spernit, arat novus accola; max ubi cultam—*'"

Gaydon tore his arm away from Misset. "I'll hear no more of it," he cried. "Poetry is none of my business."

A. E. W. Mason

"There, Dick, you are wrong," said O'Toole, sententiously. Both Misset and Gaydon came to a dead stop and stared. Never had poetry so strange an advocate. O'Toole set his great legs apart and his arms akimbo. He rocked himself backwards and forwards on his heels and toes, while a benevolent smile of superiority wrinkled across his broad face from ear to ear. "Yes, I've done it," said he; "I've written poetry. It is a thing a polite gentleman should be able to do. So I did it. It wasn't in Latin, because the young lady it was written to didn't understand Latin. Her name was Lucy, and I rhymed her to 'juicy,' and the pleasure of it made her purple in the face. There were to have been four lines, but there were never more than three and a half because I could not think of a suitable rhyme to O'Toole. Lucy said she knew one, but she would never tell it me."

Wogan's poetry, however, was of quite a different kind, and had Gaydon looked at it a trifle more closely, he would have experienced some relief. It was all about the sorrows and miseries of his unfortunate race and the cruel oppression of England. England owed all its great men to Ireland and was currish enough never to acknowledge the debt. Wogan always grew melancholy and grave-faced on that subject when he had the leisure to be idle. He thought bitterly of the many Irish officers sent into exile and killed in the service of alien countries; his sense of injustice grew into a passionate sort of despair, and the despair tumbled out of him in sonorous Latin verse written in the Virgilian measure. He wrote a deal of it during this month of waiting, and a long while afterwards sent an extract to Dr. Swift and received the great man's compliments upon its felicity, as anyone may see for himself in the doctor's correspondence.

How the month passed for James Stuart in Rome may be partly guessed from a letter which was brought to Wogan by Michael Vezozzi, the Chevalier's body-servant.

The letter announced that King George of England had offered the Princess Clementina a dowry of L100,000 if she would marry the Prince of Baden, and that the Prince of Baden with a numerous following was already at Innspruck to prosecute his suit.

"I do not know but what her Highness," he wrote, "will receive the best consolation for her sufferings on my account if she accepts so favourable a proposal, rather than run so many hazards as she must needs do as my wife. For myself, I have been summoned most urgently into Spain and am travelling thither on the instant."

Wogan could make neither head nor tail of the letter. Why should the King go to Spain at the time when the Princess Clementina might be expected at Bologna? It was plain that he did not expect Wogan would succeed. He was disheartened. Wogan came to the conclusion that there was the whole meaning of the letter. He was, however, for other reasons glad to receive it.

"It is very well I have this letter," said he, "for until it came I had no scrap of writing whatever to show either to her Highness or, what I take to be more important, to her Highness's mother," and he went back to his poetry.

Misset and his wife, on the other hand, drove forward to the town of Colmar, where they bought a travelling carriage and the necessaries for the journey. Misset left his wife at Colmar, but returned every twenty-four hours himself. They made the excuse that Misset had won a deal of money at play and was minded to lay it out in presents to his wife. The stratagem had a wonderful success at Schlestadt, especially amongst the ladies, who could do nothing day and night but praise in their husbands' hearing so excellent a mode of disposing of one's winnings.

A. E. W. Mason

O'Toole spent his month in polishing his pistols and sharpening his sword. It is true that he had to persuade Jenny to bear them company, but that was the work of an afternoon. He told her the story of the rich Austrian heiress, promised her a hundred guineas and a damask gown, gave her a kiss, and the matter was settled.

Jenny passed her month in a delicious excitement. She was a daughter of the camp, and had no fears whatever. She was a conspirator; she was trusted with a tremendous secret; she was to help the beautiful and enormous O'Toole to a rich and beautiful wife; she was to outwit an old curmudgeon of an uncle; she was to succour a maiden heart-broken and imprisoned. Jenny was quite uplifted. Never had a maid-servant been born to so high a destiny. Her only difficulty was to keep silence, and when the silence became no longer endurable she would run on some excuse or another to Wogan and divert him with the properest sentiments.

"To me," she would cry, "there's nothing sinful in changing clothes with the beautiful mistress of O'Toole. Christian charity says we are to make others happy. I am a Christian, and as to the uncle he can go to the devil! He can do nothing to me but talk, and I don't understand his stupid language."

Jenny was the one person really happy during this month. It was Wogan's effort to keep her so, for she was the very pivot of his plan.

There remains yet one other who had most reason of all to repine at the delay, the Princess Clementina. Her mother wearied her with perpetual complaints, the Prince of Baden, who was allowed admittance to the villa, persecuted her with his attentions; she knew nothing of what was planned for her escape, and the rigorous confinement was not relaxed. It was not a happy time for Clementina. Yet she was not entirely unhappy. A thought had come to her and stayed with her which called the colour to her cheeks and a smile to her lips. It accounted to her for the delay; her pride was restored by it; because of it she became yet more patient with her mother, more gentle with the Prince of Baden, more good-humoured to her gaolers. It sang at her heart like a bird; it lightened in her grey eyes. It had come to her one sleepless night, and the morning had not revealed it as a mere phantasy born of the night. The more she pondered it, the more certain was she of its truth. Her King was coming himself at the hazard of his life to rescue her.

A. E. W. Mason

# CHAPTER XI

## THE PRINCE OF BADEN VISITS CLEMENTINA

Therefore she waited in patience. It was still winter at Innspruck, though the calendar declared it to be spring. April was budless and cold, a month of storms; the snow drifted deep along the streets and M. Chateaudoux was much inconvenienced during his promenades in the afternoon. He would come back with most reproachful eyes for Clementina in that she so stubbornly clung to her vagabond exile and refused so fine a match as the Prince of Baden. On the afternoon of the 25th, however, Clementina read more than reproach in his eyes, more than discomfort in the agitation of his manner. The little chamberlain was afraid.

Clementina guessed the reason of his fear.

"He has come!" she cried. The exultation of her voice, the deep breath she drew, the rush of blood to her face, and the sudden dancing light in her eyes showed how much constraint she had set upon herself. She was like an ember blown to a flame. "You were stopped in your walk. You have a message for me. He has come!"

The height of her joy was the depth of Chateaudoux's regret.

"I was stopped in my walk," said he, "but not by the Chevalier Wogan. Who it was I do not know."

"Can you not guess?" cried Clementina.

"I would not trust a stranger," said her mother.

"Would you not?" asked Clementina, with a smile. "Describe him to me."

"His face was wrinkled," said Chateaudoux.

"It was disguised."

"His figure was slight and not over-tall."

M. Chateaudoux gave a fairly accurate description of Gaydon.

"I know no one whom the portrait fits," said the mother, and again Clementina cried,—

"Can you not guess? Then, mother, I will punish you. For though I know—in very truth, I know—I will not tell you." She turned back to Chateaudoux. "Well, his message? He did fix a time, a day, an hour, for my escape?"

"The 27th is the day, and at eight o'clock of the night."

"I will be ready."

"He will come here to fetch your Highness. Meanwhile he prays your Highness to fall sick and keep your bed."

"I can choose my malady," said Clementina. "It will not all be counterfeit, for indeed I shall fall sick of joy. But why must I fall sick?"

"He brings a woman to take your place, who, lying in bed with the curtains drawn, will the later be discovered."

The Princess's mother saw here a hindrance to success and eagerly she spoke of it.

"How will the woman enter? How, too, will my daughter leave?"

M. Chateaudoux coughed and hemmed in a great confusion. He explained in delicate hints that he himself was to bribe the sentry at the door to let her pass for a few moments into the house. The Princess broke into a laugh.

"Her name is Friederika, I'll warrant," she cried. "My poor Chateaudoux, they *will* give you a sweetheart. It is most cruel. Well, Friederika, thanks to the sentry's fellow-feeling for a burning heart, Friederika slips in at the door."

"Which I have taken care should stand unlatched. She changes clothes with your Highness, and your Highness—"

"Slips out in her stead."

"But he is to come for you, he says," exclaimed her mother. "And how will he do that? Besides, we do not know his name. And there must be a fitting companion who will travel with you. Has he that companion?"

"Your Highness," said Chateaudoux, "upon all those points he bade me say you should be satisfied. All he asks is that you will be ready at the time."

A gust of hail struck the window and made the room tremble.

Clementina laughed; her mother shivered.

"The Prince of Baden," said she, with a sigh. Clementina shrugged her shoulders.

"A Prince," said Chateaudoux, persuasively, "with much territory to his princeliness."

"A vain, fat, pudgy man," said Clementina.

"A sober, honest gentleman," said the mother.

"A sober butler to an honest gentleman," said Clementina.

"He has an air," said Chateaudoux.

"He has indeed," replied Clementina, "as though he handed himself upon a plate to you, and said, 'Here is a miracle. Thank God for it!' Well, I must take to my bed. I am very ill. I have a fever on me, and that's truth."

She moved towards the door, but before she had reached it there came a knocking on the street door below.

Clementina stopped; Chateaudoux looked out of the window.

"It is the Prince's carriage," said he.

"I will not see him," exclaimed Clementina.

"My child, you must," said her mother, "if only for the last time."

"Each time he comes it is for the last time, yet the next day sees him still in Innspruck. My patience and my courtesy are both outworn. Besides, to-day, now that I have heard this

A. E. W. Mason

great news we have waited for—how long? Oh, mother, oh, mother, I cannot! I shall betray myself."

The Princess's mother made an effort.

"Clementina, you must receive him. I will have it so. I am your mother. I will be your mother," she said in a tremulous tone, as though the mere utterance of the command frightened her by its audacity.

Clementina was softened on the instant. She ran across to her mother's chair, and kneeling by it said with a laugh, "So you shall. I would not barter mothers with any girl in Christendom. But you understand. I am pledged in honour to my King. I will receive the Prince, but indeed I would he had not come," and rising again she kissed her mother on the forehead.

She received the Prince of Baden alone. He was a stout man of much ceremony and took some while to elaborate a compliment upon Clementina's altered looks. Before, he had always seen her armed and helmeted with dignity; now she had much ado to keep her lips from twitching into a smile, and the smile in her eyes she could not hide at all. The Prince took the change to himself. His persistent wooing had not been after all in vain. He was not, however, the man to make the least of his sufferings in the pursuit which seemed to end so suitably to-day.

"Madam," he said with his grandest air, "I think to have given you some proof of my devotion. Even on this inclement day I come to pay my duty though the streets are deep in snow."

"Oh, sir," exclaimed Clementina, "then your feet are wet. Never run such risks for me. I would have no man weep on my account though it were only from a cold in the head."

The Prince glanced at Clementina suspiciously. Was this devotion? He preferred to think so.

"Madam, have no fears," said he, tenderly, wishing to set the anxious creature at her ease. "I drove here in my carriage."

"But from the carriage to the door you walked?"

"No, madam, I was carried."

Clementina's lips twitched again.

"I would have given much to have seen you carried," she said demurely. "I suppose you would not repeat the—No, it would be to ask too much. Besides, from my windows here in the side of the house I could not see." And she sighed deeply.

The fatuous gentleman took comfort from the sigh.

"Madam, you have but to say the word and your windows shall look whichever way you will."

Clementina, however, did not say the word. She merely sighed again. The Prince thought it a convenient moment to assert his position.

"I have stayed a long while in Innspruck, setting my constancy, which bade me stay, above my dignity, which bade me go. For three months I have stayed,—a long while, madam."

"I do not think three years could have been longer," said Clementina, with the utmost sympathy.

"So now in the end I have called my pride to help me."

"The noblest gift that heaven has given a man," said Clementina, fervently.

The Prince bowed low; Clementina curtsied majestically.

"Will you give me your hand," said he, "as far as your window?"

"Certainly, sir, and out of it."

Clementina laid her hand in his. The Prince strutted to the window; Clementina solemnly kept pace with him.

"What do you see? A sentinel fixed there guarding you. At the door stands a second sentinel. Answer me as I would be answered, your window and your door are free. Refuse me, and I travel into Italy. My trunks are already packed."

"Neatly packed, I hope," said Clementina. Her cheek was flushed; her lips no longer smiled. But she spoke most politely, and the Prince was at a loss.

"Will you give me your hand," said she, "as far as my table?"

The Prince doubtfully stretched out his hand, and the couple paced in a stately fashion to Clementina's table.

"What do you see upon my table?" said she, with something of the Prince's pomposity.

"A picture," said he, reluctantly.

"Whose?"

"The Pretender's," he answered with a sneer.

"The King's," said she, pleasantly. "His picture is fixed there guarding me. Against my heart there lies a second. I wish your Highness all speed to Italy."

She dropped his hand, bowed to him again in sign that the interview was ended. The Prince had a final argument.

"You refuse a dowry of L100,000. I would have you think of that."

"Sir, you think of it for both of us."

The Prince drew himself up to his full stature.

"I have your answer, then?"

"You have, sir. You had it yesterday, and if I remember right the day before."

"I will stay yet two more days. Madam, you need not fear. I shall not importune you. I give you those two days for reflection. Unless I hear from you I shall leave Innspruck—"

"In two days' time?" suddenly exclaimed Clementina.

"On the evening of the 27th," said the Prince.

Clementina laughed softly in a way which he did not understand. She was altogether in a strange, incomprehensible mood that afternoon, and when he learnt next day that she had taken to her bed he was not surprised. Perhaps he was not altogether grieved. It seemed right that she should be punished for her stubbornness. Punishment might soften her.

But no message came to him during those two days, and on the morning of the 27th he set out for Italy.

At the second posting stage, which he reached about three of the afternoon, he crossed a hired carriage on its way to Innspruck. The carriage left the inn door as the Prince drove up to it. He noticed the great size of the coachman on the box, he saw also that a man and two women were seated within the carriage, and that a servant rode on horseback by the door. The road, however, was a busy one; day and night travellers passed up and down; the Prince gave only a passing scrutiny to that carriage rolling down the hill to Innspruck. Besides, he was acquainted neither with Gaydon, who rode within the carriage, nor with Wogan, the servant at the door, nor with O'Toole, the fat man on the box.

At nightfall the Prince came to Nazareth, a lonely village amongst the mountains with a single tavern, where he thought to sleep the night. There was but one guest-room, however, which was already bespoken by a Flemish lady, the Countess of Cernes, who had travelled that morning to Innspruck to fetch her niece.

The Prince grumbled for a little, since the evening was growing stormy and wild, but there was no remedy. He could not dispute the matter, for he was shown the Countess's berlin waiting ready for her return. A servant of the Count's household also had been left behind at Nazareth to retain the room, and this man, while using all proper civilities, refused to give up possession. The Prince had no acquaintance with the officers of Dillon's Irish regiment, so that he had no single suspicion that Captain Misset was the servant. He drove on for another stage, where he found a lodging.

Meanwhile the hired carriage rolled into Innspruck, and a storm of extraordinary violence burst over the country.

# CHAPTER XII

## THE NIGHT OF THE 27TH.
## IN THE STREETS OF INNSPRUCK

In fact, just about the time when the Prince's horses were being unharnessed from his carriage on the heights of Mount Brenner, the hired carriage stopped before a little inn under the town wall of Innspruck hard by the bridge. And half an hour later, when the Prince was sitting down to his supper before a blazing fire and thanking his stars that on so gusty and wild a night he had a stout roof above his head, a man and a woman came out from the little tavern under the town wall and disappeared into the darkness. They had the streets to themselves, for that night the city was a whirlpool of the winds. Each separate chasm in the encircling hills was a mouth to discharge a separate blast. The winds swept down into the hollow and charged in a riotous combat about the squares and lanes; at each corner was an ambuscade, and everywhere they clashed with artilleries of hail and sleet.

The man and woman staggered hand in hand and floundered in the deep snow. They were soaked to the skin, frozen by the cold, and whipped by the stinging hail. Though they bent their heads and bodies, though they clung hand in hand, though they struggled with all their strength, there were

A. E. W. Mason

times when they could not advance a foot and must needs wait for a lull in the shelter of a porch. At such times the man would perhaps quote a line of Virgil about the cave of the winds, and the woman curse like a grenadier. They, however, were not the only people who were distressed by the storm.

Outside the villa in which the Princess was imprisoned stood the two sentinels, one beneath the window, the other before the door. There were icicles upon their beards; they were so shrouded in white they had the look of snow men built by schoolboys. Their coats of frieze could not keep out the searching sleet, nor their caps protect their ears from the intolerable cold. Their hands were so numbed they could not feel the muskets they held.

The sentinel before the door suffered the most, for whereas his companion beneath the window had nothing but the house wall before his eyes, he, on his part, could see on the other side of the alley of trees the red blinds of "The White Chamois," that inn which the Chevalier de St. George had mentioned to Charles Wogan. The red blinds shone very cheery and comfortable upon that stormy night. The sentinel envied the men gathered in the warmth and light behind them, and cursed his own miserable lot as heartily as the woman in the porch did hers. The red blinds made it unendurable. He left his post and joined his companion.

"Rudolf," he said, bawling into his ear, "come with me! Our birds will not fly away to-night."

The two sentries came to the front of the house and stared at the red-litten blinds.

"What a night!" cried Rudolf. "Not a citizen would thrust his nose out of doors."

"Not even the little Chateaudoux's sweetheart," replied the other, with a grin.

They stared again at the red blinds, and in a lull of the wind a clock struck nine.

"There is an hour before the magistrate comes," said Rudolf.

"You take that hour," said his companion; "I will have the hour after the magistrate has gone."

Rudolf ran across to the inn. The sentinel at the door remained behind. Both men were pleased,—Rudolf because he had his hour immediately, his fellow-soldier because once the magistrate had come and gone, he would take as long as he pleased.

Meanwhile the man and woman hand in hand drew nearer to the villa, but very slowly. For, apart from the weather's hindrances, the woman's anger had grown. She stopped, she fell down when there was no need to fall, she wept, she struggled to free her hand, and finally, when they had taken shelter beneath a portico, she sank down on the stone steps, and with many oaths and many tears refused to budge a foot. Strangely enough, it was not so much the inclemency of the night or the danger of the enterprise which provoked this obstinacy, as some outrage and dishonour to her figure.

"You may talk all night," she cried between her sobs, "about O'Toole and his beautiful German. They can go hang for me! I am only a servant, I know. I am poor, I admit it. But poverty isn't a crime. It gives no one the right to make a dwarf of me. No, no!"—this as Wogan bent down to lift her from the ground—"plague on you all! I will sit here and die; and when I am found frozen and dead perhaps you will be sorry for your cruelty to a poor girl who wanted nothing

A. E. W. Mason

better than to serve you." Here Jenny was so moved by the piteousness of her fate that her tears broke out again. She wept loudly. Wogan was in an extremity of alarm lest someone should pass, or the people of the house be aroused. He tried most tenderly to comfort her. She would have none of the consolations. He took her in his arms and raised her to her feet. She swore more loudly than she had wept, she kicked at his legs, she struck at his head with her fist. In another moment she would surely have cried murder. Wogan had to let her sink back upon the steps, where she fell to whimpering.

"I am not beautiful, I know; I never boasted that I was; but I have a figure and limbs that a painter would die to paint. And what do you make of me? A maggot, a thing all body like a nasty bear. Oh, curse the day that I set out with such tyrants! A pretty figure of fun I should make before your beautiful German, covered with mud to the knees. No, you shall hang me first! Why couldn't O'Toole do his own work, the ninny, I hate him! He's tall enough, the great donkey; but no, I must do it, who am shorter, and even then not short enough for him and you, but you must drag me through the dirt without heels!"

Wogan let her run on; he was at his wits' end what to do. All this turmoil, these tears, these oaths and blows, came from nothing more serious than this, that Jenny, to make her height less remarkable, must wear no heels. It was ludicrous, it was absurd, but none the less the whole expedition, carried to the very point of completion, must fail, utterly and irretrievably fail, because Jenny would not for one day go without her heels. The Princess must remain in her prison at Innspruck; the Chevalier must lose his wife; the exertions of Wogan and his friends, their risks, their ingenuity, must bear no fruit because Jenny would not show herself three inches short of her ordinary height. O'Toole had warned him there would be a difficulty; but that the difficulty should become an absolute hindrance, should spoil a scheme of so much consequence, that was inconceivable.

Yet there was Jenny sobbing her heart out on the steps not half a mile from the villa; the minutes were passing; the inconceivable thing was true. Wogan could have torn his hair in the rage of his despair. He could have laughed out loudly and passionately until even on that stormy night he brought the guard. He thought of the perils he had run, the difficulties he had surmounted. He had outwitted the Countess de Berg and Lady Featherstone, he had persuaded the reluctant Prince Sobieski, he had foiled his enemies on the road to Schlestadt, he had made his plans, he had gathered his friends, he had crept out with them from Strasbourg, yet in the end they had come to Innspruck to be foiled because Jenny would not go without her heels. Wogan could have wept like Jenny.

But he did not. On the contrary, he sat down by her side on the steps and took her hand, gentle as a sheep.

"You are in the right of it, Jenny," said he, in a most remorseful voice.

Jenny looked up.

"Yes," he continued. "I was in the wrong. O'Toole is the most selfish man in the whole world. Cowardly, too! But there never was a selfish man who was not at heart a bit of a coward. Sure enough, sooner or later the cowardice comes out. It is a preposterous thing that O'Toole should think that you and I are going to rescue his heiress for him while he sits at his ease by the inn fire. No; let us go back to him and tell him to his face the selfish cowardly man he is."

It seemed, however, that Jenny was not entirely pleased to

hear her own sentiments so frankly uttered by Mr. Wogan. Besides, he seemed to exaggerate them, for she said with a little reluctance, "I would not say that he was a coward."

"But I would," exclaimed Wogan, hotly. "Moreover, I do. With all my heart I say it. A great lubberly monster of a coward. He is envious, too, Jenny."

Jenny had by this time stopped weeping.

"Why envious?" she asked with an accent of rebellion which was very much to Wogan's taste.

"It's as plain as the palm of my hand. Why should he make a dwarf of you, Jenny?—for it's the truth he has done that; he has made a little dwarf out of the finest girl in the land by robbing her of her heels." Jenny was on the point of interrupting with some indignation, but Wogan would not listen to her. "A dwarf," he continued, "it was your own word, Jenny. I could say nothing to comfort you when you spoke it, for it was so true and suitable an epithet. A little dwarf he has made of you, all body and no legs like a bear, a dwarf-bear, of course; and why, if it is not that he envies you your figure and is jealous of it in a mean and discreditable way? Sure, he wants to have all the looks and to appear quite incomparable to the eyes of his beautiful German. So he makes a dwarf of you, a little bear dwarf—"

Jenny, however, had heard this phrase often enough by now. She interrupted Wogan hotly, and it seemed her anger was now as much directed against him as it had been before against O'Toole.

"He is not envious," said she. "A fine friend he has in you, I am thinking. He has no need to be envious. Captain O'Toole could carry me to the house in his arms if he wished, which is more than you could do if you tried till midday to-morrow," and she turned her shoulder to Wogan, who, in no way abashed by her contempt, cried triumphantly,—

"But he didn't wish. He let you drag through the mud and snow without so much as a patten to keep you off the ground. Why? Tell me that, Jenny! Why didn't he wish?"

Jenny was silent.

"You see, if he is not envious, he is at all events a coward," argued Wogan, "else he would have run his own risks and come in your stead."

"But that would not have served," cried Jenny. It was her turn now to speak triumphantly. "How could O'Toole have run away with his heiress and at the same time remained behind in her bed to escape suspicion, as I am to do?"

"I had forgotten that, to be sure," said Wogan, meekly.

Jenny laughed derisively.

"O'Toole is the man with the head on his shoulders," said she.

"And a pitiful, calculating head it is," exclaimed Wogan. "Think of the inconvenience of your position when you are discovered to-morrow. Think of the angry uncle! O'Toole has thought of him and so keeps out of his way. Here's a nice world, where hulking, shapeless giants like O'Toole hide themselves from angry uncles behind a dwarf-girl's petticoats. Bah! We will go back and kick O'Toole."

Wogan rose to his feet. Jenny did not move; she sat and laughed scornfully.

"*You* kick O'Toole! You might once, if he happened to be asleep. But he would take you up by the scruff of the neck and the legs and beat your face against your knees until you were dead. Besides, what do I care for an angry uncle! I am well paid to put up with his insults."

"Well paid!" said Wogan, with a sneer. "A hundred guineas and a damask gown! Three hundred guineas and a gown all lace and gold tags would not be enough. Besides, I'll wager he has not paid you a farthing. He'll cheat you, Jenny. He's a rare bite is O'Toole. Between you and me, Jenny, he is a beggarly fellow!"

"He has already paid me half," cried Jenny. It was no knowledge to Wogan, who, however, counterfeited a deal of surprise.

"Well," said he, "he has only done it to cheat you the more easily of the other fifty. We will go straight back and tell him that it costs three hundred guineas, money down, and the best gown in Paris to turn a fine figure of a girl into a dwarf-bear."

He leaned down and took Jenny by the arm. She sprang to her feet and twisted herself free.

"No," she said, "you can go back if you will and show him what a good friend you are to him. But I go on. The poor captain shall have one person in the world, though she's only a servant, to help him when he wants."

Thus Wogan won the victory. But he was most careful to conceal it. He walked by her side humble as a whipped dog. If he had to point out the way, he did it with the most penitent air; when he offered his hand to help her over a snow-heap and she struck it aside, he merely bowed his head as though her contempt was well deserved. He even whispered in her ear in a trembling voice, "Jenny, you will not say a word to O'Toole about the remarks I made of him? He is a strong, hasty man. I know not what might come of it."

Jenny sneered and shrugged her shoulders. She would not speak to Wogan any more, and so they came silently into the avenue of trees between "The White Chamois" and the villa. The windows in the front of the villa were dark, and through the blinding snow-storm Wogan could not have distinguished the position of the house at all but for the red blinds of the tavern opposite which shone out upon the night and gave the snow falling before them a tinge of pink. Wogan crept nearer to the house and heard the sentinel stamping in the snow. He came back to Jenny and pointed the sentinel out to her.

"Give me a quarter of an hour so far as you can judge. Then pass the sentinel and go up the steps into the house. The sentinel is prepared for your coming, and if he stops you, you must say 'Chateaudoux' in a whisper, and he will understand. You will find the door of the house open and a man waiting for you."

Jenny made no answer, but Wogan was sure of her now. He left her standing beneath the dripping trees and crept towards the side of the house. A sentry was posted beneath her Highness's windows, and through those windows he had to climb. He needed that quarter of an hour to wait for a suitable moment when the sentry would be at the far end of his beat. But that sentry was fuddling himself with a vile spirit distilled from the gentian flower in the kitchen of "The White Chamois." Wogan, creeping stealthily through the snow-storm, found the side of the house unguarded. The windows on the ground floor were dark; those on the first floor which lighted her Highness's apartments were ablaze.

He noticed with a pang of dismay that one of those lighted windows was wide open to the storm. He wondered whether it meant that the Princess had been removed to another lodging. He climbed on the sill of the lower window; by the side of that window a stone pillar ran up the side of the house to the windows on the first floor. Wogan had taken note of that pillar months back when he was hawking chattels in Innspruck. He set his hands about it and got a grip with his foot against the sash of the lower window. He was just raising himself when he heard a noise above him. He dropped back to the ground and stood in the fixed attitude of a sentinel.

A head appeared at the window, a woman's head. The light was behind, within the room, so that Wogan could not see the face. But the shape of the head, its gracious poise upon the young shoulders, the curve of the neck, the bright hair drawn backwards from the brows,—here were marks Wogan could not mistake. They had been present before his eyes these many months. The head at the open window was the head of the Princess. Wogan felt a thrill run through his blood. To a lover the sight of his mistress is always unexpected, though he foreknows the very moment of her coming. To Wogan the sight of his Queen had the like effect. He had not seen her since he had left Ohlau two years before with her promise to marry the Chevalier. It seemed to him, though for this he had lived and worked up early and down late for so long, a miraculous thing that he should see her now.

She leaned forward and peered downwards into the lane. The light streamed out, bathing her head and shoulders. Wogan could see the snow fall upon her dark hair and whiten it; it fell, too, upon her neck, but that it could not whiten. She leaned out into the darkness, and Wogan set foot again upon the lower window-sill. At the same moment another head appeared beside Clementina's, and a sharp cry rang out, a cry of terror. Then both heads disappeared, and a heavy curtain swung across the window, shutting the light in.

Wogan remained motionless, his heart sinking with alarm. Had that cry been heard? Had the wind carried it to the sentry at the door? He waited, but no sound of running footsteps came to his ears; the cry had been lost in the storm. He was now so near to success that dangers which a month ago would have seemed of small account showed most menacing and fatal.

"It was the Princess-mother who cried out," he thought, and was reminded that the need of persuasions was not ended for the night with the conquest of Jenny. He had to convince the Princess-mother of his authority without a line of Prince Sobieski's writing to support him; he had to overcome her timidity. But he was prepared for the encounter; he had foreseen it, and had an argument ready for the Princess-mother, though he would have preferred to wring the old lady's neck. Her cry might spoil everything. However, it had not been heard, and since it had not been heard, Wogan was disposed to forgive it.

For the window was still open, and now that the curtain was drawn no ray of light escaped from the room to betray the man who climbed into it.

# CHAPTER XIII

## THE NIGHT OF THE 27TH. IN CLEMENTINA'S APARTMENTS

Meanwhile within the room the Princess-mother clung to Clementina. The terror which her sharp cry had expressed was visible in her strained and startled face. Her eyes, bright with terror, stared at the drawn curtain; she could not avert them; she still must gaze, fascinated by her fears; and her dry, whispering lips were tremulous.

"Heaven have mercy!" she whispered; "shut the window! Shut it fast!" and as Clementina moved in surprise, she clung the closer to her daughter. "No, do not leave me! Come away! Jesu! here are we alone,—two women!"

"Mother," said Clementina, soothing her and gently stroking her hair, as though she in truth was the mother and the mother her daughter, "there's no cause for fear."

"No cause for fear! I saw him—the sentry—he is climbing up. Ah!" and again her voice rose to a cry as Wogan's foot grated on the window-ledge.

"Hush, mother! A cry will ruin us. It's not the sentinel,"

said Clementina.

Clementina was laughing, and by her laughter the Princess-mother was in some measure reassured.

"Who is it, then?" she asked.

"Can you not guess?" said Clementina, incredulously. "It is so evident. Yet I would not have you guess. It is my secret, my discovery. I'll tell you." She heard a man behind the curtain spring lightly from the window to the floor. She raised her voice that he might know she had divined him. "Your sentinel is the one man who has the right to rescue me. Your sentinel's the King."

At that moment Wogan pushed aside the curtain.

"No, your Highness," said he, "but the King's servant."

The Princess-mother dropped into a chair and looked at her visitor with despair. It was not the sentinel, to be sure, but, on the other hand, it was Mr. Wogan, whom she knew for a very insistent man with a great liking for his own way. She drew little comfort from Mr. Wogan's coming.

It seemed, too, that he was not very welcome to Clementina; for she drew back a step and in a voice which dropped and had a tremble of disappointment, "Mr. Wogan," she said, "the King is well served;" and she stood there without so much as offering him her hand. Wogan had not counted on so cold a greeting, but he understood the reason, and was not sure but what he approved of it. After all, she had encountered perils on the King's account; she had some sort of a justification to believe the King would do the like for her. It had not occurred to him or indeed to anyone before; but now that he saw the chosen woman so plainly wounded, he felt a trifle hot against his King for having disappointed her. He set his wits to work to dispel the disappointment.

"Your Highness, the truth is there are great matters brewing in Spain. His Majesty was needed there most urgently. He had to decide between Innspruck and Cadiz, and it seemed that he would honour your great confidence in him and at the same time serve you best—"

Clementina would not allow him to complete the sentence. Her cheek flushed, and she said quickly,—

"You are right, Mr. Wogan. The King is right. Mine was a girl's thought. I am ashamed of it;" and she frankly gave him her hand. Wogan was fairly well pleased with his apology for his King. It was not quite the truth, no doubt, but it had spared Clementina a trifle of humiliation, and had re-established the King in her thoughts. He bent over her hand and would have kissed it, but she stopped him.

"No," said she, "an honest handclasp, if you please; for no woman can have ever lived who had a truer friend," and Wogan, looking into her frank eyes, was not, after all, nearly so well pleased with the untruth he had told her. She was an uncomfortable woman to go about with shifts and contrivances. Her open face, with its broad forehead and the clear, steady eyes of darkest blue, claimed truth as a prerogative. The blush which had faded from her cheeks appeared on his, and he began to babble some foolish word about his unworthiness when the Princess-mother interrupted him in a grudging voice,—

"Mr. Wogan, you were to bring a written authority from the Prince my husband."

Wogan drew himself up straight.

"Your Highness," said he, with a bow of the utmost respect, "I was given such an authority."

The Princess-mother held out her hand. "Will you give it me?"

"I said that I was given such an authority. But I have it no longer. I was attacked on my way from Ohlau. There were five men against me, all of whom desired that letter. The room was small; I could not run away; neither had I much space wherein to resist five men. I knew that were I killed and that letter found on me, your Highness would thereafter be too surely guarded to make escape possible, and his Highness Prince Sobieski would himself incur the Emperor's hostility. So when I had made sure that those five men were joined against me, I twisted that letter into a taper and before their faces lit my pipe with it."

Clementina's eyes were fixed steadily and intently upon Wogan's face. When he ended she drew a deep breath, but otherwise she did not move. The Princess-mother, however, was unmistakably relieved. She spoke with a kindliness she had never shown before to Wogan; she even smiled at him in a friendly way.

"We do not doubt you, Mr. Wogan, but that written letter, giving my daughter leave to go, I needs must have before I let her go. A father's authority! I cannot take that upon myself."

Clementina took a quick step across to her mother's side.

"You did not hear," she said.

"I heard indeed that Mr. Wogan had burnt the letter."

"But under what stress, and to spare my father and to leave

me still a grain of hope. Mother, this gentleman has run great risks for me,—how great I did not know; even now in this one instance we can only guess and still fall short of the mark."

The Princess-mother visibly stiffened with maternal authority.

"My child, without some sure sign the Prince consents, you must not go."

Clementina looked towards Wogan for assistance. Wogan put his hand into his pocket.

"That sure sign I have," said he. "It is a surer sign than any written letter; for handwriting may always be counterfeit. This could never be," and he held out on the palm of his hand the turquoise snuff-box which the Prince had given him on New Year's day. "It is a jewel unique in all the world, and the Prince gave it me. It is a jewel he treasured not only for its value, but its history. Yet he gave it me. It was won by the great King John of Poland, and remains as a memorial of the most glorious day in all that warrior's glorious life; yet his son gave it me. With his own hands he put it into mine to prove to me with what confidence he trusted your Highness's daughter to my care. That confidence was written large in the letter I burnt, but I am thinking it is engraved for ever upon this stone."

The Princess-mother took the snuff-box reluctantly and turned it over and over. She was silent. Clementina answered for her.

"I am ready," she said, and she pointed to a tiny bundle on a chair in which a few clothes were wrapped. "My jewels are packed in the bundle, but I can leave them behind me if needs be."

Wogan lifted up the bundle and laughed.

"Your Highness teaches a lesson to soldiers; for there is never a knapsack but can hold this and still have half its space to spare. The front door is unlatched?"

"M. Chateaudoux is watching in the hall."

"And the hall's unlighted?"

"Yes."

"Jenny should be here in a minute, and before she comes I must tell you she does not know the importance of our undertaking. She is the servant to Mrs. Misset, who attends your Highness into Italy. We did not let her into the secret. We made up a comedy in which you have your parts to play. Your Highness," and he turned to Clementina, "is a rich Austrian heiress, deeply enamoured of Captain Lucius O'Toole."

"Captain Lucius O'Toole!" exclaimed the mother, in horror. "My daughter enamoured of a Captain Lucius O'Toole!"

"He is one of my three companions," said Wogan, imperturbably. "Moreover, he is six foot four, the most creditable lover in the world."

"Well," said Clementina, with a laugh, "I am deeply enamoured of the engaging Captain Lucius O'Toole. Go on, sir."

"Your parents are of a most unexampled cruelty. They will not smile upon the fascinating O'Toole, but have locked you up on bread and water until you shall agree to marry a wealthy but decrepit gentleman of eighty-three."

"I will not," cried Clementina; "I will starve myself to death first. I will marry my six feet four or no other man in Christendom."

"Clementina!" cried her mother, deprecatingly.

"But at this moment," continued Wogan, "there very properly appears the fairy godmother in the person of a romantical maiden aunt."

"Oh!" said Clementina, "I have a romantical maiden aunt."

"Yes," said Wogan, and turning with a bow to the Princess-mother; "your Highness."

"I?" she exclaimed, starting up in her chair.

"Your Highness has written an encouraging letter to Captain O'Toole," resumed Wogan. The Princess-mother gasped, "A letter to Captain O'Toole," and she flung up her hands and fell back in her chair.

"On the receipt of the letter Captain O'Toole gathers his friends, borrows a horse here, a carriage there, and a hundred guineas from Heaven knows whom, comes to the rescue like a knight-errant, and retells the old story of how love laughs at locksmiths."

As Wogan ended, the mother rose from her chair. It may have been that she revolted at the part she was to play; it may have been because a fiercer gust shook the curtain and bellied it inwards. At all events she flung the curtain aside; the snow drifted through the open window onto the floor; outside the open window it was falling like a cascade, and the air was icy.

"Mr. Wogan," she said, stubbornly working herself into a heat to make more sure of her resolution, "my daughter cannot go to-night. To-morrow, if the sky clears, yes, but to-night, no. You do not know, sir, being a man. But my daughter has fasted through this Lent, and that leaves a woman weak. I do forbid her going, as her father would. The very dogs running the streets for food keep kennel on such a night. She must not go."

Wogan did not give way, though he felt a qualm of despair, knowing all the stubbornness of which the weak are capable, knowing how impervious to facts or arguments.

"Your Highness," he said quickly, "we are not birds of passage to rule our flight by seasons. We must take the moment when it comes, and it comes now. To-night your daughter can escape; for here's a night made for an escape."

"And for my part," cried Clementina, "I would the snow fell faster." She crossed to the open window and held out her hands to catch the flakes. "Would they did not melt! I believe Heaven sends the snow to shelter me. It's the white canopy spread above my head, that I may go in state to meet my King." She stood eager and exultant, her eyes shining, her cheek on fire, her voice thrilling with pride. She seemed not to feel the cold. She welcomed the hardships of wind and falling snow as her opportunity. She desired not only for escape, but also to endure.

Wogan looked her over from head to foot, filled with pride and admiration. He had made no mistake; he had plucked this rose of the world to give to his King. His eyes said it; and the girl, reading them, drew a breath and rippled out a laugh of gladness that his trusted servant was so well content

A. E. W. Mason

with her. But the Princess-mother stood unmoved.

"My daughter cannot go to-night," she repeated resentfully. "I do forbid it."

Wogan had his one argument. This one argument was his last resource. He had chosen it carefully with an eye to the woman whom it was to persuade. It was not couched as an inducement; it did not claim the discharge of an obligation; it was not a reply to any definite objection. Such arguments would only have confirmed her in her stubbornness. He made accordingly an appeal to sentiment.

"Your Highness's daughter," said he, "spoke a minute since of the hazards my friends and I have run to compass her escape. As regards four of us, the words reached beyond our deserts. For we are men. Such hazards are our portion; they are seldom lightened by so high an aim. But the fifth! The words, however kind, were still below that fifth one's merits; for the fifth is a woman."

"I know. With all my heart I thank her. With all my heart I pity her."

"But there is one thing your Highness does not know. She runs our risks,—the risk of capture, the risk of the night, the storm, the snow, she a woman by nature timid and frail,—yet with never in all her life so great a reason for timidity, or so much frailty of health as now. We venture our lives, but she ventures more."

The mother bowed her head; Clementina looked fixedly at Wogan.

"Speak plainly, my friend," she said. "There are no children here."

"Madam, I need but quote to you the words her husband used. For my part, I think that nobler words were never spoken, and with her whole heart she repeats them. They are these: 'The boy would only live to serve his King; why should he not serve his King before he lives?'"

The mother was still silent, but Wogan could see that the tears overbrimmed her eyes and rolled down her cheeks. Clementina was silent for a while too, and stood with her eyes fixed thoughtfully on Wogan. Then she said gently,—

"Her name."

Wogan told her it, and she said no more; but it was plain that she would never forget it, that she had written it upon her heart.

Wogan waited, looking to the Princess, who drying her tears rose from her chair and said with great and unexpected dignity,—

"How comes it, sir, that with such servants your King still does not sit upon his throne? My daughter shall not fall below the great example set to her. My fears are shamed by it. My daughter goes with you to-night."

It was time that she consented, for even as Wogan flung himself upon his knee and raised her hand, M. Chateaudoux appeared at the door with a finger on his lips, and behind him one could hear a voice grumbling and cursing on the stairs.

"Jenny," said Wogan, and Jenny stumbled into the room. "Quiet," said he; "you will wake the house."

"Well, if you had to walk upstairs in the dark in these horrible shoes—"

A. E. W. Mason

"Oh, Jenny, your cloak, quick!"

"Take the thing! A good riddance to it; it's dripping wet, and weighs a ton."

"Dripping wet!" moaned the mother.

"I shall not wear it long," said Clementina, advancing from the embrasure of the window. Jenny turned and looked her over critically from head to foot. Then she turned away without a word and let the cloak fall to the ground. It fell about her feet; she kicked it viciously away, and at the same time she kicked off one of those shoes of which she so much complained. Jenny was never the woman to mince her language, and to-night she was in her surliest mood. So she swore simply and heartily, to the mother's utter astonishment and indignation.

"Damn!" she said, hobbling across the room to the corner, whither her shoe had fallen. "There, there, old lady; don't hold your hands to your ears as though a clean oath would poison them!"

The Princess-mother fell back in her chair.

"Does she speak to me?" she asked helplessly.

"Yes," said Wogan; and turning to Jenny, "This is the kind-hearted aunt."

Jenny turned to Clementina, who was picking the cloak from the floor.

"And you are the beautiful heiress," she said sourly. "Well, if you are going to put that wet cloak on your shoulders, I wish you joy of the first kiss O'Toole gives you when you jump into his arms."

The Princess-mother screamed; Wogan hastened to interfere.

"Jenny, there's the bedroom; to bed with you!" and he took out his watch. At once he uttered an exclamation of affright. Wogan had miscalculated the time which he would require. It had taken longer than he had anticipated to reach the villa against the storm; his conflict with Jenny in the portico had consumed valuable minutes; he had been at some pains to over-persuade the Princess-mother; Jenny herself amongst the trees in the darkness had waited more than the quarter of an hour demanded of her; Wogan himself, absorbed each moment in that moment's particular business,—now bending all his wits to vanquish Jenny, now to vanquish the Princess-mother,—even Wogan had neglected how the time sped. He looked at his watch. It was twenty-five minutes to ten, and at ten the magistrate would be knocking at the door.

"I am ready," said Clementina, drawing the wet cloak about her shoulders and its hood over her head. She barely shivered under its wet heaviness.

"There's one more thing to be done before you go," said Wogan; but before he could say what that one thing was, Jenny, who had now recovered her shoe, ran across the room and took the beautiful heiress by both hands. Jenny was impulsive by nature. The Princess-mother's distress and Clementina's fearlessness made her suddenly ashamed that she had spoken so sourly.

"There, there, old lady," she said soothingly; "don't you fret. They are very good friends your niece is going with." Then she drew Clementina close to her. "I don't wonder they are all mad about you, for I can't but say you are very handsome and richly worth the pains you have occasioned us." She kissed Clementina plump upon the cheek and whispered in her ear, "O'Toole won't mind the wet cloak, my dear, when he sees you."

Clementina laughed happily and returned her kiss with no less sincerity, if with less noise.

"Quick, Jenny," said Wogan, "to bed with you!"

He pointed to the door which led to the Princess's bedroom.

"Now you must write a letter," he added to Clementina, in a low voice, as soon as the door was shut upon Jenny. "A letter to your mother, relieving her of all complicity in your escape. Her Highness will find it to-morrow night slipped under the cover of her toilette."

Clementina ran to a table, and taking up a pen, "You think of everything," she said. "Perhaps you have written the letter."

Wogan pulled a sheet of paper from his fob.

"I scribbled down a few dutiful sentiments," said he, "as we drove down from Nazareth, thinking it might save time."

"Mother," exclaimed Clementina, "not content with contriving my escape, he will write my letters to you. Well, sir, let us hear what you have made of it."

Wogan dictated a most beautiful letter, in which a mother's claims for obedience were strongly set out—as a justification, one must suppose, for a daughter's disobedience. But Clementina was betrothed to his Majesty King James, and that engagement must be ever the highest consideration with her, on pain of forfeiting her honour. It was altogether a noble and stately letter, written in formal, irreproachable phrases which no daughter in the world would ever have written to a mother. Clementina laughed over it, but said that it would serve. Wogan looked at his watch again. It was then a quarter to ten.

"Quick!" said he. "Your Highness will wait for me under the fourth tree of the avenue, counting from the end."

He left the mother and daughter alone, that his presence might not check the tenderness of their farewell, and went down the stairs into the dark hall. M. Chateaudoux was waiting there, with his teeth chattering in the extremity of his alarm. Wogan unlatched the door very carefully and saw through the chink the sentry standing by the steps. The snow still fell; he was glad to note the only light was a white glimmering from the waste of snow upon the ground.

"You must go out with her," Wogan whispered to Chateaudoux, "and speak a word to the sentry."

"At any moment the magistrate may come," said Chateaudoux, though he trembled so that he could hardly speak.

"All the more reason for the sentinel to let your sweetheart run home at her quickest step," said Wogan, and above him he heard Clementina come out upon the landing. He crept up the stairs to her.

"Here is my hand," said he, in a low voice. She laid her own in his, and bending towards him in the darkness she whispered,—

"Promise me it shall always be at my service. I shall need friends. I am young, and I have no knowledge. Promise me!"

She was young indeed. The freshness of her voice, its little tremble of modesty, the earnestness of its appeal, carried her youth quite home to Mr. Wogan's heart. She was sweet with youth. Wogan felt it more clearly as they stood together in the darkness than when he had seen her plainly in the lighted room, with youth mantling her cheeks and visible in the buoyancy of her walk. Then she had been always the chosen woman. Wogan could just see her eyes, steady and mysteriously dark, shining at him out of the gloom, and a pang of remorse suddenly struck through him. That one step she was to take was across the threshold of a prison, it was true, but a prison familiar and warm, and into a night of storm and darkness and ice. The road lay before her into Italy, but it was a road of unknown perils, through mountains deep in snow. And this escape of to-night from the villa, this thunderous flight, with its hardships and its dangers, which followed the escape, was only the symbol of her life. She stepped from the shelter of her girlhood, as she stepped across the threshold of the villa, into a womanhood dark with many trials, storm-swept and wandering. She might reach the queendom which was her due, as the berlin in which she was to travel might—nay, surely would—rush one day from the gorges into the plains and the sunlight of Italy; but had Wogan travelled to Rome in Gaydon's place and talked with Whittington outside the Caprara Palace, it is very likely that she would never have been allowed by him to start. Up till now he had thought only of her splendid courage, of the humiliation of her capture, of her wounded pride; she was the chosen woman. Now he thought of the girl, and wondered of her destiny, and was stricken with remorse.

"Promise me," she repeated, and her hand tightened upon his and clung to it. Wogan had no fine sentiments wherewith to answer her; but his voice took a depth of sincerity and tenderness quite strange to her. Her fingers ceased to tremble.

They went down into the hall. Chateaudoux, who had been waiting in an agony of impatience, opened the door and slipped out; Clementina followed him.

The door was left ajar behind them, and Wogan in the hall saw Chateaudoux speak with the sentinel, saw the sentinel run hurriedly to Clementina, saw Clementina disappear into the snow. Chateaudoux ran back into the hall.

"And you!" he asked, as he barred and locked the door. "The magistrate is coming. I saw the lights of the guard across the avenue."

Clementina was outside in the storm; Wogan was within the house, and the lights of the guard were already near.

"I go by the way I came," said he; "I have time;" and he ran quickly up the stairs. In the room he found the Princess-mother weeping silently, and again, as he saw this weak elderly woman left alone to her fears and forebodings, remorse took hold on him.

"Courage, madam," said he, as he crossed the room; "she goes to wed a king."

"Sir, I am her mother," replied the Princess, gaining at this moment a suitable dignity from her tears. "I was wondering not of the King, but of the man the King conceals."

"You need not, madam," said Wogan, who had no time for eulogies upon his master. "Take his servant's loyalty as the measure of his merits."

He looked out of the window and suddenly drew back. He stood for a moment with a look of great fear upon his face. For the sentinel was back at his post; Wogan dared not at this moment risk a struggle, and perhaps an outcry. Clementina was waiting under the avenue of trees; Wogan was within the house, and the lights of the guard were already flaring in the roadway. Even as Wogan stood in the embrasure of the window, he heard a heavy knocking on the door.

# CHAPTER XIV

## THE ESCAPE

Wogan closed the window cautiously. The snow had drifted through and lay melting in a heap beneath the sill. He drew the curtain across the embrasure, and then he crossed to the bedroom door.

"Jenny," he whispered, "are you in bed?"

"Yes."

"Lie close! Do not show your face nor speak. Only groan, and groan most delicately, or we are lost."

He closed the door upon Jenny, and turning about came face to face with the Princess-mother. She stood confronting him, a finger on her lips, and terror in her eyes; and he heard the street-door open and clang to below.

"The magistrate!" she whispered.

"Courage, your Highness. Keep them from the bed! Say that her eyes are weak and cannot bear the light."

He slipped behind the curtain into the embrasure, picturing

A. E. W. Mason

to himself the disposition of the room, lest he should have left behind a trifle to betray him. He had in a supreme degree that gift of recollection which takes the form of a mental vision. He did not have to count over the details of the room; he summoned a picture of it to his mind, and saw it and its contents from corner to corner. And thus while the footsteps yet sounded on the stair, he saw Clementina's bundle lying forgotten on a couch. He darted from his hiding-place, seized it, and ran back. He had just sufficient and not a second more time, for the curtain had not ceased to swing when the magistrate knocked, and without waiting for an answer entered. He was followed by two soldiers, and these he ordered to wait without the door.

"Your Highness," he said in a polite voice, and stopped abruptly. It seemed to Wogan behind the curtain that his heart stopped at the same moment and with no less abruptness. There was no evidence of Clementina's flight to justify that sudden silence. Then he grew faint, as it occurred to him that he had made Lady Featherstone's mistake,—that his boot protruded into the room. He clenched his teeth, expecting a swift step and the curtain to be torn aside. The window was shut; he would never have time to open it and leap out and take his chance with the sentry underneath. He was caught in a trap, and Clementina waited for him in the avenue, under the fourth tree. All was lost, it seemed, and by his own folly, his own confidence. Had he only told her of the tavern under the city wall, where the carriage stood with its horses harnessed in the shafts, she might still have escaped, though he was trapped. The sweat passed down his face. Yet no swift step was taken, nor was the curtain torn aside.

For within the room the magistrate, a kindly citizen of Innspruck who had no liking for this addition to his duties, stood gazing at the Princess-mother with a respectful pity. It was the sight of her tear-stained face which had checked his words. For two days Clementina had kept her bed, and the mother's tears alarmed him.

"Her Highness, your daughter, suffers so much?" said he.

"Sir, it is little to be wondered at."

The magistrate bowed. That question was not one with which he had a mind to meddle.

"She still lies in bed?" said he, and he crossed to the door. The mother flung herself in the way.

"She lies in pain, and you would disturb her; you would flash your lanterns in her eyes, that if perchance she sleeps, she may wake into a world of pain. Sir, you will not."

"Your Highness—"

"It is the mother who beseeches you. Sir, would you have me on my knees?"

Wogan, but this moment recovered from his alarm, became again uneasy. Her Highness protested too much; she played her part in the comedy too strenuously. He judged by the ear; the magistrate had the quivering, terror-stricken face before his eyes, and his pity deepened.

"Your Highness," he said, "I must pray you to let me pass. I have General Heister's orders to obey."

The Princess-mother now gave Wogan reason to applaud her. She saw that the magistrate, for all his politeness, was quite inflexible.

"Go, then," she said with a quiet dignity which once before she had shown that evening. "Since there is no humiliation to be spared us, take a candle, sir, and count the marks of suffering in my daughter's face;" and with her own hand she opened the bedroom door and stood aside.

"Madam, I would not press my duty an inch beyond its limits," said the magistrate. "I will stand in the doorway, and do you bid your daughter speak."

The Princess-mother did not move from her position.

"My child," she said.

Jenny in the bedroom groaned and turned from one side to the other.

"You are in pain?"

Jenny groaned again. The magistrate himself closed the door.

"Believe me," said he, "no one could more regret than I the incivilities to which I am compelled."

He crossed the room. Wogan heard him and his men descending the stairs. He heard the door open and shut; he heard Chateaudoux draw the bolts. Then he stepped out from the curtain.

"Your Highness, that was bravely done," said he, and kneeling he kissed her hand. He went back into the embrasure, slipped the bundle over his arm, and opened the window very silently. He saw the snow was still falling, the wind still moaning about the crannies and roaring along the streets. He set his knee upon the window-ledge, climbed out, and drew the window to behind him.

The Princess-mother waited in the room with her hand upon her heart. She waited, it seemed to her, for an eternity. Then she heard the sound of a heavy fall, and the clang of a musket against the wall of the villa. But she heard no cry. She ran to the window and looked out. But strain her eyes as she might, she could distinguish nothing in that blinding storm. She could not see the sentinel; nor was this strange, for the sentinel lay senseless on the snow against the house-wall, and Mr. Wogan was already running down the avenue.

Under the fourth tree he found Clementina; she took his arm, and they set off together, wrestling with the wind, wading through the snow. It seemed to Clementina that her companion was possessed by some new fear. He said no single word to her; he dragged her with a fierce grip upon her wrist; if she stumbled, he jerked her roughly to her feet. She set her teeth and kept pace with him. Only once did she speak. They had come to a depression in the road where the melted snow had made a wide pool. Wogan leaped across it and said,—

"Give me your hand! There's a white stone midway where you can set your foot."

The Princess stepped as he bade her. The stone yielded beneath her tread and she stood ankle-deep in the water. Wogan sprang to her side and lifted her out. She had uttered no cry, and now she only laughed as she stood shivering on the further edge. It was that low musical, good-humoured laugh to which Wogan had never listened without a thrill of gladness, but it waked no response in him now.

"You told me of a white stone on which I might safely set my foot," she said. "Well, sir, your white stone was straw."

They were both to remember these words afterwards and to

make of them a parable, but it seemed that Wogan barely heard them now. "Come!" he said, and taking her arm he set off running again.

Clementina understood that something inopportune, something terrible, had happened since she had left the villa. She asked no questions; she trusted herself without reserve to these true friends who had striven at such risks for her, she desired to prove to them that she was what they would have her be,—a girl who did not pester them with inconvenient chatter, but who could keep silence when silence was helpful, and face hardships with a buoyant heart.

They crossed the bridge and stopped before a pair of high folding doors. They were the doors of the tavern. Wogan drew a breath of relief, pulled the bobbin, and pushed the doors open. Clementina slipped through, and in darkness she took a step forward and bruised herself against the wheels of a carriage. Wogan closed the door and ran to her side.

"This way," said he, and held out his hand. He guided Clementina round the carriage to a steep narrow stairway—it was more a ladder than a stair—fixed against the inner wall. At the top of this stairway shone a horizontal line of yellow light. Wogan led the Princess up the stairs. The line of light shone out beneath a door. Wogan opened the door and stood aside. Clementina passed into a small bare room lighted by a single candle, where Mrs. Misset, Gaydon, and O'Toole waited for her coming. Not a word was said; but their eyes spoke their admiration of the woman, their knees expressed their homage to the Queen. There was a fire blazing on the hearth, Mrs. Misset had a dry change of clothes ready and warm. Wogan laid the Princess's bundle on a chair, and with Gaydon and O'Toole went down the stairs.

"The horses?" he asked.

"I have ordered them," said Gaydon, "at the post-house. I will fetch them;" and he hurried off upon his errand.

Wogan turned to O'Toole.

"And the bill?"

"I have paid it."

"There is no one awake in the house?"

"No one but the landlady."

"Good! Can you keep her engaged until we are ready?"

"To be sure I can. She shall never give a thought to any man of you but myself."

O'Toole passed through a door at the bottom of the staircase into the common-room of the inn. Wogan gently opened the big doors and dragged the carriage out into the road. Gaydon with the horses galloped silently up through the snow, and together the two men feverishly harnessed them to the carriage. There were six for the carriage, and a seventh for O'Toole to ride. The expedition which Wogan and Gaydon showed was matched by the Princess. For while they were fastening the last buckles, the door at the top of the stairs opened, and again that night Clementina whispered,—

"I am ready."

"Come!" replied Wogan. She wore a scarlet cloak upon her shoulders, and muffling it about her head she ran down with Mrs. Misset. Wogan opened the lower door of the inn and called for O'Toole. O'Toole came running out before Wogan had ended his words, and sprang into his saddle. Gaydon was already on the box with the reins gathered in his hand. Wogan had the carriage door open before Clementina had reached the foot of the stairs; it was shut upon her and her companion almost before they were aware they were within it; the carriage started almost before the door was shut. Yet when it did start, Wogan was beside Gaydon upon the box. Their movements, indeed, occurred with so exact a rapidity, that though the hostess at once followed O'Toole to bid her guests farewell, when she reached the big doors she saw only the back of the carriage lurching through the ruts of snow.

"Quick!" cried Wogan; "we have lost too much time."

"A bare twenty minutes," said Gaydon.

"A good twelve hours," said Wogan.

Gaydon lashed the horses into a gallop, the horses strained at their collars, the carriage raced out of the town and up the slopes of the Brenner. The princess Clementina had been rescued from her prison.

"But we must keep her free!" cried Wogan, as he blew through his gloves upon his frozen fingers. "Faster! Faster!"

The incline was steep, the snow clogged the wheels, the horses sank deep in it. Gaydon might ply his whip as he would, the carriage might lurch and leap from side to side; the pace was all too slow for Wogan.

"We have lost twelve hours," he cried. "Oh, would to God we were come to Italy!" And turning backwards he strained his eyes down through the darkness and snow to the hidden roofs of Innspruck, almost fearing to see the windows from one end of the town to the other leap to a blaze of light, and to hear a roar of many voices warn him that the escape was discovered. But the only cry that he heard came from the lips of Mrs. Misset, who put her head from the carriage and bade him stop.

Gaydon brought the horses to a standstill three miles out of Innspruck.

A. E. W. Mason

## CHAPTER XV

## THE FLIGHT TO ITALY:
## WOGAN'S CITY OF DREAMS

Wogan jumped down from his box and ran to the carriage-door.

"Her Highness is ill?" he cried in suspense.

"Not the least bit in the world," returned Clementina, whose voice for once in a way jarred upon Wogan's ears. Nothing short of a positive sickness could justify the delay.

"What is it, then?" he asked curtly, almost roughly, of Mrs. Misset.

"You carried a packet for her Highness. It is left behind at the tavern."

Wogan stamped impatiently on the ground.

"And for this, for a petticoat or two, you hinder us," he cried in a heat. "There's no petticoat in the world, though it were so stiff with gold that it stood on end of itself, that's worth a single second of the next forty-eight hours."

"But it contains her Highness's jewels."

Wogan's impatience became an exasperation. Were all women at heart, then, no better than Indian squaws? A string of beads outweighed the sacrifices of friends and the chance of a crown! There was a blemish in his idol, since at all costs she must glitter. Wogan, however, was the master here.

"Her Highness must lose her jewels," he said roughly, and was turning away when her Highness herself spoke.

"You are unjust, my friend," she said. "I would lose them very willingly, were there a chance no one else would discover them. But there's no chance. The woman of the tavern will find the bundle, will open it; very likely she has done so already. We shall have all Innspruck on our heels in half an hour;" and for the first time that night Wogan heard her voice break, and grieved to know that the tears were running down her cheeks. He called to O'Toole,—

"Ride back to the tavern! Bring the packet without fail!"

O'Toole galloped off, and Gaydon drove the carriage to the side of the road. There was nothing to do but to wait, and they waited in silence, counting up the chances. There could be no doubt that the landlady, if once she discovered the jewels hidden away in a common packet of clothing, must suspect the travellers who had left them behind. She would be terrified by their value; she would be afraid to retain them lest harm should come to her; and all Innspruck would be upon the fugitives' heels. They waited for half an hour,— thirty minutes of gloom and despair. Clementina wept over this new danger which her comrades ran; Mrs. Misset wept for that her negligence was to blame; Gaydon sat on the box in the falling snow with his arms crossed upon his breast, and felt his head already loose upon his shoulders. The only

A. E. W. Mason

one of the party who had any comfort of that half-hour was Wogan. For he had been wrong,—the chosen woman had no wish to glitter at all costs, though, to be sure, she could not help glittering with the refulgence of her great merits. His idol had no blemish. Wogan paced up and down the road, while he listened for O'Toole's return, and that thought cheated the time for him. At last he heard very faintly the sound of galloping hoofs below him on the road. He ran back to Gaydon.

"It might be a courier to arrest us. If I shout, drive fast as you can to Nazareth, and from Nazareth to Italy."

He hurried down the road and was hailed by O'Toole.

"I have it," said he. Wogan turned and ran by O'Toole's stirrup to the carriage.

"The landlady has a good conscience and sleeps well," said O'Toole. "I found the house dark and the doors shut. They were only secured, however, by a wooden beam dropped into a couple of sockets on the inside."

"But how did you open them?" asked Clementina.

"Your Highness, I have, after all, a pair of arms," said O'Toole. "I just pressed on the doors till—"

"Till the sockets gave?"

"No, till the beam broke," said he, and Clementina laughed.

"That's my six foot four!" said she. O'Toole did not understand. But he smiled with great condescension and dignity, and continued his story.

"I groped my way up the stairs into the room and found the bundle untouched in the corner."

He handed it to the Princess; Wogan sprang again onto the box, and Gaydon whipped up the horses. They reached the first posting stage at two, the second at four, the third at six, and at each they wasted no time. All that night their horses strained up the mountain road amid the whirling sleet. At times the wind roaring down a gorge would set the carriage rocking; at times they stuck fast in drifts; and Wogan and Gaydon must leap from the box and plunging waist-deep in the snow, must drag at the horses and push at the wheels. The pace was too slow; Wogan seemed to hear on every gust of wind the sound of a galloping company.

"We have lost twelve hours, more than twelve hours now," he repeated and repeated to Gaydon. All the way to Ala they would still be in the Emperor's territory. It needed only a single courier to gallop past them, and at either Roveredo or Trent they would infallibly be taken. Wogan fingered his pistols, straining his eyes backwards down the road.

At daybreak the snow stopped; the carriage rolled on high among the mountains under a grey sky; and here and there, at a wind of the road, Wogan caught a glimpse of the towers and chimney-tops of Innspruck, or had within his view a stretch of the slope they had climbed. But there was never a black speck visible upon the white of the snow; as yet no courier was overtaking them, as yet Innspruck did not know its captive had escaped. At eight o'clock in the morning they came to Nazareth, and found their own berlin ready harnessed at the post-house door, the postillion already in his saddle, and Misset waiting with an uncovered head.

"Her Highness will breakfast here, no doubt?" said Gaydon.

A. E. W. Mason

"Misset will have seen to it," cried Wogan, "that the berlin is furnished. We can breakfast as we go."

They waited no more than ten minutes at Nazareth. The order of travelling was now changed. Wogan and Gaydon now travelled in the berlin with Mrs. Misset and Clementina. Gaydon, being the oldest of the party, figured as the Count of Cernes, Mrs. Misset as his wife, Clementina as his niece, and Wogan as a friend of the family. O'Toole and Misset rode beside the carriage in the guise of servants. Thus they started from Nazareth, and had journeyed perhaps a mile when without so much as a moan Clementina swooned and fell forward into Wogan's arms. Mrs. Misset uttered a cry; Wogan clasped the Princess to his breast. Her head fell back across his arm, pale as death; her eyes were closed; her bosom, strained against his, neither rose nor fell.

"She has fasted all Lent," he said in a broken voice. "She has eaten nothing since we left Innspruck."

Mrs. Misset burst into tears; she caught Clementina's hand and clasped it; she had no eyes but for her. With Gaydon it was different. Wogan was holding the Princess in a clasp too loverlike, though, to be sure, it was none of his business.

"We must stop the carriage," he said.

"No," cried Wogan, desperately; "that we must not do;" and he caught her still closer to him. He had a fear that she was dying. Even so, she should not be recaptured. Though she were dead, he would still carry her dead body into Bologna and lay it white and still before his King. Europe from London to the Bosphorus should know the truth of her and ring with the wonder of her, though she were dead. O'Toole, attracted by the noise of Mrs. Misset's lamentations, bent down over his horse's neck and looked into the carriage.

"Her Highness is dead!" he cried.

"Drive on," replied Wogan, through his clenched teeth.

Upon the other side of the carriage, Misset shouted through the window, "There is a spring by the roadside."

"Drive on," said Wogan.

Gaydon touched him on the arm.

"You will stifle her, man."

Wogan woke to a comprehension of his attitude, and placed Clementina back on her seat. Mrs. Misset by good fortune had a small bottle of Carmelite water in her pocket; she held it to the Princess's nostrils, who in a little opened her eyes and saw her companions in tears about her, imploring her to wake.

"It is nothing," she said. "Take courage, my poor marmosets;" and with a smile she added, "There's my six feet four with the tears in his eyes. Did ever a woman have such friends?"

The sun came out in the sky as she spoke. They had topped the pass and were now driving down towards Italy. There was snow about them still on the mountain-sides and deep in drifts upon the roads. The air was musical with the sound of innumerable freshets: they could be seen leaping and sparkling in the sunlight; the valleys below were green with the young green of spring, and the winds were tempered with the warmth of Italy. A like change came upon the fugitives. They laughed, where before they had wept; from under the seat they pulled out chickens which Misset had cooked with his own hands at Nazareth, bottles of the wine of St. Laurent, and bread; and Wogan allowed a halt long enough to get water from a spring by the roadside.

"There is no salt," said Gaydon.

"Indeed there is," replied Misset, indignant at the aspersion on his catering. "I have it in my tobacco-box." He took his tobacco-box from his pocket and passed it into the carriage. Clementina made sandwiches and passed them out to the horsemen. The chickens turned out to be old cocks, impervious to the soundest tooth. No one minded except Misset, who had brought them. The jolts of the carriage became matter for a jest. They picnicked with the merriment of children, and finally O'Toole, to show his contempt for the Emperor, fired off both his loaded pistols in the air.

At that Wogan's anxiety returned. He blazed up into anger. He thrust his head from the window.

"Is this your respect for her Highness?" he cried. "Is this your consideration?"

"Nay," interposed Clementina, "you shall not chide my six feet four."

"But he is mad, your Highness. I don't say but what a trifle of madness is salt to a man; but O'Toole's clean daft to be firing his pistols off to let the whole world know who we are. Here are we not six stages from Innspruck, and already we have lost twelve hours."

"When?"

"Last night, before we left Innspruck, between the time when you escaped from the villa and when I joined you in the avenue. I climbed out of the window to descend as I had entered, but the sentinel had returned. I waited on the window-ledge crouched against the wall until he should show me his back. After five minutes or so he did. He stamped on the snow and marched up the lane. I let myself down and hung by my hands, but he turned on his beat before I could drop. He marched back; I clung to the ledge, thinking that in the darkness he would pass on beneath me and never notice. He did not notice; but my fingers were frozen and numbed with the cold. I felt them slipping; I could cling no longer, and I fell. Luckily I fell just as he passed beneath me; I dropped feet foremost upon his shoulders, and he went down without a cry. I left him lying stunned there on the snow; but he will be found, or he will recover. Either way our escape will be discovered, and no later than this morning. Nay, it must already have been discovered. Already Innspruck's bells are ringing the alarm; already the pursuit is begun—" and he leaned his head from the window and cried, "Faster! faster!" O'Toole, for his part, shouted, "Trinkgeldt!" It was the only word of German which he knew. "But," said he, "there was a Saracen lady I learned about at school who travelled over Europe and found her lover in an alehouse in London, with no word but his name to help her over the road. Sure, it would be a strange thing if I couldn't travel all over Germany with the help of 'Trinkgeldt.'"

The word certainly had its efficacy with the postillion. "Trinkgeldt!" cried O'Toole, and the berlin rocked and lurched and leaped down the pass. The snow was now less deep, the drifts fewer. The road wound along a mountain-side: at one window rose the rock; from the other the travellers looked down hundreds of feet to the bed of the valley and the boiling torrent of the Adige. It was a mere narrow ribbon of a road made by the Romans, without a thought for the convenience of travellers in a later day; and as the carriage turned a corner, O'Toole, mounted on his horse, saw ahead a heavy cart crawling up towards them.

A. E. W. Mason

The carter saw the berlin thundering down towards him behind its four maddened horses, and he drew his cart to the inside of the road against the rock. The postillion tugged at his reins; he had not sufficient interval of space to check his team; he threw a despairing glance at O'Toole. It seemed impossible the berlin could pass. There was no use to cry out; O'Toole fell behind the carriage with his mind made up. He looked down the precipice; he saw in his imagination the huge carriage with its tangled, struggling horses falling sheer into the foam of the river. He could not ride back to Bologna with that story to tell; he and his horse must take the same quick, steep road.

The postillion drove so close to the cart that he touched it as he passed. "We are lost!" he shouted in an agony; and O'Toole saw the hind wheel of the berlin slip off the road and revolve for the fraction of a second in the air. He was already putting his horse at the precipice as though it was a ditch to be jumped, when the berlin made, to his astonished eyes, an effort to recover its balance like a live thing. It seemed to spring sideways from the brink of the precipice. It not only seemed, it did spring; and O'Toole, drawing rein, in the great revulsion of his feelings, saw, as he rocked unsteadily in his saddle, the carriage tearing safe and unhurt down the very centre of the road.

O'Toole set his spurs to his horse and galloped after it. The postillion looked back and laughed.

"Trinkgeldt!" he cried.

O'Toole swore loudly, and getting level beat him with his whip. Wogan's head popped out of the window.

"Silence!" said he in a rage. "Mademoiselle is asleep;" and then seeing O'Toole's white and disordered face he asked,

"What is it?" No one in the coach had had a suspicion of their danger. But O'Toole still saw before his eyes that wheel slip over the precipice and revolve in air, he still felt his horse beneath him quiver and refuse this leap into air. In broken tones he gasped out his story to Wogan, and as he spoke the Princess stirred.

"Hush!" said Wogan; "she need not know. Ride behind, O'Toole! Your blue eyes are green with terror. Your face will tell the story, if once she sees it."

O'Toole fell back again behind the carriage, and at four that afternoon they stopped before the post-house at Brixen. They had crossed the Brenner in a storm of snow and howling winds; they had travelled ten leagues from Innspruck. Wogan called a halt of half an hour. The Princess had eaten barely a mouthful since her supper of the night before. Wogan forced her to alight, forced her to eat a couple of eggs, and to drink a glass of wine. Before the half-hour had passed, she was anxious to start again.

From Brixen the road was easier; and either from the smoothness of the travelling or through some partial relief from his anxieties, Wogan, who had kept awake so long, suddenly fell fast asleep, and when he woke up again the night was come. He woke up without a start or even a movement, as was his habit, and sat silently and bitterly reproaching himself for that he had yielded to fatigue. It was pitch-dark within the carriage; he stared through the window and saw dimly the moving mountain-side, and here and there a clump of trees rush past. The steady breathing of Gaydon, on his left, and of Mrs. Misset in the corner opposite to Gaydon, showed that those two guardians slept as well. His reproaches became more bitter and then suddenly ceased, for over against him in the darkness a young, fresh voice was singing very sweetly and very low. It was the Princess

A. E. W. Mason

Clementina, and she sang to herself, thinking all three of her companions were asleep. Wogan had not caught the sound at first above the clatter of the wheels, and even now that he listened it came intermittently to his ears. He heard enough, however, to know and to rejoice that there was no melancholy in the music. The song had the clear bright thrill of the blackbird's note in June. Wogan listened, entranced. He would have given worlds to have written the song with which Clementina solaced herself in the darkness, to have composed the melody on which her voice rose and sank.

The carriage drew up at an inn; the horses were changed; the flight was resumed. Wogan had not moved during this delay, neither had Misset nor O'Toole come to the door. But an ostler had flashed a lantern into the berlin, and for a second the light had fallen upon Wogan's face and open eyes. Clementina, however, did not cease; she sang on until the lights had been left behind and the darkness was about them. Then she stopped and said,—

"How long is it since you woke?"

Wogan was taken by surprise.

"I should never have slept at all," stammered he. "I promised myself that. Not a wink of sleep betwixt Innspruck and Italy; and here was I fast as a log this side of Trent. I think our postillion sleeps too;" and letting down the window he quietly called Misset.

"We have fresh relays," said he, "and we travel at a snail's-pace."

"The relays are only fresh to us," returned Misset. "We can go no faster. There is someone ahead with three stages' start of us,—someone of importance, it would seem, and who travels with a retinue, for he takes all the horses at each stage."

Wogan thrust his head out of the window. There was no doubt of it; the horses lagged. In this hurried flight the most trifling hindrance was a monumental danger, and this was no trifling hindrance. For the hue and cry was most certainly raised behind them; the pursuit from Innspruck had begun twelve hours since, on the most favourable reckoning. At any moment they might hear the jingle of a horse's harness on the road behind. And now here was a man with a great retinue blocking their way in front.

"We can do no more, but make a fight of it in the end," said he. "They may be few who follow us. But who is he ahead?"

Misset did not know.

"I can tell you," said Clementina, with a slight hesitation. "It is the Prince of Baden, and he travels to Italy."

Wogan remembered a certain letter which his King had written to him from Rome; and the hesitation in the girl's voice told him the rest of the story. Wogan would have given much to have had his fingers about the scruff of that pompous gentleman's neck with the precipice handy at his feet. It was intolerable that the fellow should pester the Princess in prison and hinder her flight when she had escaped from it.

"Well, we can do no more," said he, and he drew up the window. Neither Gaydon nor Mrs. Misset were awakened; Clementina and Wogan were alone in the darkness.

She leaned forward to him and said in a low voice,—

　　　　　A. E. W. Mason

"Tell me of the King. I shall make mistakes in this new world. Will he have patience with me while I learn?"

She had spoken upon the same strain in the darkness of the staircase only the night before. Wogan gently laughed her fears aside.

"I will tell you the truest thing about the King. He needs you at his side. For all his friends, he is at heart a lonely man, throned upon sorrows. I dare to tell you that, knowing you. He needs not a mere wife, but a mate, a helpmate, to strive with him, her hand in his. Every man needs the helpmate, as I read the world. For it cannot but be that a man falls below himself when he comes home always to an empty room."

The Princess was silent. Wogan hoped that he had reassured her. But her thoughts were now turned from herself. She leaned yet further forward with her elbows upon her knees, and in a yet lower voice she asked a question which fairly startled him.

"Does she not love you?"

Wogan, indeed, had spoken unconsciously, with a deep note of sadness in his voice, which had sounded all the more strange and sad to her from its contrast with the quick, cheerful, vigorous tones she had come to think the mark of him. He had spoken as though he looked forward with a poignant regret through a weary span of days, and saw himself always in youth and middle years and age coming home always to an empty room. Therefore she put her question, and Wogan was taken off his guard.

"There is no one," he said in a flurry.

Clementina shook her head.

"I wish that I may hear the King speak so, and in that voice; I shall be very sure he loves me," she said in a musing voice, and so changing almost to a note of raillery. "Tell me her name!" she pleaded. "What is amiss with her that she is not thankful for a true man's love like yours? Is she haughty? I'll bring her on her knees to you. Does she think her birth sets her too high in the world? I'll show her so much contempt, you so much courtesy, that she shall fall from her arrogance and dote upon your steps. Perhaps she is too sure of your devotion? Why, then, I'll make her jealous!"

Wogan interrupted her, and the agitation of his voice put an end to her raillery. Somehow she had wounded him who had done so much for her.

"Madam, I beg you to believe me, there is no one;" and casting about for a sure argument to dispel her conjectures, he said on an impulse, "Listen; I will make your Highness a confidence." He stopped, to make sure that Gaydon and Mrs. Misset were still asleep. Then he laughed uneasily like a man that is half-ashamed and resumed,—"I am lord and king of a city of dreams. Here's the opening of a fairy tale, you will say. But when I am asleep my city's very real; and even now that I am awake I could draw you a map of it, though I could not name its streets. That's my town's one blemish. Its streets are nameless. It has taken a long while in the building, ever since my boyhood; and indeed the work's not finished yet, nor do I think it ever will be finished till I die, since my brain's its architect. When I was asleep but now, I discovered a new villa, and an avenue of trees, and a tavern with red blinds which I had never remarked before. At the first there was nothing but a queer white house of which the original has fallen to ruins at Rathcoffey in Ireland. This house stood alone in a wide flat emerald plain that stretched like an untravelled sea to a circle of curving sky. There was room to build, you see, and when I left Rathcoffey and became a

A. E. W. Mason

wanderer, the building went on apace. There are dark lanes there from Avignon between great frowning houses, narrow climbing streets from Meran, arcades from Verona, and a park of many thickets and tall poplar-trees with a long silver stretch of water. One day you will see that park from the windows of St. James. It has a wall too, my city,—a round wall enclosing it within a perfect circle; and from whatever quarter of the plain you come towards it, you only see this wall, there's not so much as a chimney visible above it. Once you have crowded with the caravans and traders through the gates,—for my town is busy,—you are at once in the ringing streets. I think my architect in that took Aigues Mortes for his model. Outside you have the flat, silent plain, across which the merchants creep in long trailing lines, within the noise of markets, the tramp of horses' hoofs, the talk of men and women, and, if you listen hard, the whispers, too, of lovers. Oh, my city's populous! There are quiet alleys with windows opening onto them, where on summer nights you may see a young girl's face with the moonlight on it like a glory, and in the shadow of the wall beneath, the cloaked figure of a youth. Well, I have a notion—" and then he broke off abruptly. "There's a black horse I own, my favourite horse."

"You rode it the first time you came to Ohlau," said the Princess.

"Do you indeed remember that?" cried Wogan, with so much pleasure that Gaydon stirred in his corner, and Clementina said, "Hush!"

Wogan waited in a suspense lest Gaydon should wake up, which, to be sure, would be the most inconsiderate thing in the world. Gaydon, however, settled himself more comfortably, and in a little his regular breathing might be heard again.

"Well," resumed Wogan, "I have a notion that the lady I shall marry will come riding some sunrise on my black horse across the plain and into my city of dreams. And she has not."

"Ah," said Clementina, "here's a subterfuge, my friend. The lady you shall marry, you say. But tell me this! Has the lady you love ridden on your black horse into your city of dreams?"

"No," said Wogan; "for there is no lady whom I love." There Wogan should have ended, but he added rather sadly, "Nor is there like to be."

"Then I am sure," said Clementina.

"Sure that I speak truth?"

"No, sure that you mislead me. It is not kind; for here perhaps I might give you some small token of my gratitude, would you but let me. Oh, it is no matter. I shall find out who the lady is. You need not doubt it. I shall set my wits and eyes to work. There shall be marriages when I am Queen. I will find out!"

Wogan's face was not visible in the darkness; but he spoke quickly and in a startled voice,—

"That you must never do. Promise that you never will! Promise me that you will never try;" and again Gaydon stirred in his corner.

Clementina made no answer to the passionate words. She did not promise, but she drew a breath, and then from head to foot she shivered. Wogan dared not repeat his plea for a promise, but he felt that though she had not given it, none the

A. E. W. Mason

less she would keep it. They sat for awhile silent. Then Clementina came back to her first question.

"Tell me of the King," she said very softly. And as the carriage rolled down the mountain valley through the night and its wheels struck flashes of fire from the stones, Wogan drew a picture for her of the man she was to marry. It was a relief to him to escape from the dangerous talk of the last hour, and he spoke fervently. The poet in him had always been sensitive to the glamour of that wandering Prince; he had his countrymen's instinctive devotion for a failing cause. This was no suitable moment for dwelling upon the defects and weaknesses. Wogan told her the story of the campaign in Scotland, of the year's residence in Avignon. He spoke most burningly. A girl would no doubt like to hear of her love's achievements; and if James Stuart had not so many to his name as a man could wish, that was merely because chance had served him ill. So a fair tale was told, not to be found in any history book, of a night attack in Scotland and how the Chevalier de St. George, surprised and already to all purposes a prisoner, forced a way alone through nine grenadiers with loaded muskets and escaped over the roof-tops. It was a good breathless story as he told it, and he had just come to an end of it when the carriage drove through the village of Wellishmile and stopped at the posting-house. Wogan opened the door and shook Gaydon by the shoulder.

"Let us try if we can get stronger horses here," said he, and he got out. Gaydon woke up with surprising alacrity.

"I must have fallen asleep," said he. "I beseech your Highness's forgiveness; I have slept this long while." It was no business of his if Wogan chose to attribute his own escape from Newgate as an exploit of the King's. The story was a familiar one at Bologna, whither they were hurrying; it was sufficiently known that Charles Wogan was its hero. All this was Wogan's business, not Gaydon's. Nor had Gaydon anything to do with any city of dreams or with any lady that might ride into it, or with any black horse that chanced to carry her. Poets no doubt talked that way. It was their business. Gaydon was not sorry that he had slept so heartily through those last stages. He got down from the carriage and met Wogan coming from the inn with a face of dismay.

"We are stopped here. There is no help for it. We have gained on the Prince of Baden, who is no more than two stages ahead. The relays which carried him from here to the next stage have only this instant come back. They are too tired to move. So we must stay until they are refreshed. And we are still three posts this side of Trent!" he cried. "I would not mind were Trent behind us. But there's no help for it. I have hired a room where the Countess and her niece can sleep until such time as we can start."

Clementina and Mrs. Misset descended and supped in company with Gaydon and Wogan, while Misset and O'Toole waited upon them as servants. It was a silent sort of supper, very different from the meal they had made that morning. For though the fare was better, it lacked the exhilaration. This delay weighed heavily upon them all. For the country was now for a sure thing raised behind them, and if they had gained on the Prince of Baden, their pursuers had no less certainly gained on them.

"Would we were t'other side of Trent!" exclaimed Wogan; and looking up he saw that Clementina was watching him with a strange intentness. Her eyes were on him again while they sat at supper; and when he led her to the door of her room and she gave him her hand, she stood for a little while looking deep into his eyes. And though she had much need of sleep, when she had got into the room and the door was closed behind her, she remained staring at the logs of the fire.

For she knew his secret, and to her eyes he was now another man. Before, Wogan was the untiring servant, the unflinching friend; now he was the man who loved her. The risks he had run, his journeyings, his unswerving confidence in the result, his laborious days and nights of preparation, and the swift execution,—love as well as service claimed a share in these. He was changed for ever to her eyes; she knew his secret. There was the cloud no bigger than a man's hand. For she must needs think over all that he had said and done by the new light the secret shed. When did he first begin to care? Why? She recalled his first visit long ago to Ohlau, when he rode across the park on his black horse charged with his momentous errand. She had been standing, she remembered, before the blazing log-fire in the great stone hall, much as she was standing now. Great changes had come since then. She was James Stuart's chosen wife—and this man loved her. He had no hope of any reward; he desired even that she should not know. She should no doubt have been properly sorry and compassionate, but she was a girl simple and frank. To be loved by a man who could so endure and strive and ask no guerdon,—that lifted her. She thought the more worthily of herself because he loved her. She was raised thereby. She could not be sorry; her blood pulsed, her heart sang, the starry eyes shone with a brighter light. He loved her. She knew his secret. A little clock chimed the hour upon the mantel-shelf, and lifting her eyes she saw that just twenty-four hours had passed since she had driven out of Innspruck up the Brenner.

As she got into bed a horse galloped up to the inn and stopped. She remembered that she had not ridden on his black horse out of the sunrise across the plain. He loved her, and since he loved her, surely—She fell asleep puzzled and wondering why. She was waked up some two hours afterwards by a rapping on the door, and she grew hot and she recognised Wogan's voice cautiously whispering to her to rise with all speed. For in her dreams from which she had wakened, she had ridden across the flat green plain into the round city of dreams.

A. E. W. Mason

# CHAPTER XVI

## THE FLIGHT TO ITALY: THE POTENT
## EFFECTS OF A WATER-JUG

When the horse galloped up to the door, the Princess turned on her side and went to sleep. In the common-room below Gaydon and Wogan were smoking a pipe of tobacco over the fire. Both men rose on the instant; Wogan stealthily opened the door an inch or so and looked down the passage. Gaydon raised a corner of the blind and peered through the window. The two remaining members of the party, Misset and O'Toole, who as lackeys had served the supper of the Princess, were now eating their own. When the Princess turned over on her side, and Wogan stepped on tiptoe to the door and Gaydon peeped through the window, Misset laid down his knife and fork, and drawing a flask from his pocket emptied its contents into an earthenware water-jug which stood upon the table. O'Toole, for his part, simply continued to eat.

"He is getting off his horse," said Gaydon.

"Has he ridden hard, do you think?" asked Misset.

"He looks in a mighty ill-humour."

O'Toole looked up from his plate, and became gradually aware that something was occurring. Before he could speak, however, Gaydon dropped the blind.

"He is coming in. It will never do for him to find the four of us together. He may not be the courier from Innspruck; on the other hand, he may, and seeing the four of us he will ask questions of the landlord. Seeing no more than two, he will very likely ask none."

O'Toole began to understand. He understood, at all events, that for him there was to be no more supper. If two were to make themselves scarce, he knew that he would be one of the two.

"Very well," said he, heaving a sigh which made the glasses on the table dance, and laying his napkin down he got up. To his surprise, however, he was bidden to stay.

"Gaydon and I will go," said Wogan. "Jack will find out the fellow's business."

Misset nodded his head, took up his knife and fork again. He leaned across the table to O'Toole as the others stepped out of the room.

"You speak only French, Lucius. You come from Savoy." He had no time to say more, for the new-comer stamped blustering down the passage and flung into the room. The man, as Gaydon had remarked, was in a mighty ill-humour; his clothes and his face were splashed with mud, and he seemed, moreover, in the last stage of exhaustion. For though he bawled for the landlord it was in a weak, hoarse voice, which did not reach beyond the door.

Misset looked at him with sympathy.

A. E. W. Mason

"You have no doubt come far," said he; "and the landlord's a laggard. Here's something that may comfort you till he comes;" and he filled a glass half full with red Tyrol wine from the bottle at his elbow.

The man thanked him and advanced to the table.

"It is a raw hot wine," continued Misset, "and goes better with water;" and he filled up the glass from the water-jug. The courier reached out his hand for it.

"I am the thirstiest man in all Germany," said he, and he took a gulp of the wine and immediately fell to spluttering.

"Save us," said he, "but this wine is devilishly strong."

"Try some more water," said Misset, and again he filled up the glass. The courier drank it all in a single draught, and stood winking his eyes and shaking his head.

"That warms a man," said he. "It does one good;" and again he called for the landlord, and this time in a strange voice. The landlord still lagged, however, and Misset did not doubt that Wogan had found a means to detain him. He filled up the courier's glass again, half wine, half water. The courier sat heavily down in a chair.

"I take the liberty, gentlemen," said he. "I am no better than a dung-heap to sit beside gentlemen. But indeed I can stand no longer. Never have I stridden across such vile slaughter-house cattle as they keep for travellers on the Brenner road. I have sprained my legs with spurring 'em. Seven times," he cried with an oath,—"seven times has a horse dropped under me to-day. There's not an inch of me unbruised, curse me if there is! I'm a cake of mud."

Misset knew very well why the courier had suffered these falls. The horses he had ridden had first been tired by the Prince of Baden, and then had the last spark of fire flogged out of them by the Princess's postillions. He merely shrugged his shoulders, however, and said, "That looks ill for us."

The courier gazed suddenly at Misset, then at O'Toole, with a dull sort of suspicion in his eyes.

"And which way might you gentlemen be travelling?"

"To Innspruck; we're from Trent," said Misset, boldly.

The courier turned to O'Toole.

"And you too, sir?"

O'Toole turned a stolid, uncomprehending face upon the courier.

"Pour moi, monsieur, je suis Savoyard. Monsieur qui vous parle, c'est mon compagnon de negoce."

The courier gazed with blank, heavy eyes at O'Toole. He had the appearance of a man fuddled with drink. He heaved a sigh or two.

"Will you repeat that," he said at length, "and slowly?"

O'Toole repeated his remark, and the courier nodded at him. "That's very strange," said he, solemnly, wagging his head. "I do not dispute its truth, but it is most strange. I will tell my wife of it." He turned in his chair, and a twinge from his bruises made him cry out. "I shall be as stiff as a mummy in the morning," he exclaimed, and swore loudly at "the bandits" who had caused him this deplorable journey. Misset

A. E. W. Mason

and O'Toole exchanged a quick glance, and Misset pushed the glass across the table. The courier took it, and his eyes lighted up.

"You have come from Trent," said he. "Did you pass a travelling carriage on the road?"

"Yes," said Misset; "the Prince of Baden with a large following drove into Trent as we came out."

"Yes, yes," said the courier. "But no second party behind the Prince?"

Misset shook his head; he made a pretence of consulting O'Toole in French, and O'Toole shook his head.

"Then I shall have the robbers," cried the courier. "They are to be flayed alive, and they deserve it," he shouted fiercely to Misset. "Gallows-birds!"

He dropped his head upon his arms and muttered "gallows-birds" again. It seemed that he was falling asleep, but he suddenly sat up and beat on the table with his fist.

"I have eaten nothing since the morning. Ah—gallows-birds—flayed alive, and hanged—no, hanged and flayed alive—no, that's impossible." He drank off the wine which Misset had poured out for him, and rose from his chair. "Where's the landlord? I want supper. I want besides to speak to him;" and he staggered towards the door.

"As for supper," said Misset, "we shall be glad if you will share ours. Travellers should be friendly."

O'Toole caught the courier by the arm and with a polite speech in French drew him again down into his chair. The courier stared at O'Toole and forgot all about the landlord. He had eaten nothing all day, and the wine and the water-jug had gone to his head. He put a long forefinger on O'Toole's knee.

"Say that again," said he, and O'Toole obeyed. A slow, fat smile spread all over the courier's face.

"I'll tell my wife about it," said he. He tried to clap O'Toole on the back, and missing him fell forward with his face on the table. The next minute he was snoring. Misset walked round the table and deftly picked his pockets. There was a package in one of them superscribed to "Prince Taxis, the Governor of Trent." Misset deliberately broke the seal and read the contents. He handed the package to O'Toole, who read it, and then flinging it upon the ground danced upon it. Misset went out of the room and found Wogan and Gaydon keeping watch by Clementina's door. To them he spoke in a whisper.

"The fellow brings letters from General Heister to the Governor of Trent to stop us at all costs. But his letters are destroyed, and he's lying dead-drunk on the table."

The three men quickly concerted a plan. The Princess must be roused; a start must be made at once; and O'Toole must be left behind to keep a watch upon the courier, Wogan rapped at the door and waked Clementina; he sent Gaydon to the stables to bribe the ostlers, and with Misset went down to inform O'Toole.

O'Toole, however, was sitting with his eyes closed and his head nodding, surrounded by scraps of the letter which he had danced to pieces. Wogan shook him by the shoulder, and he opened his eyes and smiled fatuously.

A. E. W. Mason

"He means to tell his wife," he said with a foolish gurgle of laughter. "He must be an ass. I don't think if I had a wife I should tell her. Would you, Wogan, tell your wife if you had one? Misset wouldn't tell his wife."

Misset interrupted him.

"What have you drank since I went out of the room?" he asked roughly. He took up the water-jug and turned it topsy-turvy. It was quite empty.

"Only water," said O'Toole, dreamily, and he laughed again. "Now I wouldn't mind telling my wife that," said he.

Misset let him go and turned with a gesture of despair to Wogan.

"I poured my flask out into the water-bottle. It was full of burnt Strasbourg brandy, of double strength. It is as potent as opium. Neither of them will have his wits before to-morrow. It will not help us to leave O'Toole to guard the courier."

"And we cannot take him," said Wogan. "There is the Princess to be thought of. We must leave him, and we cannot leave him alone, for his neck's in danger,—more than in danger if the courier wakes before him."

He picked up carefully the scraps of the letter and placed them in the middle of the fire. They were hardly burnt before Gaydon came into the room with word that horses were already being harnessed to the berlin. Wogan explained their predicament.

"We must choose which of us three shall stay behind," said he.

"Which of us two," Misset corrected, pointing to Gaydon and himself. "When the Princess drives into Bologna, Charles Wogan, who first had the high heart to dare this exploit, the brain to plot, the hand to execute it,—Charles Wogan must ride at her side, not Misset, not Gaydon. I take no man's honours." He shook Wogan by the hand as he spoke, and he had spoken with an extraordinary warmth of admiration. Gaydon could do no less than follow his companion's example, though there was a shade of embarrassment in his manner of assenting. It was not that he had any envy of Wogan, or any desire to rob him of a single tittle of his due credit. There was nothing mean in Gaydon's nature, but here was a halving of Clementina's protectors, and he could not stifle a suspicion that the best man of the four to leave behind was really Charles Wogan himself. Not a word, however, of this could he say, and so he nodded his assent to Misset's proposal.

"It is I, then, who stay behind with O'Toole and the courier," he said. "Misset has a wife; the lot evidently falls to me. We will make a shift somehow or another to keep the fellow quiet till sundown to-morrow, which time should see you out of danger." He unbuckled the sword from his waist and laid it on the table, and that simple action somehow touched Wogan to the heart. He slipped his arm into Gaydon's and said remorsefully,—

"Dick, I do hate to leave you, you and Lucius. I swept you into the peril, you two, my friends, and now I leave you in the thick of it to find a way out for yourselves. But there is no remedy, is there? I shall not rest until I see you both again. Goodbye, Lucius." He looked at O'Toole sprawling with outstretched legs upon his groaning chair. "My six feet four," said he, turning to Gaydon; "you must give me the passport. Have a good care of him, Dick;" and he gripped O'Toole affectionately by the arms for a second, and then

A. E. W. Mason

taking the passport hurried from the room. Gaydon had seldom seen Wogan so moved.

The berlin was brought round to the door; the Princess, rosy with sleep, stepped into it; Wogan had brought with him a muff, and he slipped it over Clementina's feet to keep her warm during the night; Misset took Gaydon's place, and the postillion cracked his whip and set off towards Trent. Gaydon, sitting before the fire in the parlour, heard the wheels grate upon the road; he had a vision of the berlin thundering through the night with a trail of sparks from the wheels; and he wondered whether Misset was asleep or merely leaning back with his eyes shut, and thus visiting incognito Woman's fairy-land of dreams. However, Gaydon consoled himself with the reflection that it was none of his business.

# CHAPTER XVII

## THE FLIGHT TO ITALY: A GROWING CLOUD

But Gaydon was out of his reckoning. There were no fairy tales told for Misset to overhear, and the Princess Clementina slept in her corner of the carriage. If a jolt upon a stone wakened her, a movement opposite told her that her sentinel was watchful and alert. Three times the berlin stopped for a change of horses; and on each occasion Wogan was out of the door and hurrying the ostlers before the wheels had ceased to revolve.

"You should sleep, my friend," said she.

"Not till we reach Italy," he replied; and with the confidence of a child she nestled warmly in her cloak again and closed her eyes. This feeling of security was a new luxury to her after the months of anxiety and prison. The grey light of the morning stole into the berlin and revealed to her the erect and tireless figure of her saviour. The sun leaped down the mountain-peaks, and the grey of the light was now a sparkling gold. Wogan bade her Highness look from the carriage window, and she could not restrain a cry of delight. On her left, mountain-ridge rose behind mountain-ridge, away to the towering limestone cliffs of Monte Scanupia; on her right, the white peaks of the Orto d'Abram flashed to the

A. E. W. Mason

sun; and between the hills the broad valley of the Adige rolled southwards,—a summer country of villages and vines, of mulberry-trees and fields of maize, in the midst of which rose the belfries of an Italian town.

"This is Italy," she cried.

"But the Emperor's Italy," answered Wogan; and at half-past nine that morning the carriage stopped in the public square of Trent. As Wogan stepped onto the ground, he saw a cloud of dust at the opposite side of the square, and wrapped in that cloud men on horseback like soldiers in the smoke of battle; he heard, too, the sound of wheels. The Prince of Baden had that instant driven away, and he had taken every procurable horse in the town. Wogan's own horses could go no further. He came back to the door of the carriage.

"I must search through Trent," said he, "on the mere chance of finding what will serve us. Your Highness must wait in the inn;" and Clementina, muffling her face, said to him,—

"I dare not. My face is known in Trent, though this is the first time ever I saw it. But many gentlemen from Trent came to the Innspruck carnival, and of these a good number were kind enough to offer me their hearts. They were allowed to besiege me to their content. I must needs remain in the shelter of the carriage."

Wogan left Misset to stand sentinel, and hurried off upon his business. He ran from stable to stable, from inn to inn. The Prince of Baden had hired thirty-six horses; six more were nowhere to be found. Wogan would be content with four; he ended in a prayer for two. At each house the door was shut in his face. Wogan was in despair; nowhere could delay be so dangerous as at Trent, where there were soldiers, and a Governor who would not hesitate to act without orders if he suspected the Princess Clementina was escaping through his town. Two hours had passed in Wogan's vain search,—two hours of daylight, during which Clementina had sat in an unharnessed carriage in the market square. Wogan ran back to the square, half expecting to find that she had been recognised and arrested. As he reached the square, he saw that curious people were loitering about the carriage; as he pushed through them, he heard them questioning why travellers should on so hot a morning of spring sit muffled up in a close, dark carriage when they could take their ease beneath trees in the inn-garden. One man laughed out at the Princess and the comical figure she made with her scarlet cloak drawn tight about her face. Wogan himself had bought that cloak in Strasbourg to guard his Princess from the cold of the Brenner, and guessed what discomfort its ermine lining must now be costing her. And this lout dared to laugh and make her, this incomparable woman, a butt for his ridicule! Wogan took a step towards the fellow with his fists clenched, but thought the better of his impulse, and turning away ran to the palace of Prince Taxis.

This desperate course alone remained to him; he must have speech with the Prince-bishop himself. At the palace, however, he was informed that the Prince was in bed with the gout. Mr. Wogan, however, insisted.

"You will present my duties to the Prince; you will show him my passport; you will say that the Count of Cernes has business of the last importance in Italy, and begs permission, since the Prince of Baden has hired every post-horse in the town, to requisition half a dozen farm-horses from the fields."

Mr. Wogan kicked his heels in the courtyard while the message was taken. At any moment some rumour of the curious spectacle in the square might be brought to the

A. E. W. Mason

palace and excite inquiry. There might be another courier in pursuit besides the man whom Gaydon kept a prisoner. Wogan was devoured with a fever of impatience. It seemed to him hours before the Prince's secretary returned to him. The secretary handed him back his passport, and on the part of the Prince made a speech full of civilities.

"Here's a great deal of jam, sir," said Wogan. "I misdoubt me but what there's a most unpalatable pill hidden away in it."

"Indeed," said the secretary, "the Prince begs you to be content and to wait for the post-horses to return."

"Ah, ah!" cried Wogan, "but that's the one thing I cannot do. I must speak plainly, it appears." He drew the secretary out of ear-shot, and resumed: "My particular business is to catch up the Prince of Baden. He is summoned back to Innspruck. Do you understand?" he asked significantly.

"Sir, we are well informed in Trent as to the Emperor's wishes," said the secretary, with a great deal of dignity.

"No, no, my friend," said Wogan. "It is not by the Emperor the Prince of Baden is summoned, though I have no doubt the summons is much to his taste."

The secretary stepped back in surprise.

"By her Highness the Princess?" he exclaimed.

"She changes her mind; she is willing where before she was obdurate. To tell you the truth, the Prince plied her too hard, and she would have none of him. Now that he turns his back and puts the miles as fast as he can between himself and her, she cannot sleep for want of him."

The secretary nodded his head sagaciously.

"Her Highness is a woman," said he, "and that explains all. But it will do her no harm to suffer a little longer for her obstinacy, and, to tell you the truth, the Prince Taxis is so tormented with the gout that—"

"That you are unwilling to approach him a second time," interrupted Wogan. "I have no doubt of it. I have myself seen prelates in a most unprelatical mood. But here is a case where needs must. I have not told you all. There is a devil of a fellow called Charles Wogan."

The secretary nodded his head.

"A mad Irishman who has vowed to free her Highness."

"He has set out from Strasbourg with that aim."

"He will hang for it, then, but he will never rescue her;" and the secretary began to laugh. "I cannot upon my honour vex the Prince again because a gallows-bird has prated in his cups."

"No, no," said Wogan; "you do not follow me. Charles Wogan will come to the gallows over this adventure. For my part, I would have him broken on the wheel and tortured in many uncomfortable ways. These Irishmen all the world over are pestilent fellows. But the trouble is this: If her Highness hears of his attempt, she is, as you sagely discovered, a woman, a trivial, trifling thing. She will be absurd enough to imagine her rescue possible; she will again change her mind, and it is precisely that which General Heister fears. He would have her formally betrothed to the Prince of Baden before Charles Wogan is caught and hanged sky-high. Therefore, since I was pressing into Italy, he

A. E. W. Mason

charged me with this message to the Prince of Baden. Now observe this, if you please. Suppose that I do not overtake the Prince; suppose that her Highness hears of Wogan's coming and again changes her mind,—who will be to blame? Not I, for I have done my best, not Prince Taxis, for he is not informed, but Prince Taxis's secretary."

The secretary yielded to Wogan's argument. He might be in a great fear of Prince Taxis, but he was in a greater of the Emperor's wrath. He left Wogan again, and in a little while came back with the written permission which Wogan desired. Wogan wasted no time in unnecessary civilities; the morning had already been wasted. The clocks were striking one as he hurried away from the palace, and before two the Princess Clementina was able to throw back her cloak from about her face and take the air; for the berlin was on the road from Trent to Roveredo.

"Those were the four worst hours since we left Innspruck," she said. "I thought I should suffocate." The revulsion from despair, the knowledge that each beat of the hoofs brought them nearer to safety, the glow of the sun upon a country which was Italy in all but name, raised them all to the top of their spirits. Clementina was in her gayest mood; she lavished caresses upon her "little woman," as she called Mrs. Misset; she would have Wogan give her an account of his interview with Prince Taxis's secretary; she laughed with the merriest enjoyment over his abuse of Charles Wogan.

"But it was not myself alone whom I slandered," said he. "Your Highness had a share of our abuse. Our heads wagged gravely over woman's inconstancies. It was not in nature but you must change your mind. Indeed, your Highness would have laughed."

But at all events her Highness did not laugh now. On the

contrary, her eyes lost all their merriment, and her blood rushed hotly into her cheeks. She became for that afternoon a creature of moods, now talking quickly and perhaps a trifle wildly, now relapsing into long silences. Wogan was troubled by a thought that the strain of her journey was telling its tale even upon her vigorous youth. It may be that she noted his look of anxiety, but she said to him abruptly and with a sort of rebellion,—

"You would despise any woman who had the temerity to change her mind."

"Nay; I do not say that."

"But it is merely politeness that restrains you. You would despise her, judging her by men. When a man changes his mind, why, it is so, he changes his mind. But when a girl does, it may well be that for the first time she is seriously exercising her judgment. For her upbringing renders it natural that she should allow others to make up her mind for her at the first."

"That I think is very true," said Wogan.

Clementina, however, was not satisfied with his assent. She attacked him again and almost vindictively.

"You of course would never change your mind for any reason, once it was fixed. You are resolute. You are quite, quite perfect."

Mr. Wogan could not imagine what he had done thus to provoke her irony.

"Madam," he pleaded, "I am not in truth so obstinate a fellow as you make me out. I have often changed my mind. I take some pride in it on occasion."

Her Highness inclined to a greater graciousness.

"I am glad to know it. You shall give me examples. One may have a stiff neck and yet no cause for pride."

Wogan looked so woe-begone under this reproof that Clementina suddenly broke out into a laugh, and so showed herself in a fresh and more familiar mood. The good-humour continued; she sat opposite to Mr. Wogan; if she moved, her hand, her knee, her foot, must needs touch his; she made him tell her stories of his campaigns; and so the evening came upon them,—an evening of stars and mysterious quiet and a clear, dark sky.

They passed Roveredo; they drew near to Ala, the last village in the Emperor's territories. Five miles beyond Ala they would be on Venetian soil, and already they saw the lights of the village twinkling like so many golden candles. But the berlin, which had drawn them so stoutly over these rugged mountain-roads, failed them at the last. One of the hind wheels jolted violently upon a great stone, there was a sudden cracking of wood, and the carriage lurched over, throwing its occupants one against the other.

Wogan disentangled himself, opened the door, and sprang out. He sprang out into a pool of water. One glance at the carriage, dark though the night was, told him surely what had happened. The axle-tree was broken. He saw that Clementina was about to follow him.

"There is water," said he. "It is ankle-deep."

"And no white stone," she answered with a laugh, "whereon I can safely set my foot?"

"No," said he, "but you can trust without fear to my arms;" and he reached them out to her.

"Can I?" said she, in a curious voice; and when he had lifted her from the carriage, she was aware that she could not. He lifted her daintily, like a piece of porcelain; but to lift her was not enough, he must carry her. His arms tightened about her waist, hers in spite of herself about his shoulders. He took a step or two from the carriage, with the water washing over his boots, and the respectful support of a servant became the warm grip of a man. He no longer held her daintily; he clipped her close to him, straining her breasts against his chest; he was on fire with her. She could not but know it; his arms shook, his bosom heaved; she felt the quick hammering of his heart; and a murmur, an inarticulate murmur, of infinite longing trembled from his throat. And something of his madness passed into her and made a sweet tumult in her blood. He stopped still holding her; he felt her fingers clasp tighter; he looked downwards into her face upturned to his. They were alone for a moment, these two, alone in an uninhabited world. The broken carriage, the busy fingers about it, the smoking horses, the lights of Ala twinkling in the valley, had not even the substance of shadows. They simply were not, and they never had been. There were just two people alive between the Poles,—not princess and servant, but man and woman in the primitive relationship of rescuer and rescued; and they stood in the dark of a translucent night of spring, with the stars throbbing above them to the time of their passionate hearts, and the earth stretching about them rich as black velvet. He looked down into her eyes as once in the night-time he had done before; and again he marvelled at their steadiness and their mysterious depths. Her eyes were fixed on his and did not flinch; her arms were close about his neck; he bent his head towards her, and she said in a queer, toneless voice, low but as steady as her eyes,—

A. E. W. Mason

"I know. Ah, but well I know. Last night I dreamed; I rode on your black horse into your city of dreams;" and the moment of passion ended in farce. For Wogan, startled by the words, set her down there and then into the pool. She stood over her ankles in water. She uttered a little cry and shivered. Then she laughed and sprang lightly onto dry soil, making much of her companion's awkwardness. Wogan joined in the laughter, finding therein as she did a cover and a cloak.

"We must walk to Ala," said he.

"It is as well," said she. "There was a time when cavaliers laid their cloaks in the mud to save a lady's shoe-sole."

"Madam," said Wogan, "the chivalry of to-day has the same intention."

"But in its effect," said she, "it is more rheumatical."

Wogan searched in the carriage and drew out a coil of rope which he slung across his shoulders like a bandolier. Clementina laughed at him for his precautions, but Wogan was very serious. "I would not part with it," said he. "I never travelled for four days without being put to it for a piece of rope."

They left the postillion to make what he could of the berlin and walked forward in the clear night to Ala. The shock of the tumble had alarmed Mrs. Misset; the fatigue of the journey had strained her endurance to the utmost. She made no complaint, but she could walk but slowly and with many rests by the way. It took a long while for them to reach the village. They saw the lights diminish in the houses; the stars grew pale; there came a hint of morning in the air. The laughter at Wogan's awkwardness had long since died away, and they walked in silence.

Forty-eight hours had passed since the berlin left Innspruck. Twenty-four hours ago Clementina knew Wogan's secret. Now he was aware that she knew it. They could not look into each other's faces, but their eyes conversed of it. If they turned their heads sharply away, that aversion of their gaze spoke no less clearly. There was a link between them now, and a secret link, the sweeter on that account, perhaps,— certainly the more dangerous. The cloud had grown much bigger than a man's hand. Moreover, she had never seen James Stuart; she had his picture, it is true, but the picture could not recall. It must create, not revivify his image to her thoughts, and that it could not do; so that he remained a shadowy figure to her, a mere number of features, almost an abstraction. On the other hand the King's emissary walked by her side, sat sleepless before her, had held her in his arms, had talked with her, had risked his life for her; she knew him. What she knew of James Stuart, she knew chiefly from the lips of this emissary. On this walk to Ala he spoke of his master, and remorsefully in the highest praise. But she knew his secret, she knew that he loved her, and therefore every remorseful, loyal word he spoke praised him more than it praised his master. And it happened that just as they came to the outskirts of the village, she dropped a handkerchief which hung loosely about her neck. For a moment she did not remark her loss; when she did and turned, she saw that her companion was rising from the ground on which no handkerchief longer lay, and that he had his right hand in his breast. She turned again without a word, and walked forward. But she knew that kerchief was against his heart, and the cloud still grew.

A. E. W. Mason

# CHAPTER XVIII

## WOGAN AND CLEMENTINA CONTINUE
## THEIR JOURNEY ALONE

They reached Ala towards two o'clock of the morning. The town had some reputation in those days for its velvets and silks, and Wogan made no doubt that somewhere he would procure a carriage to convey them the necessary five miles into Venetian territory. The Prince of Baden was still ahead of them, however. The inn of "The Golden Lion" had not a single horse fit for their use in its stables. Wogan, however, obtained there a few likely addresses and set out alone upon his search. He returned in a couple of hours with a little two-wheeled cart drawn by a pony, and sent word within that he was ready. Clementina herself with her hood thrown back from her face came out to him at the door. An oil lamp swung in the passage and lit up her face. Wogan could see that the face was grave and anxious.

"Your Highness and Mrs. Misset can ride in the cart. It has no springs, to be sure, and may shake to pieces like plaster. But if it carries you five miles, it will serve. Misset and I can run by the side."

"But Lucy Misset must not go," said Clementina. "She is ill, and no wonder. She must not take one step more to-night. There would be great danger, and indeed she has endured enough for me." The gravity of the girl's face, as much as her words, convinced Wogan that here was no occasion for encouragement or resistance. He said with some embarrassment,—

"Yet we cannot leave her here alone; and of us two men, her husband must stay with her."

"Dare we wait till the morning?" asked Clementina. "Lucy may be recovered then."

Wogan shook his head.

"The courier we stopped at Wellishmile was not the only man sent after us. Of that we may be very sure. Here are we five miles from safety, and while those five miles are still unbridged—Listen!"

Wogan leaned his head forward and held up his hand for silence. In the still night they could hear far away the galloping of a horse. The sound grew more distinct as they listened.

"The rider comes from Italy," said Clementina. "But he might have come from Trent," cried Wogan. "We left Trent behind twelve hours ago, and more. For twelve hours we crept and crawled along the road; these last miles we have walked. Any moment the Emperor's troopers might come riding after us. Ah, but we are not safe! I am afraid!"

Clementina turned sharply towards him as he spoke this unwonted confession.

"You!" she exclaimed with a wondering laugh. Yet he had

spoken the truth. His face was twitching; his eyes had the look of a man scared out of his wits.

"Yes, I am afraid," he said in a low, uneasy voice. "When I have all but won through the danger, then comes my moment of fear. In the thick of it, perils tread too close upon the heels of peril for a man to count them up. Each minute claims your hands and eyes and brain,—claims you and inspires you. But when the danger's less, and though less still threatens; when you're just this side of safety's frontier and not safe,—indeed, indeed, one should be afraid. A vain spirit of confidence, and the tired head nods, and the blow falls on it from nowhere. Oh, but I have seen examples times out of mind. I beg you, no delay!"

The hoofs of the approaching horse sounded ever louder while Wogan spoke; and as he ended, a man rode out from the street into the open space before the inn. The gallop became a trot.

"He is riding to the door," said Wogan. "The light falls on your face;" and he drew Clementina into the shadow of the wall. But at the same moment the rider changed his mind. He swerved; it seemed too that he used his spurs, for his horse bounded beneath him and galloped past the inn. He disappeared into the darkness, and the sound of the horse diminished. Wogan listened until they had died away.

"He rides into Austria!" said he. "He rides to Trent, to Brixen, to Innspruck! And in haste. Let us go! I had even a fancy that I knew his voice."

"From a single oath uttered in anger! Nay, you are all fears. For my part, I was afraid that he had it in his mind to stay here at this inn where my little woman lies. What if suspicion fall on her? What if those troopers of the Emperor find her and guess the part she played!"

"You make her safe by seeking safety," returned Wogan. "You are the prey the Emperor flies at. Once you are out of reach, his mere dignity must hold him in from wreaking vengeance on your friends."

Wogan went into the inn, and calling Misset told him of his purpose. He would drive her Highness to Peri, a little village ten miles from Ala, but in Italy. At Peri, Mrs. Misset and her husband were to rejoin them in the morning, and from Peri they could travel by slow stages to Bologna. The tears flowed from Clementina's eyes when she took her farewell of her little woman. Though her reason bowed to Wogan's argument, she had a sense of cowardice in deserting so faithful a friend. Mrs. Misset, however, joined in Wogan's prayer; and she mounted into the trap and at Wogan's side drove out of the town by that street along which the horseman had ridden.

Clementina was silent; her driver was no more talkative. They were alone and together on the road to Italy. That embarrassment from which Wogan's confession of fear had procured them some respite held them in a stiff constraint. They were conscious of it as of a tide engulfing them. Neither dared to speak, dreading what might come of speech. The most careless question, the most indifferent comment, might, as it seemed to both, be the spark to fire a mine. Neither had any confidence to say, once they had begun to talk, whither the talk would lead; but they were very much afraid, and they sat very still lest a movement of the one should provoke a question in the other. She knew his secret, and he was aware that she knew it. She could not have found it even then in her heart to part willingly with her knowledge. She had thought over-much upon it during the last day. She had withdrawn herself into it from the company of her fellow-travellers, as into a private chamber; it was familiar and near. Nor would Wogan have desired, now that she had the knowledge, to deprive her of it, but he knew it instinctively for a dangerous thing. He drove on in silence while the stars paled in the heavens and a grey, pure light crept mistily up from the under edges of the world, and the morning broke hard and empty and cheerless. Wogan suddenly drew in the reins and stopped the cart.

"There is a high wall behind us. It stretches across the fields from either side," said he. "It makes a gateway of the road."

Clementina turned. The wall was perhaps ten yards behind them.

"A gateway," said she, "through which we have passed."

"The gateway of Italy," answered Wogan; and he drew the lash once or twice across the pony's back and so was silent. Clementina looked at his set and cheerless face, cheerless as that chill morning, and she too was silent. She looked back along the road which she had traversed through snow and sunshine and clear nights of stars; she saw it winding out from the gates of Innspruck over the mountains, above the foaming river, and after a while she said very wistfully,—

"There are worse lives than a gipsy's."

"Are there any better?" answered Wogan.

So this was what Mr. Wogan's fine project had come to. He remembered another morning when the light had welled over the hills, sunless and clear and cold, on the road to Bologna,— the morning of the day when he had first conceived the rescue of Clementina. And the rescue had been effected, and here was Clementina safe out of Austria, and Wogan sure of a deathless renown, of the accomplishment of an endeavour held absurd and preposterous; and these two short sentences were their summary and comment,—

"There are worse lives than a gipsy's."

"Are there any better?"

Both had at this supreme crisis of their fortunes but the one thought,—that the only days through which they had really lived were those last two days of flight, of hurry, of hope alternating with despair, of light-hearted companionship, days never to be forgotten, when each snatched meal was a picnic seasoned with laughter, days of unharnessed freedom lived in the open air.

Clementina was the first to perceive that her behaviour fell below the occasion. She was safe in Italy, journeying henceforward safely to her betrothed. She spurred herself to understand it, she forced her lips to sing aloud the Te Deum. Wogan looked at her in surprise as the first notes were sung, and the woful appeal in her eyes compelled him to as brave a show as he could make of joining in the hymn. But the words faltered, the tune wavered, joyless and hollow in that empty morning.

"Drive on," said Clementina, suddenly; and she had a sense that she was being driven into bondage,—she who had just been freed. Wogan drove on towards Peri.

It was the morning of Sunday, the 30th of April; and as the little cart drew near to this hamlet of thirty cottages, the travellers could hear the single bell in the church belfry calling the villagers to Mass. Wogan spoke but once to Clementina, and then only to point out a wooden hut which stood picturesquely on a wooded bluff of Monte Lessini,

A. E. W. Mason

high up upon the left. A narrow gorge down which a torrent foamed led upwards to the bluff, and the hut of which the windows were shuttered, and which seemed at that distance to have been built with an unusual elegance, was to Wogan's thinking a hunting-box. Clementina looked up at the bluff indifferently and made no answer. She only spoke as Wogan drove past the church-door, and the sound of the priest's voice came droning out to them.

"Will you wait for me?" she asked. "I will not be long."

Wogan stopped the pony.

"You would give thanks?" said he. "I understand."

"I would pray for an honest heart wherewith to give honest thanks," said Clementina, in a low voice; and she added hastily, "There is a life of ceremonies, there is a life of cities before me. I have lived under the skies these last two days."

She went into the church, shrouding her face in her hood, and kneeled down before a rush chair close to the door. A sense of gratitude, however, was not that morning to be got by any prayers, however earnest. It was merely a distaste for ceremonies and observances, she strenuously assured herself, that had grown upon her during these ten days. She sought to get rid of that distaste, as she kneeled, by picturing in her thoughts the Prince to whom she was betrothed. She recalled the exploits, the virtues, which Wogan had ascribed to him; she stamped them upon the picture. "It is the King," she said to herself; and the picture answered her, "It is the King's servant." And, lo! the face of the picture was the face of Charles Wogan. She covered her cheeks with her hands in a burning rush of shame; she struck in her thoughts at the face of that image with her clenched fists, to bruise, to annihilate it. "It is the King! It is the King! It is the King!" she cried in her remorse, but the image persisted. It still wore the likeness of Charles Wogan; it still repeated, "No, it is the King's servant." There was more of the primitive woman in this girl bred in the rugged country-side of Silesia than even Wogan was aware of, and during the halts in their journey she had learned from Mrs. Misset details which Wogan had been at pains to conceal. It was Wogan who had conceived the idea of her rescue—in the King's place. In the King's place, Wogan had come to Innspruck and effected it. In the King's place, he had taken her by the hand and cleft a way for her through her enemies. He was the man, the rescuer; she was the woman, the rescued.

She became conscious of the futility of her attitude of prayer. She raised her head and saw that a man kneeling close to the altar had turned and was staring fixedly towards her. The man was the Prince of Baden. Had he recognised her? She peered between her fingers; she remarked that his gaze was puzzled; he was not then sure, though he suspected. She waited until he turned his head again, and then she silently rose to her feet and slipped out of the church. She found Wogan waiting for her in some anxiety.

"Did he recognise you?" he asked.

"He was not sure," answered Clementina. "How did you know he was at Mass?"

"A native I spoke with told me."

Clementina climbed up into the cart.

"The Prince is not a generous man," she said hesitatingly.

Wogan understood her. The Prince of Baden must not know that she had come to Peri escorted by a single cavalier. He would talk bitterly, he would make much of his good fortune in that he had not married the Princess Clementina, he would pity the Chevalier de St. George,—there was a fine tale there. Wogan could trace it across the tea-tables of Europe, and hear the malicious inextinguishable laughter which winged it on its way. He drove off quickly from the church door.

"He leaves Peri at nine," said Wogan. "He will have no time to make inquiries. We have but to avoid the inn he stays at. There is a second at the head of the village which we passed."

To this second inn Wogan drove, and was welcomed by a shrewish woman whose sour face was warmed for once in a way into something like enthusiasm.

"A lodging indeed you shall have," cried she, "and a better lodging than the Prince of Baden can look back upon, though he pay never so dearly for it. Poor man, he will have slept wakefully this night! Here, sir, you will find honest board and an honest bed for yourself and your sweet lady, and an honest bill to set you off in a sweet humour in the morning."

"Nay, my good woman," interrupted Wogan, hastily. "This is no sweet lady of mine, nor are we like to stay until the morrow. The truth is, we are a party of four, but our carriage snapped its axle some miles back. The young lady's uncle and aunt are following us, and we wait only for their arrival."

Wogan examined the inn and thought the disposition of it very convenient. It made three sides of a courtyard open to the road. On the right and the bottom were farm-buildings and a stable; the inn was the wing upon the left hand. The guest rooms, of which there were four, were all situated upon the first floor and looked out upon a little thicket of fir-trees at the back of the wing. They were approached by a staircase, which ran up with a couple of turns from the courtyard itself and on the outside of the house-wall. Wogan was very pleased with that staircase; it was narrow. He was pleased, too, because there were no other travellers in the inn. He went back to the landlady.

"It is very likely," said he, "that my friends when they come will, after all, choose to stay here for the night. I will hire all the rooms upon the first floor."

The landlady was no less pleased than Mr. Wogan. She had a thought that they were a runaway couple and served them breakfast in a little parlour up the stairs with many sly and confusing allusions. She became confused, however, when after breakfast Clementina withdrew to bed, and Wogan sauntered out into the high-road, where he sat himself down on a bank to watch for Captain Misset. All day he sat resolutely with his back towards the inn. The landlady inferred that here were lovers quarrelling, and she was yet more convinced of it when she entered the parlour in the afternoon to lay the table for dinner and saw Clementina standing wistfully at the window with her eyes upon that unmoving back. Wogan meanwhile for all his vigilance watched the road but ill. Merchants, pedlars, friars, and gentlemen travelling for their pleasure passed down the road into Italy. Mr. Wogan saw them not, or saw them with unseeing eyes. His eyes were turned inwards, and he gazed at a picture that his heart held of a room in that inn behind him, where after all her dangers and fatigues a woman slept in peace. Towards evening fewer travellers passed by, but there came one party of six well-mounted men whose leader suddenly bowed his head down upon his horse's neck as he rode past. Wogan had preached a sermon on the carelessness which comes with danger's diminutions, but he was very tired. The head was nodding; the blow might fall from nowhere, and he not know.

At nightfall he returned and mounted to the parlour, where Clementina awaited him.

"There is no sign of Captain Misset," said he.

Wogan was puzzled by the way in which Clementina received the news. For a moment he thought that her eyes lightened, and that she was glad; then it seemed to him that her eyes clouded and suddenly as if with pain. Nor was her voice a guide to him, for she spoke her simple question without significance,—

"Must we wait, then, till the morning?"

"There is a chance that they may come before the morning. I will watch on the top stair, and if they come I will make bold to wake your Highness."

Their hostess upon this brought their supper into the room, and Wogan became at once aware of a change in her demeanour. She no longer embarrassed them with her patronage, nor did she continue her sly allusions to the escapades of lovers. On the contrary, she was of an extreme deference. Under the deference, too, Wogan seemed to remark a certain excitement.

"Have you other lodgers to-night?" he asked carelessly.

"No, sir," said she. "Travellers are taken by a big house and a bustle of servants. They stay at the Vapore Inn when they stay at Peri, and to their cost."

As soon as she had left the room Wogan asked of Clementina,—

"When did her manner change?"

"I had not remarked the change till now," replied Clementina.

Wogan became uneasy. He went down into the courtyard, and found it empty. There was a light in the kitchen, and he entered the room. The landlady was having her supper in company with her few servants, and there were one or two peasants from the village. Wogan chatted with them for a few minutes and came out again much relieved of his fears. He thought, however, it might be as well to see that his pony was ready for an emergency. He crossed silently to the stable, which he found dark as the courtyard. The door was latched, but not locked. He opened it and went in. The building was long, with many stalls ranged side by side. Wogan's pony stood in the end stall opposite to the door. Wogan took down the harness from the pegs and began to fix it ready on the pony. He had just put the collar over its head when he heard a horse stamping in one of the stalls at the other end of the stables. Now he had noticed in the morning that there were only two horses in the building, and those two were tied up in the stalls next to that which his pony occupied. He walked along the range of stalls. The two horses were there, then came a gap of empty stalls, and beyond the gap he counted six other horses. Wogan became at once curious about those six other horses. They might of course be farm-horses, but he wished to know. It was quite dark within the building; he had only counted the horses by the noise of their movements in their stalls, the rattle of their head-ropes, and the pawing of their feet. He dared not light a lamp, but horses as a rule knew him for a friend. He went into the stall of the first, petted it for a moment and ran his hand down its legs. He repeated the process with the second, and with so much investigation he was content. No farm-horse that ever Wogan had seen had such a smooth sleek

A. E. W. Mason

skin or such fine legs as had those two over which he had passed his hands. "Now where are the masters of those horses?" he asked himself. "Why do they leave their cattle at this inn and not show themselves in the kitchen or the courtyard? Why do they not ask for a couple of my rooms?" Wogan stood in the dark and reflected. Then he stepped out of the door with even more caution than he had used when entering by it. He stole silently along to the shed where his trap was housed, and felt beneath the seat. From beneath the seat he drew out a coil of rope, and a lamp. The rope he wound about him under his coat. Then he went back to his staircase and the parlour.

Clementina could read in his face that something was amiss, but she had a great gift of silence. She waited for him to speak. Wogan unwound the coil of rope from his body.

"Your Highness laughed at me for that I would not part with my rope. I have a fear this night will prove my wisdom." And with that he began deliberately to break up the chairs in the room. Clementina asked no questions; she watched him take the rungs and bars of the chairs and test their strength. Then he cut the coil of rope in half and tied loops at intervals; into the loops he fitted the wooden rungs. Wogan worked expeditiously for an hour without opening his mouth. In an hour he had fashioned a rope-ladder. He went to the window which looked out on the back of the wing, upon the little thicket of fir-trees. He opened the window cautiously and dropped the ladder down the wall.

"Your Highness has courage," said he. "The ladder does not touch the ground, but it will not be far to drop, should there be need."

The window of Clementina's bedroom was next to that of the parlour and looked out in the same direction. Wogan fixed the rope-ladder securely to the foot of the bed and drew the bed close to the window. He left the lamp upon a chair and went back to the parlour and explained.

"Your Highness," he added, "there may be no cause for any alarm. On the other hand, the Governor of Trent may have taken a leaf from my own book. He may have it in mind to snatch your Highness out of Italy even as I did out of Austria; and of a truth it would be the easier undertaking. Here are we five miles from the border and in a small tavern set apart from a small village, instead of in the thick of an armed town."

"But we might start now," she said. "We might leave a message behind for Mrs. Misset and wait for her in Verona."

"I had thought of that. But if my mere suspicion is the truth, the six men will not be so far from their six horses that we could drive away unnoticed by any one of them. Nor could we hope to outpace them and six men upon an open road; indeed, I would sooner face them at the head of my staircase here. And while I hold them back your Highness can creep down that ladder."

"And hide in the thicket," she interrupted. "Yet—yet—that leaves you alone. I could give you some help;" and her face coloured. "You were so kind as to tell me I had courage. I could at the least load your pistols."

"You would do that?" cried Wogan. "Aye, but you would, you would!"

For the first time that day he forgot to address her with the ceremony of her title. All that day he had schooled his tongue to the use of it. They were not man and woman, though his heart would have it so; they were princess and

A. E. W. Mason

servant, and every minute he must remember it. But he forgot it now. Delicate she was to look upon as any princess who had ever adorned a court, delicate and fresh, rich-voiced and young, but here was the rare woman flashing out like a light over stormy seas, the spirit of her and her courage!

"You would load my pistols!" he repeated, his whole face alight. "To be sure, you would do that. But I ask you, I think, for a higher courage. I ask you to climb down that ladder, to run alone, taking shelter when there's need, back to that narrow gorge we saw where the path leads upwards to the bluff. There was a hut; two hours would take you to it, and there you should be safe. I will keep the enemy back till you are gone. If I can, when all is over here I'll follow you. If I do not come, why, you must—"

"Ah, but you will come," said she, with a smile. "I have no fears but that you will come;" and she added, "Else would you never persuade me to go."

"Well, then, I will come. At all events, Captain Misset and his wife will surely come down the road to-morrow. If I rap twice upon your door, you will take that for my signal. But it is very likely I shall not rap at all."

Wogan shivered as he spoke. It was not for the first time during that conversation, and a little later, as they stood together in the passage by the stair-head, Clementina twice remarked that he shivered again. There was an oil lamp burning against the passage wall, and by its light she could see that on that warm night of spring his face was pinched with cold. He was in truth chilled to the bone through lack of sleep; his eyes had the strained look of a man strung to the breaking point, and at the sight of him the mother in her was touched.

"What if I watched to-night?" she said. "What if you slept?"

Wogan laughed the suggestion aside.

"I shall sleep very well," said he, "upon that top stair. I can count upon waking, though only the lowest step tremble beneath a foot." This he said, meaning not to sleep at all, as Clementina very well understood. She leaned over the balustrade by Wogan's side and looked upwards to the sky. The night was about them like a perfume of flowers. A stream bubbled and sang over stones behind the inn. The courtyard below was very silent. She laid a hand upon his sleeve and said again in a pleading voice,—

"Let me watch to-night. There is no danger. You are racked by sleeplessness, and phantoms born of it wear the face of truth to you. We are safe; we are in Italy. The stars tell me so. Let me watch to-night." And at once she was startled. He withdrew his arm so roughly that it seemed he flung off his hand; he spoke in a voice so hoarse and rough she did not know it for his. And indeed it was a different man who now confronted her,—a man different from the dutiful servant who had rescued her, different even from the man who had held her so tenderly in his arms on the road to Ala.

"Go to your room," said he. "You must not stay here."

She stepped back in her surprise and faced him.

"Every minute," he cried in a sort of exasperation, "I bid myself remember the great gulf between you and me; every minute you forget it. I make a curtain of your rank, your title, and—let us be frank—your destiny; I hang the curtain up between us, and with a gentle hand you tear it down. At the end of it all I am flesh and blood. Why did I sit the whole long dreary day out on the bank by the roadside there? To watch? I could not describe to you one traveller out of them all who passed. Why, then? Ask yourself! It was not that I might stand by your side afterwards in the glamour of an Italian night with the stars pulsing overhead like a smile upon your lips, and all the world whispering! You must not stay here!"

His eyes burnt upon her; his hands shook; from head to foot he was hot and fierce with passion, and in spite of herself she kindled to it. That he loved she knew before, but his description of his city of dreams had given to him in her thoughts a touch of fancifulness, had led her to conceive of his love as something dreamlike, had somehow spiritualised him to the hindrance of her grasp of him as flesh and blood. Thus, she understood, she might well have seemed to be trifling with him, though nothing was further from her thoughts. But now he was dangerous; love had made him dangerous, and to her. She knew it, and in spite of herself she gloried in the knowledge. Her heart leaped into her eyes and shone there responsive, unafraid. The next moment she lowered her head. But he had seen the unmistakable look in her eyes. Even as she stood with her bowed head, he could not but feel that every fibre in her body thrilled; he could not but know the transfigured expression of her face.

"I had no thought to hurt you," she said, and her voice trembled, and it was not with fear or any pain. Wogan took a step towards her and checked himself. He spoke sharply between clenched teeth.

"Lock your door," said he.

The curtain between them was down. Wogan had patched and patched it before; but it was torn down now, and they had seen each other without so much as that patched semblance of a screen to veil their eyes. Clementina did not answer him or raise her head. She went quietly into her room. Wogan did not move until she had locked the door.

Then he disposed himself for the night. He sat down across the top step of the stairs with his back propped against the passage wall. Facing him was the door of Clementina's room, on his left hand the passage with the oil lamp burning on a bracket, stretched to the house-wall; on his right the stairs descended straight for some steps, then turned to the left and ran down still within view to a point where again they turned outwards into the courtyard. Wogan saw to the priming of his pistols and laid them beside him. He looked out to his right over the low-roofed buildings opposite, and saw the black mountains with their glimmering crests, and just above one spur a star which flashed with a particular brightness. He was very tired and very cold; he drew his cloak about him; he leaned back against the wall and watched that star. So long as he saw that, he was awake, and therefore he watched it. At what time sleep overtook him he could never discover. It seemed to him always that he did not even for a second lose sight of that star. Only it dilated, it grew brighter, it dropped towards earth, and he was not in any way surprised. He was merely pleased with it for behaving in so attractive and natural a way. Then, however, the strange thing happened. When the star was hung in the air between earth and sky and nearer to the earth, it opened like a flower and disclosed in its bright heart the face of a girl, which was yet brighter. And that girl's face, with the broad low brows and the dark eyes and the smile which held all earth and much of heaven, stooped and stooped out of fire through the cool dark towards him until her lips touched his. It was then that he woke, quietly as was his wont, without any start, without opening his eyes, and at once he was aware of someone breathing.

He raised his eyelids imperceptibly and peered through his

A. E. W. Mason

eyelashes. He saw close beside him the lower part of a woman's frock, and it was the frock which Clementina wore. One wild question set his heart leaping within his breast. "Was there truth in the dream?" he asked himself; and while he was yet formulating the question, Clementina's breathing was suddenly arrested. It seemed to him, too, from the little that he saw between his closed eyes, that she stiffened from head to foot. She stood in that rigid attitude, very still. Something new had plainly occurred, something that brought with it a shock of surprise. Wogan, without moving his head or opening his eyes a fraction wider, looked down the staircase and saw just above the edge of one of the steep stairs a face watching them,—a face with bright, birdlike eyes and an indescribable expression of cunning.

Wogan had need of all his self-control. He felt that his eyelids were fluttering on his cheeks, that his breath had stopped even as Clementina's had. For the face which he saw was one quite familiar to him, though never familiar with that expression. It was the face of an easy-going gentleman who made up for the lack of his wit by the heartiness of his laugh, and to whom Wogan had been drawn because of his simplicity. There was no simplicity in Henry Whittington's face now. It remained above the edge of the step staring at them with a look of crafty triumph, a very image of intrigue. Then it disappeared silently.

Wogan remembered the voice of the man who had spurred past the doorway of the inn at Ala. He knew now why he had thought to recognise it. The exclamation had been one of anger,—because he had seen Clementina and himself in Italy? He had spurred onwards—towards Trent? There were those six horses in the stables. Whittington's face had disappeared very silently. "An honest man," thought Wogan, "does not take off his boots before he mounts the stairs."

Clementina was still standing at his side. Without changing his attitude he rapped with his knuckles gently twice upon the boards of the stair. She turned towards him with a gasp of the breath. He rapped again twice, fearful lest she should speak to him. She understood that he had given her the signal to go. She turned on her heel and slipped back into her room.

A. E. W. Mason

# CHAPTER XIX

## THE ATTACK AT PERI

Wogan did not move. In a few minutes he heard voices whispering in the courtyard below. By that time the Princess should have escaped into the thicket. The stairs creaked, and again he saw a face over the edge of a step. It was the flabby face of a stranger, who turned and whispered in German to others behind him. The face rose; a pair of shoulders, a portly body, and a pair of unbooted legs became visible. The man carried a drawn sword; between his closed eyelashes Wogan saw that four others with the like arms followed. There should have been six; but the sixth was Harry Whittington, who, to be sure, was not likely to show himself to Wogan awake. The five men passed the first turn of the stairs without noise. Wogan was very well pleased with their noiselessness. Men without boots to their feet were at a very great disadvantage when it came to a fight. He allowed them to come up to the second turn, he allowed the leader to ascend the last straight flight until he was almost within sword-reach, and then he quietly rose to his feet.

"Gentlemen," said he, "I grieve to disappoint you; but I have hired this lodging for the night."

The leader stopped, discountenanced, and leaned back

against his followers. "You are awake?" he stammered.

"It is a habit of mine."

The leader puffed out his cheeks and assumed an appearance of dignity.

"Then we are saved some loss of time. For we were coming to awake you."

"It was on that account, no doubt," said Wogan, folding his arms, "that you have all taken off your boots. But, pardon me, your four friends behind appear in spite of what I have said to be thrusting you forward. I beg you to remain on the step on which you stand. For if you mount one more, you will put me to the inconvenience of drawing my sword."

Wogan leaned back idly against the wall. The Princess should now be on the road and past the inn—unless perhaps Whittington was at watch beneath the windows. That did not seem likely, however. Whittington would work in the dark and not risk detection. The leader of the four had stepped back at Wogan's words, but he said very bravely,—

"I warn you to use no violence to officers in discharge of their duty. We hold a warrant for your arrest."

"Indeed?" said Wogan, with a great show of surprise. "I cannot bring myself to believe it. On what counts?"

"Firstly, in that you stole away her Highness the Princess Clementina from the Emperor's guardianship on the night of the 27th of April at Innspruck."

"Did I indeed do that?" said Wogan, carelessly. "Upon my word, this cloak of mine is frayed. I had not noticed it;" and he picked at the fringe of his cloak with some annoyance.

"In the second place, you did kill and put to death, at a wayside inn outside Stuttgart, one Anton Gans, servant to the Countess of Berg."

Wogan smiled amicably.

"I should be given a medal for that with a most beautiful ribbon of salmon colour, I fancy, salmon or aquamarine. Which would look best, do you think, on a coat of black velvet? I wear black velvet, as your relations will too, my friend, if you forget which step your foot is on. Shall we say salmon colour for the ribbon? The servant was a noxious fellow. We will."

The leader of the four, who had set his foot on the forbidden step, withdrew it quickly. Wogan continued in the same quiet voice,—

"You say you have a warrant?" And a voice very different from his leader's—a voice loud and decisive, which came from the last of the four—answered him,—

"We have. The Emperor's warrant."

"And how comes it," asked Wogan, "that the Emperor's warrant runs in Venice?"

"Because the Emperor's arm strikes in Venice," cried the hindermost again, and he pushed past the man in front of him.

"That we have yet to see," cried Wogan, and his sword flashed naked in his hand. At the same moment the man who had spoken drew a pistol and fired. He fired in a hurry; the bullet cut a groove in the rail of the stair and flattened itself against the passage wall.

"The Emperor's arm shakes, it seems," said Wogan, with a laugh. The leader of the party, thrust forward by those behind him, was lifted to the forbidden step.

"I warned you," cried Wogan, and his sword darted out. But whether from design or accident, the man uttered a cry and stumbled forward on his face. Wogan's sword flashed over his shoulder, and its point sank into the throat of the soldier behind him. That second soldier fell back, with the blood spurting from his wound, upon the man with the smoking pistol, who thrust him aside with an oath.

"Make room," he cried, and lunged over the fallen leader.

"Here's a fellow in the most desperate hurry," said Wogan, and parrying the thrust he disengaged, circled, disengaged again, and lunging felt the soldier's leather coat yield to his point. "The Emperor's arm is weak, too, one might believe," he laughed, and he drove his sword home. The man fell upon the stairs; but as Wogan spoke the leader crouched on the step plucked violently at his cloak below his knees. Wogan had not recovered from his lunge; the jerk at the cloak threw him off his balance, his legs slipped forward under him, in another moment he would have come crashing down the stairs upon his back, and at the bottom of the flight there stood one man absolutely unharmed supporting his comrade who had been wounded in the throat. Wogan felt the jerk, understood the danger, and saw its remedy at the same instant. He did not resist the impetus, he threw his body into it, he sprang from the stairs forwards, tearing his cloak from the leader's hands, he sprang across the leader, across the soldier who had fired at him, and he dropped with all his weight into the arms of the third man with the pierced throat.

A. E. W. Mason

The blood poured out from the wound over Wogan's face and breast in a blinding jet. The fellow uttered one choking cry and reeling back carried the comrade who supported him against the balustrade at the turn of the stairs. Wogan did not give that fourth man time to disengage himself, but dropping his sword caught him by the throat as the third wounded man slipped between them to the ground. Wogan bent his new opponent backwards over the balustrade, and felt the muscles of his back resist and then slacken. Wogan bent him further and further over until it seemed his back must break. But it was the balustrade which broke. Wogan heard it crack. He had just time to loose his hands and step back, and the railing and the man poised on the rail fell outwards into the courtyard. Wogan stepped forward and peered downwards. The soldier had not broken his neck, for Wogan saw him writhe upon the ground. He bent his head to see the better; he heard a report behind him, and a bullet passed through the crown of his hat. He swung round and saw the leader of the four with one of his own pistols smoking in his hand.

"You!" cried Wogan. "Sure, here's a rabbit attacking a terrier dog;" and he sprang up the stairs. The man threw away the pistol, fell on his knees, and held up his hands for mercy.

"Now what will I do to you?" said Wogan. "Did you not fire at my back? That's reprehensible cowardice. And with my own pistol, too, which is sheer impertinence. What will I do with you?" The man's expression was so pitiable, his heavy cheeks hung in such despairing folds, that Wogan was stirred to laughter. "Well, you have put me to a deal of inconvenience," said he; "but I will be merciful, being strong, being most extraordinary strong. I'll send you back to your master the Emperor with a message from me that four men are no manner of use at all. Come in here for a bit."

Wogan took the unfortunate man and led him into the

parlour. Then he lit a lamp, and making his captive sit where he could see any movement that he made, he wrote a very polite note to his Most Catholic Majesty the Emperor wherein he pointed out that it was a cruel thing to send four poor men who had never done harm to capture Charles Wogan; that no King or Emperor before who had wanted to capture Charles Wogan, of whom there were already many, and by God's grace he hoped there would be more, had ever despatched less than a regiment of horse upon so hazardous an expedition; and that when Captain O'Toole might be expected to be standing side by side with Wogan, it was usually thought necessary to add seven batteries of artillery and a field marshal. Wogan thereupon went on to point out that Peri was in Venetian territory, which his Most Catholic Majesty had violated, and that Charles Wogan would accordingly feel it his bounden duty not to sleep night or day until he had made a confederation of Italian states to declare war and captivity upon his Most Catholic Majesty. Wogan concluded with the assurances of his profoundest respects and was much pleased by his letter, which he sealed and compelled his prisoner upon his knees to promise to deliver into the Emperor's own hands.

"Now where is that pretty warrant?" said Wogan, as soon as this important function was accomplished.

"It is signed by the Governor of Trent," said the man.

"Who in those regions is the Emperor's deputy. Hand it over."

The man handed it over reluctantly.

"Now," continued Wogan, "here is paper and ink and a chair. Sit down and write a full confession of your audacious incursion into a friendly country, and just write, if you

A. E. W. Mason

please, how much you paid the landlady to hear nothing of what was doing."

"You will not force me to that," cried the fellow.

"By no means. The confession must be voluntary and written of your own free will. So write it, my friend, without any compulsion whatever, or I'll throw you out of the window."

Then followed a deal of sighing and muttering. But the confession was written and handed to Wogan, who glanced over it.

"But there's an omission," said he. "You make mention of only five men."

"There were only five men on the staircase."

"But there are six horses in the stables. Will you be good enough to write down at what hour on what day Mr. Harry Whittington knocked at the Governor's door in Trent and told the poor gout-ridden man that the Princess and Mr. Wogan had put up at the Cervo Inn at Ala."

The soldier turned a startled face on Wogan.

"So you knew!" he cried.

"Oh, I knew," answered Wogan, suddenly. "Look at me! Did you ever see eyes so heavy with want of sleep, a face so worn by it, a body so jerked upon strings like a showman's puppet? Write, I tell you! We who serve the King are trained to wakefulness. Write! I am in haste!"

"Yet your King does not reign!" said the man, wonderingly, and he wrote. He wrote the truth about Harry Whittington;

for Wogan was looking over his shoulder.

"Did he pay you to keep silence as to his share in the business?" asked Wogan, as the man scattered some sand over the paper. "There is no word of it in your handwriting."

The man added a sentence and a figure.

"That will do," said Wogan. "I may need it for a particular purpose;" and he put the letter carefully away in the pocket of his coat. "For a very particular purpose," he added. "It will be well for you to convey your party back with all haste to Trent. You are on the wrong side of the border."

A. E. W. Mason

# CHAPTER XX

## THE GOD OF THE MACHINE DOES NOT APPEAR

Wogan went from the parlour and climbed out of the house
by the rope-ladder. He left it hanging at the window and
walked up the glimmering road, a ribbon of ghostly white
between dim hills. It was then about half-past twelve of the
night, and not a feather of cloud stained the perfection of the
sky. It curved above his head spangled like a fair lady's fan,
and unfathomably blue like Clementina's eyes when her
heart stirred in their depths. He reached the little footway and
turned into the upward cleft of the hills. He walked now into
the thick night of a close-grown clump of dwarf-oaks, which
weaved so dense a thatch above his head that he knocked
against the boles. The trees thinned, he crossed here and
there a dimpled lawn in the pure starshine, he traversed a
sparse grove of larches in the dreamy twilight, he came out
again upon the grassy lip of a mountain torrent which
henceforth kept him company, and which, speaking with
many voices, seemed a friend trying to catch his mood. For
here it leaped over an edge of rock, and here in a tiny
waterfall, and splashed into a pellucid pool, and the
reverberating noise filled the dell with a majestic din; there it
ran smoothly kissing its banks with a murmur of contentment, embosoming the stars; beyond, it chafed hoarsely
between narrow walls; and again half a mile higher up it

sang on shallows and evaded the stones with a tinkling laugh. But Wogan was deaf to the voices; he mounted higher, the trees ceased, he came into a desolate country of boulders; and the higher he ascended, the more heavily he walked. He stopped and washed his face and hands clean of blood-stains in the stream. Above him and not very far away was the lonely hut.

He came upon it quite suddenly. For the path climbed steeply at the back, and slipping from the mouth of a narrow gully he stood upon the edge of a small plateau in the centre of which stood the cabin, a little house of pinewood built with some decoration and elegance. One unglazed window was now unshuttered, and the light from a lantern streamed out of it in a yellow fan, marking the segment of a circle upon the rough rocky ground and giving to the dusk of the starshine a sparkle of gold. Through the window Wogan could see into the room. It was furnished simply, but with an eye to comfort. He saw too the girl he had dared to bear off from the thick of a hostile town. She was lying upon a couch, her head resting upon her folded arms. She was asleep, and in a place most solitary. Behind the cabin rose a black forest of pines, pricking the sky with their black spires, and in front of it the ground fell sharply to the valley, in which no light gleamed; beyond the valley rose the dim hills again. Nor was there any sound except the torrent. The air at this height was keen and fresh with a smell of primeval earth. Wogan hitched his cloak about his throat, and his boots rang upon the rock. The Princess raised her head; Wogan walked to the door and stood for a little with his hand upon the latch. He lifted it and entered. Clementina looked at him for a moment, and curiously. She had no questions as to how his struggle with the Governor of Trent's emissaries had fared. Wogan could understand by some unspoken sympathy that that matter had no place in her thoughts. She stood up in an attitude of expectation.

A. E. W. Mason

"It grows towards morning?" said she.

"In two hours we shall have the dawn," he replied; and there was a silence between them.

"You found this cabin open?" said Wogan.

"The door was latched. I loosed a shutter. The night is very still."

"One might fancy there were no others alive but you and me across all the width of the world."

"One could wish it," she said beneath her breath, and crossed to the window where she stayed, breathing the fresh night. The sigh, however, had reached to Wogan's ears. He took his pistols from his belt, and to engage his thoughts, loaded the one which had been fired at him. After a little he looked up and saw that Clementina's eyes dwelt upon him with that dark steady look, which held always so much of mystery and told always one thing plainly, her lack of fear. And she said suddenly,—

"There was trouble at Peri. I climbed from the window. I had almost forgotten. As I ran down the road past the open court, I saw a little group of men gathered about the foot of the staircase! I was in two minds whether to come back and load your pistols or to obey you. I obeyed, but I was in much fear for you. I had almost forgotten, it seems so long ago. Tell me! You conquered; it is no new thing. Tell me how!"

She did not move from the window, she kept her eyes fixed upon Wogan while he told his story, but it was quite clear to him that she did not hear one half of it. And when he had done she said,—

"How long is it till the morning?"

Wogan had spun his tale out, but half an hour enclosed it, from the beginning to the end. He became silent again; but he was aware at once that silence was more dangerous than speech, for in the silence he could hear both their hearts speaking. He began hurriedly to talk of their journey, and there could be no more insidious topic for him to light upon. For he spoke of the Road, and he had already been given a warning that to the romance of the Road her heart turned like a compass-needle to the north. They were both gipsies, for all that they had no Egyptian blood. That southward road from Innspruck was much more than a mere highway of travel between a starting-place and a goal, even to these two to whom the starting-place meant peril and the goal the first opportunity of sleep.

"Even in our short journey," said Clementina, "how it climbed hillsides angle upon angle, how it swept through the high solitudes of ice where no trees grow, where silence lives; how it dropped down into green valleys and the noise of streams! And it still sweeps on, through dark and light, a glimmer at night, a glare in the midday, between lines of poplars, hidden amongst vines, through lighted cities, down to Venice and the sea. If one could travel it, never retracing a step, pitching a tent by the roadside when one willed! That were freedom!" She stopped with a remarkable abruptness. She turned her eyes out of the window for a little. Then again she asked,—

"How long till morning?"

"But one more hour."

She came back into the room and seated herself at the table.

"You gave me some hint at Innspruck of an adventurous ride from Ohlau," and she drew her breath sharply at the word, as though the name with all its associations struck her a blow, "into Strasbourg. Tell me its history. So will this hour pass."

He told her as he walked about the room, though his heart was not in the telling, nor hers in the hearing, until he came to relate the story of his escape from the inn a mile or so beyond Stuttgart. He described how he hid in the garden, how he crossed the rich level of lawn to the lighted window, how to his surprise he was admitted without a question by an old bookish gentleman—and thereupon he ceased so suddenly that Clementina turned her head aside and listened.

"Did you hear a step?" she asked in a low voice.

"No."

And they both listened. No noise came to their ears but the brawling of the torrent. That, however, filled the room, drowning all the natural murmurs of the night.

"Indeed, one would not hear a company of soldiers," said Clementina. She crossed to the window.

"Yet you heard my step, and it waked you," said Wogan, as he followed her.

"I listened for it in my sleep," said she.

For a second time that night they stood side by side looking upon darkness and the spangled sky. Only there was no courtyard with its signs of habitation. Clementina drew herself away suddenly from the sill. Wogan at once copied her example.

"You saw—?" he began.

"No one," said she, bending her dark eyes full upon him. "Will you close the shutter?"

Wogan drew back instinctively. He had a sense that this open window, though there was no one to spy through it, was in some way a security. Suppose that he closed it! That mere act of shutting himself and her apart, though it gave not one atom more of privacy, still had a semblance of giving it. He was afraid. He said,—

"There is no need. Who should spy on us? What would it matter if we were spied upon?"

"I ask you to close that shutter."

From the quiet, level voice he could infer nothing of the thought behind the request; and her unwavering eyes told him nothing.

"Why?"

"Because I am afraid, as you are," said she, and she shivered. "You would not have it shut. I am afraid while it stays open. There is too much expectation in the night. Those great black pines stand waiting; the stars are very bright and still, they wait, holding their breath. It seems to me the whirl of the earth has stopped. Never was there a night so hushed in expectation;" and these words too she spoke without a falter or a lifting note, breathing easily like a child asleep, and not changing her direct gaze from Wogan's face. "I am afraid," she continued, "of you and me. I am the more afraid;" and Wogan set the shutter in its place and let the bar fall. Clementina with a breath of relief came back to her seat at the table.

"How long is it till dawn?" she said.

"We have half an hour," said Wogan.

"Well, that old man—Count von Ahlen, you said—received you, heaped logs upon his fire, stanched your wounds, and asked no questions. Well? You stopped suddenly. Tell me all!"

Wogan looked doubtfully at her and then quickly seated himself over against her.

"All? I will. It will be no new thing to you;" and as Clementina raised her eyes curiously to his, he met her gaze and so spoke the rest looking at her with her own direct gaze.

"Why did he ask no question, seeing me disordered, wounded, a bandit, for all he knew, with a murder on my hands? Because thirty years before Count Philip Christopher von Koenigsmarck had come in just that same way over the lawn to the window, and had sat by that log-fire and charmed the old gentleman into an envy by his incomparable elegance and wit."

"Koenigsmarck!" exclaimed the girl. She knew the history of that brilliant and baleful adventurer at the Court of Hanover. "He came as you did, and wounded?"

"The Princess Sophia Dorothea was visiting the Duke of Wuertemberg," Wogan explained, and Clementina nodded.

"Count Otto von Ahlen, my host," he continued, "had a momentary thought that I was Koenigsmarck mysteriously returned as he had mysteriously vanished; and through these thirty years' retention of his youth, Count Otto could never think of Koenigsmarck but as a man young and tossed in a froth of passion. He would have it to the end that I had escaped from such venture as had Koenigsmarck; he would have it my wounds were the mere offset to a love well worth them; he *would* envy me. 'Passion,' said he, 'without passion there can be no great thing.'"

"And the saying lived in your thoughts," cried Clementina. "I do not wonder. 'Without passion there can be no great thing!' Can books teach a man so much?"

"Nay, it was an hour's talk with Koenigsmarck which set the old man's thoughts that way; and though Koenigsmarck talked never so well, I would not likely infer from his talk an eternal and universal truth. Count Otto left me alone while he fetched me food, and he left me in a panic."

"A panic?" said Clementina, with a little laugh. "You!"

"Yes. That first mistake of me for Koenigsmarck, that insistence that my case was Koenigsmarck's—"

"There was a shadow of truth in it—even then?" said Clementina, suddenly leaning across the table towards him. Wogan strove not to see the light of her joy suddenly sparkling in her eyes.

"I sat alone, feeling the ghost of Koenigsmarck in the room with me," he resumed quickly, and his voice dropped, and he looked round the little cabin. Clementina looked round quickly too. Then their eyes met again. "I heard his voice menacing me. 'For love of a queen I lived. For love of a queen I died most horribly; and it would have gone better with the queen had she died the same death at the same time—'" And Clementina interrupted him with a cry which was fierce.

A. E. W. Mason

"Ah, who can say that, and know it for the truth—except the Queen? You must ask her in her prison at Ahlden, and that you cannot do. She has her memories maybe. Maybe she has built herself within these thirty years a world of thought so real, it makes her gaolers shadows, and that prison a place of no account, save that it gives her solitude and is so more desirable than a palace. I can imagine it;" and then she stopped, and her voice dropped to the low tone which Wogan had used.

"You looked round you but now and most fearfully. Is Koenigsmarck's spirit here?"

"No," exclaimed Wogan; "I would to God it were! I would I felt its memories chilling me as they chilled me that night! But I cannot. I cannot as much as hear a whisper. All the heavens are dumb," he cried.

"And the earth waits," said Clementina.

She did not move, neither did Wogan. They both sat still as statues. They had come to the great crisis of their destiny. A change of posture, a gesture, an assumed expression which might avert the small, the merely awkward indiscretions of the tongue, they both knew to be futile. It was in the mind of each of them that somehow without their participation the truth would out that night; for the dawn was so long in coming.

"All the way up from Peri," said Wogan, suddenly, "I strove to make real to myself the ignominy, the odium, the scandal."

"But you could not," said Clementina, with a nod of comprehension, as though that inability was a thing familiar to her.

"When I reached the hut, and saw that fan of light spreading from the window, as it spread over the lawn beyond Stuttgart, I remembered Otto von Ahlen and his talk of Koenigsmarck. I tried to hear the menaces."

"But you could not."

"No. I saw you through the window," he cried, "stretched out upon that couch, supple and young and sweet. I saw the lamplight on your hair, searching out the gold in its dark brown. I could only remember how often I have at nights wakened and reached out my hands in the vain dream that they would meet in its thick coils, that I should feel its silk curl and nestle about my fingers. There's the truth out, though it's a familiar truth to you ever since I held you in my arms beneath the stars upon the road to Ala."

"It was known to me a day before," said she; "but it was known to you so long ago as that night in the garden."

"Oh, before then," cried Wogan.

"When? Let the whole truth be known, since we know so much."

"Why, on that first day at Ohlau."

"In the great hall. I stood by the fire and raised my head, and our eyes met. I do remember."

"But I had no thought ever to let you know. I was the King's man-at-arms, as I am now;" and he burst into a harsh laugh. "Here's madness! The King's man-at-arms dumps him down in the King's chair! I had a thought to live to you, if you understand, as a man writes a poem to his mistress, to make my life the poem, an unsigned poem that you would never

A. E. W. Mason

read, and yet unsigned, unread, would make its creator glad and fill his days. And here's the poem!" and at that a great cry of terror leaped from Clementina's lips and held them both aghast.

Wogan had risen from his seat; with a violent gesture he had thrown back his cloak, and his coat beneath was stained and dark with blood. Clementina stood opposite to him, all her quiet and her calmness gone. There was no longer any mystery in her eyes. Her bosom rose and fell; she pointed a trembling hand towards his breast.

"You are hurt. Again for love of me you are hurt."

"It is not my wound," he answered. "It is blood I spilt for you;" he took a step towards her, and in a second she was between his arms, sobbing with all the violence of passion which she had so long restrained. Wogan was wrung by it. That she should weep at all was a thought strange to him; that he should cause the tears was a sorrow which tortured him. He touched her hair with his lips, he took her by the arms and would have set her apart; but she clung to him, hiding her face, and the sobs shook her. Her breast was strained against him, he felt the beating of her heart, a fever ran through all his blood. And as he held her close, a queer inconsequential thought came into his mind. It shocked him, and he suddenly held her off.

"The blood upon my coat is wet," he cried. The odium, the scandal of a flight which would make her name a byword from London to Budapest, that he could envisage; but that this blood upon his coat should stain the dress she wore—no! He saw indeed that the bodice was smeared a dark red.

"See, the blood stains you!" he cried.

"Why, then, I share it," she answered with a ringing voice of pride. "I share it with you;" and she smiled through her tears and a glowing blush brightened upon her face. She stood before him, erect and beautiful. Through Wogan's mind there tripped a procession of delicate ladies who would swoon gracefully at the sight of a pricked finger.

"That's John Sobieski speaking," he exclaimed, and with an emphasis of despair, "Poland's King! But I was mad! Indeed, I blame myself."

"Blame!" she cried passionately, her whole nature rising in revolt against the word. "Are we to blame? We are man and woman. Who shall cast the stone? Are you to blame for that you love me? Who shall blame you? Not I, who thank you from my heart. Am I to blame? What have we hearts for, then, if not to love? I have a thought—it may be very wrong. I do not know. I do not trouble to think—that I should be much more to blame did I not love you too. There's the word spoken at the last," and she lowered her head.

Even at that moment her gesture struck upon Wogan as strange. It occurred to him that he had never before seen her drop her eyes from his. He had an intuitive fancy that she would never do it but as a deliberate token of submission. Nor was he wrong. Her next words told him it was her white flag of surrender.

"I believe the spoken truth is best," she said simply in a low voice which ever so slightly trembled. "Unspoken and yet known by both of us, I think it would breed thoughts and humours we are best without. Unspoken our eyes would question, each to other, at every meeting; there would be no health in our thoughts. But here's the truth out, and I am glad—in whichever way you find its consequence."

She stood before him with her head bent. She made no movement save with her hands, which worked together slowly and gently.

"In whichever way—I—?" repeated Wogan.

"Yes," she answered. "There is Bologna. Say that Bologna is our goal. I shall go with you to Bologna. There is Venice and the sea. Bid me go, then; hoist a poor scrap of a sail in an open boat. I shall adventure over the wide seas with you. What will you do?"

Wogan drew a long breath. The magnitude of the submission paralysed him. The picture which she evoked was one to blind him as with a glory of sunlight. He remained silent for a while. Then he said timidly,—

"There is Ohlau."

The girl shivered. The name meant her father, her mother, their grief, the disgrace upon her home. But she answered only with her question,—

"What will you do?"

"You would lose a throne," he said, and even while he spoke was aware that such a plea had not with her now the weight of thistledown.

"You would become the mock of Europe,—you that are its wonder;" and he saw the corner of her lip curve in a smile of scorn.

"What will you do?" she asked, and he ceased to argue. It was he who must decide; she willed it so. He turned towards the door of the hut and opened it. As he passed through, he heard her move behind, and looking over his shoulder, he saw that she leaned down upon the table and kissed the pistol which he had left loaded there. He stepped out of the cabin and closed the door behind him.

The dark blue of the sky had faded to a pure and pearly colour; a colourless grey light invaded it; the pale stars were drowning; and all about him the trees shivered to the morning. Wogan walked up and down that little plateau, torn by indecision. Inside the sheltered cabin sat waiting the girl, whose destiny was in his hands. He had a sentence to speak, and by it the flow of all her years would be irrevocably ordered. She had given herself over to him,—she, with her pride, her courage, her endurance. Wogan had seen too closely into her heart to bring any foolish charge of unmaidenliness against her. No, the very completeness of her submission raised her to a higher pinnacle. If she gave herself, she did so without a condition or a reserve, body and bone, heart and soul. Wogan knew amongst the women of his time many who made their bargain with the world, buying a semblance of esteem with a double payment of lies. This girl stood apart from them. She loved, therefore she entrusted herself simply to the man she loved, and bade him dispose of her. That very simplicity was another sign of her strength. She was the more priceless on account of it. He went back into the hut. Through the chinks of the shutter the morning stretched a grey finger; the room was filled with a vaporous twilight.

"We travel to Bologna," said he. "I will not have you wasted. Other women may slink into kennels and stop their ears—not you. The King is true to you. You are for the King."

As she had not argued before, she did not argue now. She nodded her head and fastened her cloak about her throat. She followed him out of the hut and down the gorge. In the

A. E. W. Mason

northeast the sky already flamed, and the sun was up before they reached the road. They walked silently towards Peri, and Wogan was wondering whether in her heart she despised him when she stopped.

"I am to marry the King," said she.

"Yes," said Wogan.

"But you?" she said with her brows in a frown; "there is no compulsion on you to marry—anyone."

Wogan was relieved of his fears. He broke into a laugh, to which she made no reply. She still waited frowning for his answer.

"No woman," he said, "will ride on my black horse into my city of dreams. You may be very sure I will not marry."

"No. I would not have you married."

Wogan laughed again, but Clementina was very serious. That she had no right to make any such claim did not occur to her. She was merely certain and resolved that Wogan must not marry. She did not again refer to the matter, nor could she so have done had she wished. For a little later and while they were not yet come to Peri, they were hailed from behind, and turning about they saw Gaydon and O'Toole riding after them. O'Toole had his story to tell. Gaydon and he had put the courier to bed and taken his clothes and his money, and after the fellow had waked up, they had sat for a day in the bedroom keeping him quiet and telling the landlord he was very ill. O'Toole finished his story as they came to Peri. They went boldly to the Cervo Inn, where all traces of the night's conflict had been removed, and neither Wogan nor the landlady thought it prudent to make any mention of the matter; they waited for Misset and his wife, who came the next day. And thus reunited they passed one evening into the streets of Bologna and stopped at the Pilgrim Inn.

A. E. W. Mason

# CHAPTER XXI

## COMPLICATIONS AT BOLOGNA

In the parlour of the Pilgrim Inn the four friends took their leave of the Princess. She could not part from them lightly; she spoke with a faltering voice:—

"Five days ago I was in prison at Innspruck, perpetually harassed and with no hope of release but in you. Now I am in Bologna, and free. I could not believe that any girl could find such friends except in fairyland. You make the world very sweet and clean to me. I should thank you. See my tears fall! Will you take them for my thanks? I have no words which can tell as much of my thoughts towards you. My little woman I keep with me, but to you gentlemen I would gladly give a token each, so that you may know I will never forget, and so that you too may keep for me a home within your memories." To Major Gaydon she gave a ring from off her finger, to Captain Misset a chain which she wore about her neck, to O'Toole, "her six feet four," as she said between laughter and tears, her watch. Each with a word of homage took his leave. Clementina spoke to Wogan last of all, and when the room was empty but for these two.

"To you, my friend," said she, "I give nothing. There is no need. But I ask for something. I would be in debt to you still deeper than I am. I ask for a handkerchief which I dropped from my shoulders one evening under the stars upon the road to Ala."

Wogan bowed to her without a word. He drew the handkerchief from his breast slowly.

"It is true," said he; "I have no right to it;" and he gave it back. But his voice showed that he was hurt.

"You do not understand," said she, with a great gentleness. "You have every right which the truest loyalty can confer. I ask you for this handkerchief, because I think at times to wear it in memory of a white stone on which I could safely set my foot, for the stone was not straw."

Wogan could not trust his voice to answer her. He took her hand to lift it to his lips.

"No," said she; "as at Innspruck, an honest handclasp, if you please."

Wogan joined his three companions in the road, and they stood together for a little, recounting to one another the incidents of the flight.

"Here's a great work ended," said Gaydon at last.

"We shall be historical," said O'Toole. "It is my one ambition. I want to figure in the history-books and be a great plague and nuisance to children at school. I would sooner be cursed daily by schoolboys than have any number of golden statues in galleries. It means the more solid reputation;" and then he became silent. Gaydon had, besides his joy at the rescue of Clementina, a private satisfaction that matters which were none of his business had had no uncomfortable

A. E. W. Mason

issue. Misset, too, was thankful for that his wife had come safely to the journey's end. O'Toole alone had a weight upon his mind; and when Gaydon said, "Well, we may go to bed and sleep without alarms till sundown to-morrow," he remarked,—

"There's Jenny. It was on my account she ventured with us."

"That's true," said Wogan; "but we shall put an end to her captivity, now we are safe at Bologna. I have friends here who can serve me so far, I have no doubt."

O'Toole was willing to leave the matter in Wogan's hands. If Wogan once pledged himself to Jenny's release, why, Jenny *was* released; and he went to bed now with a quite equable mind. Wogan hurried off to the palace of the Cardinal Origo, whom he found sitting at his supper. The Cardinal welcomed Wogan back very warmly.

"I trust, your Eminence," said Wogan, "that Farini is now at Bologna."

"You come in the nick of time," replied the Cardinal. "This is his last week. There is a great demand for the seats; but you will see to it, Mr. Wogan, that the box is in the first tier."

"There was to be a dinner, too, if I recollect aright. I have not dined for days. Your Eminence, I shall be extraordinarily hungry."

"You will order what you will, Mr. Wogan. I am a man of a small appetite and have no preferences."

"Your Eminence's cook will be the better judge of what is seasonable. Your Eminence will be the more likely to secure the box in the first tier. Shall we fix a day? To-morrow, if it please you. To-morrow I shall have the honour, then, to be your Eminence's guest."

The Cardinal started up from the table and stared at his visitor.

"You are jesting," said he.

"So little," replied Wogan, "that her Highness, the Princess Clementina, is now at the Pilgrim Inn at Bologna."

"In Bologna!" cried the Cardinal; and he stood frowning in a great perturbation of spirit. "This is great news," he said, but in a doubtful voice which Wogan did not understand. "This is great news, to be sure;" and he took a turn or two across the room.

"Not wholly pleasant news, one might almost think," said Wogan, in some perplexity.

"Never was better news," exclaimed the Cardinal, hastily,—a trifle too hastily, it seemed to Wogan. "But it surprises one. Even the King did not expect this most desirable issue. For the King's in Spain. It is that which troubles me. Her Highness comes to Bologna, and the King's in Spain."

"Yes," said Wogan, with a wary eye upon his Eminence. "Why is the King in Spain?"

"There is pressing business in Spain,—an expedition from Cadiz. The King's presence there was urged most earnestly. He had no hope you would succeed. I myself have some share in the blame. I did not hide from you my thought, Mr. Wogan."

Wogan was not all reassured. He could not but remember

that the excuse for the King's absence which the Cardinal now made to him was precisely that which he himself had invented to appease Clementina at Innspruck. It was the simple, natural excuse which came first of all to the tongue's tip, but—but it did not satisfy. There was, besides, too much flurry and agitation in the Cardinal's manner. Even now that he was taking snuff, he spilled the most of it from the trembling of his fingers. Moreover, he must give reason upon reason for his perturbation the while he let his supper get cold.

"Her Highness I cannot but feel will have reason to think slightly of our welcome. A young girl, she will expect, and rightly, something more of ceremony as her due."

"Your Eminence does not know her," interrupted Wogan, with some sharpness. His Eminence was adroit enough to seize the occasion of ending a conversation which was growing with every minute more embarrassing.

"I shall make haste to repair my defect," said he. "I beg you to present my duty to her Highness and to request her to receive me to-morrow at ten. By that, I will hope to have discovered a lodging more suitable to her dignity."

Wogan made his prayer for the Pope's intervention on Jenny's behalf and then returned to the Pilgrim Inn, dashed and fallen in spirit. He had thought that their troubles were at an end, but here was a new difficulty at which in truth he rather feared to guess. The Chevalier's departure to Spain had been a puzzle to him before; he remembered now that the Chevalier had agreed with reluctance to his enterprise, and had never been more than lukewarm in its support. That reluctance, that lukewarmness, he had attributed to a natural habit of discouragement; but the evasiveness of Cardinal Origo seemed to propose a different explanation. Wogan would not guess at it.

"The King is to marry the Princess," said he, fiercely. "I brought her out of Innspruck to Bologna. The King must marry the Princess;" and, quite unawares, he set off running towards the inn. As he drew near to it, he heard a confused noise of shouting. He quickened his pace, and rushing out of the mouth of a side street into the square where the inn stood, came suddenly to a stop. The square was filled with a great mob of people, and in face of the inn the crowd was so thick Wogan could have walked upon the shoulders. Many of the people carried blazing torches, which they waved in the air, dropping the burning resin upon their companions; others threw their hats skywards; here were boys beating drums, and grown men blowing upon toy trumpets; and all were shouting and cheering with a deafening enthusiasm. The news of the Princess's arrival had spread like wildfire through the town. Wogan's spirits rose at a bound. Here was a welcome very different from the Cardinal's. Wogan rejoiced in the good sense of the citizens of Bologna who could appreciate the great qualities of his chosen woman. Their enthusiasm did them credit; he could have embraced them one by one.

He strove to push his way towards the door, but he would hardly have pierced through that throng had not a man by the light of a torch recognised him and bawled out his name. He was lifted shoulder high in a second; he was passed from hand to hand over the heads of the people; he was set tenderly down in the very doorway of the Pilgrim Inn, and he found Clementina at the window of an unlighted room gazing unperceived at the throng.

"Here's a true welcome, madam," said he, cordially, with his thoughts away upon that bluff of hillside where the acclamations had seemed so distant and unreal. It is possible

A. E. W. Mason

that they seemed of small account to Clementina now, for though they rang in ears and were visible to her eyes, she sat quite unmoved by them.

"This is one tiny square in a little town," he continued. "But its shouts will ring across Europe;" and she turned her head to him and said quietly,—

"The King is still in Spain, is he not?"

Wogan's enthusiasm was quenched in alarm. Her voice had rung, for all its quietude, with pride. What if she guessed what he for one would not let his wildest fancy dwell upon? Wogan repeated to himself the resolve which he had made, though with an alteration. "The King must marry the Princess," he had said; now he said, "The Princess must marry the King."

He began hurriedly to assure her that the King had doubted his capacity to bring the enterprise to a favourable issue, but that now he would without doubt return. Cardinal Origo would tell her more upon that head if she would be good enough to receive him at ten in the morning; and while Wogan was yet speaking, a torch waved, and amongst that close-pressed throng of faces below him in the street, one sprang to his view with a remarkable distinctness, a face most menacing and vindictive. It was the face of Harry Whittington. Just for a second it shone out, angles and lines so clearly revealed that it was as though the crowd had vanished, and that one contorted face glared alone at the windows in a flare of hell-fire.

Clementina saw the face too, for she drew back instinctively within the curtains of the window.

"The man at Peri," said she, in a whisper.

"Your Highness will pardon me," exclaimed Wogan, and he made a movement towards the door. Then he stopped, hesitated for a second, and came back. He had a question to put, as difficult perhaps as ever lips had to frame.

"At Peri," he said in a stumbling voice, "I waked from a dream and saw that man, bird-like and cunning, watching over the rim of the stairs. I was dreaming that a star out of heaven stooped towards me, that a woman's face shone out of the star's bright heart, that her lips deigned to bend downwards to my earth. And I wonder, I wonder whether those cunning eyes had cunning enough to interpret my dream."

And Clementina answered him simply,—

"I think it very likely that they had so much skill;" and Wogan ran down the stairs into the street. He forced his way through the crowd to the point where Whittington's face had shown, but his hesitation, his question, had consumed time. Whittington had vanished. Nor did he appear again for some while in Bologna. Wogan searched for him high and low. Here was another difficulty added to the reluctance of his King, the pride of his Queen. Whittington had a piece of dangerous knowledge, and could not be found. Wogan said nothing openly of the man's treachery, though he kept very safely the paper in which that treachery was confessed. But he did not cease from his search. He was still engaged upon it when he received the summons from Cardinal Origo. He hurried to the palace, wondering what new thing had befallen, and was at once admitted to the Cardinal. It was no bad thing, at all events, as Wogan could judge from the Cardinal's smiling face.

"Mr. Wogan," said he, "our Holy Father the Pope wishes to testify his approbation of your remarkable enterprise on behalf of a princess who is his god-daughter. He bids me hand you, therefore, your patent of Roman Senator, and request you to present yourself at the Capitol in Rome on June 15, when you will be installed with all the ancient ceremonies."

Wogan thanked his Eminence dutifully, but laid the patent on the table.

"You hardly know what you refuse," said his Eminence. "The Holy Father has no greater honour to bestow, and, believe me, he bestows it charily."

"Nay, your Eminence," said Wogan, "I do not undervalue so high a distinction. But I had three friends with me who shared every danger. I cannot accept an honour which they do not share; for indeed they risked more than I did. For they hold service under the King of France."

The Cardinal was pleased to compliment Wogan upon his loyalty to his friends.

"They shall not be the losers," said he. "I think I may promise indeed that each will have a step in rank, and I do not doubt that when the Holy Father hears what you have said to me, I shall have three other patents like to this;" and he locked Wogan's away in a drawer.

"And what of the King in Spain?" asked Wogan.

"I sent a messenger thither on the night of your coming," said the Cardinal; "but it is a long journey into Spain. We must wait."

To Wogan it seemed the waiting would never end. The Cardinal had found a little house set apart from the street with a great garden of lawns and cedar-trees and laurels; and in that garden now fresh with spring flowers and made private by high walls, the Princess passed her days. Wogan saw her but seldom during this time, but each occasion sent him back to his lodging in a fever of anxiety. She had grown silent, and her silence alarmed him. She had lost the sparkling buoyancy of her spirits. Mrs. Misset, who attended her, told him that she would sit for long whiles with a red spot burning in each cheek. Wogan feared that her pride was chafing her gentleness, that she guessed there was reluctance in the King's delay. "But she must marry the King," he still persevered in declaring. Her hardships, her imprisonment, her perilous escape, the snows of Innspruck,—these were known now; and if at the last the end for which they had been endured—Wogan broke off from his reflections to hear the world laughing. The world would not think; it would laugh. "For her own sake she must marry," he cried, as he paced about his rooms. "For ours, too, for a country's sake;" and he looked northwards towards England. But "for her own sake" was the reason uppermost in his thoughts.

But the days passed. The three promised patents came from Rome, and Cardinal Origo unlocked the drawer and joined Wogan's to them. He presented all four at the same time.

"The patents carry the titles of 'Excellency,'" said he.

O'Toole beamed with delight.

"Sure," said he, "I will have a toga with the arms of the O'Tooles embroidered on the back, to appear in at the Capitol. It is on June 15, your Eminence. Upon my soul, I have not much time;" and he grew thoughtful.

"A toga will hardly take a month, even with the embroidery, which I do not greatly recommend," said the Cardinal, drily.

A. E. W. Mason

"I was not at the moment thinking of the toga," said O'Toole, gloomily.

"And what of the King in Spain?" asked Wogan.

"We must wait, my friend," said the Cardinal.

In a week there was brought to Wogan one morning a letter in the King's hand. He fingered it for a little, not daring to break the seal. When he did break it, he read a great many compliments upon his success, and after the compliments a statement that the marriage should take place at Montefiascone as soon as the King could depart from Spain, and after that statement, a declaration that since her Highness's position was not meanwhile one that suited either her dignity or the love the King had for her, a marriage by proxy should take place at Bologna. The Chevalier added that he had written to Cardinal Origo to make the necessary arrangements for the ceremony, and he appointed herewith Mr. Charles Wogan to act as his proxy, in recognition of his great services.

Wogan felt a natural distaste for the part he was to take in the ceremony. To stand up before the Cardinal and take Clementina's hand in his, and speak another's marriage vows and receive hers as another's deputy,—there was a certain mockery in the situation for which he had no liking. The memory of the cabin on the mountain-side was something too near. But, at all events, the King was to marry the Princess, and Wogan's distaste was swallowed up in a great relief. There would be no laughter rippling over Europe like the wind over a field of corn. He stood by his window in the spring sunshine with a great contentment of spirit, and then there came a loud rapping on his door.

He caught his breath; he grew white with a sudden fear; you

would have thought it was his heart that was knocked upon. For there was another side to the business. The King would marry the Princess; but how would the Princess take this marriage by proxy and the King's continued absence? She had her pride, as he knew well. The knocking was repeated. Wogan in a voice of suspense bade his visitor enter. The visitor was one of her Highness's new servants. "Without a doubt," thought Wogan, "she has received a letter by the same messenger who brought me mine."

The servant handed him a note from the Princess, begging him to attend on her at once. "She must marry the King," said Wogan to himself. He took his hat and cane, and followed the servant into the street.

# CHAPTER XXII

## CLEMENTINA TAKES MR. WOGAN TO
## VISIT THE CAPRARA PALACE

Wogan was guided through the streets to the mouth of a
blind alley, at the bottom of which rose a high garden wall,
and over the wall the smoking chimneys of a house among
the tops of many trees freshly green, which shivered in the
breeze and shook the sunlight from their leaves. This alley,
from the first day when the Princess came to lodge in the
house, had worn to Wogan a familiar air; and this morning,
as he pondered dismally whether, after all, those laborious
months since he had ridden hopefully out of Bologna to
Ohlau were to bear no fruit, he chanced to remember why.
He had passed that alley at the moment of grey dawn, when
he was starting out upon this adventure, and he had seen a
man muffled in a cloak step from its mouth and suddenly
draw back as his horse's hoofs rang in the silent street, as
though to elude recognition. Wogan wondered for a second
who at that time had lived in the house; but he was admitted
through a door in the wall and led into a little room with
French windows opening on a lawn. The garden seen from
here was a wealth of white blossoms and yellow, and
amongst them Clementina paced alone, the richest and the
whitest blossom of them all. She was dressed simply in a

white gown of muslin and a little three-cornered hat of straw; but Wogan knew as he advanced towards her that it was not merely the hat which threw the dark shadow on her face.

She took a step or two towards him and began at once without any friendly greeting in a cold, formal voice,—

"You have received a letter this morning from his Majesty?"

"Yes, your Highness."

"Why does the King linger in Spain?"

"The expedition from Cadiz—"

"Which left harbour a week ago. Well, Mr. Wogan," she asked in biting tones, "how does that expedition now on the high seas detain his Majesty in Spain?"

Wogan was utterly dumfounded. He stood and gazed at her, a great trouble in his eyes, and his wits with that expedition all at sea.

"Is your Highness sure?" he babbled.

"Oh, indeed, most sure," she replied with the hardest laugh which he had ever heard from a woman's lips.

"I did not know," he said in dejection, and she took a step nearer to him, and her cheeks flamed.

"Is that the truth?" she asked, her voice trembling with anger. "You did not know?"

And Wogan understood that the real trouble with her at this moment was not so much the King's delay in Spain as a

A. E. W. Mason

doubt whether he himself had played with her and spoken her false. For if he was proved untrue here, why, he might have been untrue throughout, on the stairway at Innspruck, on the road to Ala, in the hut on the bluff of the hills. He could see how harshly the doubt would buffet her pride, how it would wound her to the soul.

"It is the truth," he answered; "you will believe it. I pledge my soul upon it. Lay your hand in mine. I will repeat it standing so. Could I speak false with your hand close in mine?"

He held out his hand; she did not move, nor did her attitude of distrust relent.

"Could you not?" she asked icily.

Wogan was baffled; he was angered. "Have I ever told you lies?" he asked passionately, and she answered, "Yes," and steadily looked him in the face.

The monosyllable quenched him like a pail of cold water. He stood silent, perplexed, trying to remember.

"When?" he asked.

"In the berlin between Brixen and Wellishmile."

Wogan remembered that he had told her of his city of dreams. But it was plainly not to that that she referred. He shrugged his shoulders.

"I cannot remember."

"You told me of an attack made upon a Scottish town, what time the King was there in the year '15. He forced a passage through nine grenadiers with loaded muskets and escaped over the roof-tops, where he played a game of hide-and-seek among the chimneys. Ah, you remember the story now. There was a chain, I remember, which even then as you told of it puzzled me. He threw the chain over the head of one of those nine grenadiers, and crossing his arms jerked it tight about the man's neck, stifling his cry of warning. 'What chain?' I asked, and you answered,—oh, sir, with a practised readiness,—'The chain he wore about his neck.' Do you remember that? The chain linked your hand-locks, Mr. Wogan. It was your own escape of which you told me. Why did you ascribe your exploits to your King?"

"Your Highness," he said, "we know the King, we who have served him day in and day out for years. We can say freely to each other, 'The King's achievements, they are to come.' We were in Scotland with him, and we know they will not fail to come. But with you it's different. You did not know him. You asked what he had done, and I told you. You asked for more. You said, 'Amongst his throng of adventurers, each of whom has something to his credit, what has he, the chief adventurer?'"

"Well, sir, why not the truth in answer to the question?"

"Because the truth's unfair to him."

"And was the untruth fair to me?"

Mr. Wogan was silent.

"I think I understand," she continued bitterly; "you thought, here's a foolish girl, aflame for knights and monsters overthrown. She cries for deeds, not statecraft. Well, out of your many, you would toss her one, and call it the King's. You could afford the loss, and she, please God, would be content with it." She spoke with an extraordinary violence in a low, trembling voice, and she would not listen to Wogan's stammered interruption.

"Very likely, too, the rest of your words to me was of a piece. I was a girl, and girls are to have gallant speeches given to them like so many lollipops. Oh, but you have hurt me beyond words. I would not have thought I could have suffered so much pain!"

That last cry wrung Wogan's heart. She turned away from him with the tears brimming in her eyes. It was this conjecture of hers which he had dreaded, which at all costs he must dispel.

"Do not believe it!" he exclaimed. "Think! Should I have been at so much pains to refrain from speech, if speech was what I had intended?"

"How should I know but what that concealment was part of the gallantry, a necessary preface to the pretty speeches?"

"Should I have urged your rescue on the King had I believed you what you will have it that I did,—a mere witless girl to be pampered with follies?"

"Then you admit," she cried, "you *urged* the King."

"Should I have travelled over Europe to search for a wife and lit on you? Should I have ridden to Ohlau and pestered your father till he yielded? Should I have ridden across Europe to Strasbourg? Should I have endangered my friends in the rush to Innspruck? No, no, no! From first to last you were the chosen woman."

The vehemence and fire of sincerity with which he spoke

had its effect on her. She turned again towards him with a gleam of hopefulness in her face, but midway in the turn she stopped.

"You spoke to me words which I have not forgotten," she said doubtfully. "You said the King had need of me. I will be frank, hoping that you will match my frankness. On that morning when we climbed down the gorge, and ever since I cheered myself with that one thought. The King had need of me."

"Never was truer word spoken," said Wogan, stoutly.

"Then why is the King in Spain?"

They had come back to the first question. Wogan had no new answer to it. He said,—

"I do not know."

For a moment or two Clementina searched his eyes. It seemed in the end that she was satisfied he spoke the truth. For she said in a voice of greater gentleness,—

"Then I will acquaint you. Will you walk with me for half a mile?"

Wogan bowed, and followed her out of the garden. He could not think whither she was leading him, or for what purpose. She walked without a word to him, he followed without a question, and so pacing with much dignity they came to the steps of a great house. Then Clementina halted.

"Sir," said she, "can you put a name to the house?"

"Upon my word, your Highness, I cannot."

"It is the Caprara Palace," said she, suddenly, and suddenly she bent her eyes upon Wogan. The name, however, conveyed no meaning whatever to him, and his blank face told her so clearly. She nodded in a sort of approval. "No," she said, relenting, "you did not know."

She mounted the steps, and knocking upon the door was admitted by an old broken serving-man, who told her that the Princess Caprara was away. It was permitted him, however, to show the many curiosities and treasures of the palace to such visitors as desired it. Clementina did desire it. The old man led her and her companion to the armoury, where he was for spending much time and breath over the trophies which the distinguished General Caprara had of old rapt from the infidels. But Clementina quickly broke in upon his garrulity.

"I have a great wish to see the picture gallery," said she, and the old man tottered onwards through many shrouded and darkened rooms. In the picture gallery he drew up the blinds and then took a wand in his hand.

"Will you show me first the portrait of Mlle. de Caprara?" said Clementina.

It was a full-length portrait painted with remarkable skill. Maria Vittoria de Caprara was represented in a black dress, and the warm Italian colouring of her face made a sort of glow in the dark picture. Her eyes watched you from the canvas with so life-like a glance you had a thought when you turned that they turned after you. Clementina gazed at the picture for a long while, and the blood slowly mounted on her neck and transfused her cheeks.

"There is a face, Mr. Wogan,—a passionate, beautiful face,—which might well set a seal upon a man's heart. I do not wonder. I can well believe that though to-day that face gladdens the streets of Rome, a lover in Spain might see it through all the thick earth of the Pyrenees. There, sir, I promised to acquaint you why the King lingered in Spain. I have fulfilled that promise;" and making a present to the custodian, she walked back through the rooms and down the steps to the street. Wogan followed her, and pacing with much dignity they walked back to the little house among the trees, and so came again into the garden of blossoms.

The anger had now gone from her face, but it was replaced by a great weariness.

"It is strange, is it not," she said with a faltering smile, "that on a spring morning, beneath this sky, amongst these flowers, I should think with envy of the snows of Innspruck and my prison there? But I owe you a reparation," she added. "You said the King had need of me. For that saying of yours I find an apt simile. Call it a stone on which you bade me set my foot and step. I stepped, and found that your stone was straw."

"No, madam," cried Wogan.

"I had a thought," she continued, "you knew the stone was straw when you commended it to me as stone. But this morning I have learned my error. I acquit you, and ask your pardon. You did not know that the King had no need of me." And she bowed to him as though the conversation was at an end. Wogan, however, would not let her go. He placed himself in front of her, engrossed in his one thought, "She must marry the King." He spoke, however, none the less with sincerity when he cried,—

"Nor do I know now—no, and I shall not know."

A. E. W. Mason

"You have walked with me to the Caprara Palace this morning. Or did I dream we walked?"

"What your Highness has shown me to-day I cannot gainsay. For this is the first time that ever I heard of Mlle. de Caprara. But I am very sure that you draw your inference amiss. You sit in judgment on the King, not knowing him. You push aside the firm trust of us who know him as a thing of no account. And because once, in a mood of remorse at my own presumption, I ascribed one trivial exploit—at the best a success of muscle and not brain—to the King which was not his, you strip him of all merit on the instant." He saw that her face flushed. Here, at all events, he had hit the mark, and he cried out with a ringing confidence,—

"Your stone is stone, not straw."

"Prove it me," said she.

"What do you know of the Princess Caprara at the end of it all? You have told me this morning all you know. I will go bail if the whole truth were out the matter would take a very different complexion."

Again she said,—

"Prove that to me!" and then she looked over his shoulder. Wogan turned and saw that a servant was coming from the house across the lawn with a letter on a salver. The Princess opened the letter and read it. Then she turned again to Wogan.

"His Eminence the Cardinal fixes the marriage in Bologna here for to-day fortnight. You have thus two weeks wherein to make your word good."

Two weeks, and Wogan had not an idea in his head as to how he was to set about the business. But he bowed imperturbably.

"Within two weeks I will convince your Highness," said he, and for a good half-hour he sauntered with her about the garden before he took his leave.

A. E. W. Mason

# CHAPTER XXIII

## WOGAN LEARNS THAT HE HAS MEDDLED

But his thoughts had been busy during that half-hour, and as soon as he had come out from the mouth of the alley, he ran to Gaydon's lodging. Gaydon, however, was not in. O'Toole lodged in the same house, and Wogan mounted to his apartments, hoping there to find news of Gaydon's whereabouts. But O'Toole was taking the air, too, but Wogan found O'Toole's servant.

"Where will I find Captain O'Toole?" asked Wogan.

"You will find his Excellency," said the servant, with a reproachful emphasis upon the title, "at the little bookseller's in the Piazza."

Wogan sprang down the stairs and hurried to the Piazza, wondering what in the world O'Toole was doing at a bookseller's. O'Toole was bending over the counter, which was spread with open books, and Wogan hailed him from the doorway. O'Toole turned and blushed a deep crimson. He came to the door as if to prevent Wogan's entrance into the shop. Wogan, however, had but one thought in his head.

"Where shall I find Gaydon?" he asked.

"He went towards the Via San Vitale," replied O'Toole.

Wogan set off again, and in an hour came upon Gaydon. He had lost an hour of his fortnight; with the half-hour during which he had sauntered in the garden, an hour and a half.

"You went to Rome in the spring," said he. "There you saw the King. Did you see anyone else by any chance whilst you were in Rome?"

"Edgar," replied Gaydon, with a glance from the tail of his eye which Wogan did not fail to remark.

"Aha!" said he. "Edgar, to be sure, since you saw the King. But besides Edgar, did you see anyone else?"

"Whittington," said Gaydon.

"Oho!" said Wogan, thoughtfully. "So you saw my friend Harry Whittington at Rome. Did you see him with the King?"

Gaydon was becoming manifestly uncomfortable.

"He was waiting for the King," he replied.

"Indeed. And whereabouts was he waiting for the King?"

"Oh, outside a house in Rome," said Gaydon, as though he barely remembered the incident. "It was no business of mine, that I could see."

"None whatever, to be sure," answered Wogan, cordially. "But why in the world should Whittington be waiting for the King outside a house in Rome?"

A. E. W. Mason

"It was night-time. He carried a lantern."

"Of course, if it was night-time," exclaimed Wogan, in his most unsuspicious accent, "and the King wished to pay a visit to a house in Rome, he would take an attendant with a lantern. A servant, though, one would have thought, unless, of course, it was a private sort of visit—"

"It was no business of mine," Gaydon interrupted; "and so I made no inquiries of Whittington."

"But Whittington did not wait for inquiries, eh?" said Wogan, shrewdly. "You are hiding something from me, my friend,—something which that good honest simpleton of a Whittington blurted out to you without the least thought of making any disclosure. Oh, I know my Whittington. And I know you, too, Dick. I do not blame you. For when the King goes a-visiting the Princess Caprara privately at night-time while the girl to whom he is betrothed suffers in prison for her courageous loyalty to him, and his best friends are risking their heads to set her free, why, there's knowledge a man would be glad to keep even out of his own hearing. So you see I know more than you credit me with. So tell me the rest! Don't fob me off. Don't plead it is none of your business, for, upon my soul, it is." Gaydon suddenly changed his manner. He spoke with no less earnestness than Wogan,—

"You are in the right. It is my business, and why? Because it touches you, Charles Wogan, and you are my friend."

"Therefore you will tell me," cried Wogan.

"Therefore I will not tell you," answered Gaydon. He had a very keen recollection of certain pages of poetry he had seen on the table at Schlestadt, of certain conversations in the berlin when he had feigned to sleep.

Wogan caught him by the arm.

"I must know. Here have I lost two hours out of one poor fortnight. I must know."

"Why?"

Gaydon stood quite unmoved, and with a remarkable sternness of expression. Wogan understood that only the truth would unlock his lips, and he cried,—

"Because unless I do, in a fortnight her Highness will refuse to marry the King." And he recounted to him the walk he had taken and the conversation he had held with Clementina that morning. Gaydon listened with an unfeigned surprise. The story put Wogan in quite a different light, and moreover it was told with so much sincerity of voice and so clear a simplicity of language, Gaydon could not doubt one syllable.

"I am afraid, my friend," said he, "my thoughts have done you some wrong—"

"Leave me out of them," cried Wogan, impatiently. He had no notion and no desire to hear what Gaydon meant. "Tell me from first to last what you saw in Rome."

Gaydon told him thereupon of that secret passage from the Chevalier's house into the back street, and of that promenade to the Princess's house which he had spied upon. Wogan listened without any remark, and yet without any attempt to quicken his informant. But as soon as he had the story, he set off at a run towards the Cardinal's palace. "So the Princess," he thought, "had more than a rumour to go upon, though how she came by her knowledge the devil only knows." At the

A. E. W. Mason

palace he was told that the Cardinal was gone to the Archiginnasio.

"I will wait," said Wogan; and he waited in the library for an hour,—another priceless hour of that swiftly passing fortnight, and he was not a whit nearer to his end! He made it his business, however, to show a composed face to his Eminence, and since his Eminence's dinner was ready, to make a pretence of sharing the meal. The Cardinal was in a mood of great contentment.

"It is your presence, Mr. Wogan, puts me in a good humour," he was pleased to say.

"Or a certain letter your Eminence received from Spain to-day?" asked Wogan.

"True, the letter was one to cause all the King's friends satisfaction."

"And some few of them, perhaps, relief," said Wogan.

The Cardinal glanced at Wogan, but with a quite impassive countenance. He took a pinch of snuff and inhaled it delicately. Then he glanced at Wogan again.

"I have a hope, Mr. Wogan," said he, with a great cordiality. "You shall tell me if it is to fall. I see much of you of late, and I have a hope that you are thinking of the priesthood. We should welcome you very gladly, you may be sure. Who knows but what there is a Cardinal's hat hung up in the anteroom of the future for you to take down from its peg?"

The suggestion was sufficiently startling to Wogan, who had thought of nothing less than of entering into orders. But he was not to be diverted by this piece of ingenuity.

"Your Eminence," said he, "although I hold myself unworthy of priestly vows, I am here in truth in the character of a catechist."

"Catechise, then, my friend," said the Cardinal, with a smile.

"First, then, I would ask your Eminence how many of the King's followers have had the honour of being presented to the Princess Clementina?"

"Very few."

"Might I know the names?"

"To be sure."

Cardinal Origo repeated three or four names. They were the names of men known to Wogan for irreproachable loyalty. Not one of them would have gone about the Princess with slanders upon his master; he would have gone bail for them all,—at least, a month ago he would, he reflected, though now indeed he hardly knew where to put his trust.

"Her Highness lives, as you know, a very suitable, secluded life," continued Origo.

"But might not others have had access to her at the Pilgrim Inn?"

"Nay, she was there but the one night,—the night of her arrival. I do not think it likely. For if you remember, I myself went to her early the next morning, and by a stroke of good luck I had already come upon the little house in the garden which was offered to me by a friend of yours for her Highness's service."

A. E. W. Mason

"On the evening of our arrival? A friend of mine offered you the house," said Wogan, puzzling over who that friend could be.

"Yes. Harry Whittington."

Wogan started to his feet. So, after all, Whittington was at the bottom of the trouble. Wogan wondered whether he had done wisely not to publish the fellow's treachery. But he could not,—no, he had to make his account with the man alone. There were reasons.

"It was Harry Whittington who offered the house for her Highness's use?" Wogan exclaimed.

"It was an offer most apt and kind."

"And made on the evening of our arrival?"

"Not an hour after you left me. But you are surprised?"

Wogan was reflecting that on the evening of his arrival, and indeed just before Whittington made his offer to Origo, he had seen Whittington's face by the torchlight in the square. That face lived very plainly in Wogan's thoughts. It was certainly not for Clementina's service that Whittington had offered the house. Wogan resumed his seat, saying carelessly,—

"I was surprised, for I had a notion that Whittington lodged opposite the Torre Garisenda, and not at the house."

"Nor did he. He hired it for a friend who has now left Bologna."

"Man or woman?" asked Wogan, remembering that visitor who had drawn back into the alley one early morning of last autumn. The man might very likely have been Whittington.

"I did not trouble to inquire," said the Cardinal. "But, Mr. Wogan, why do you ask me these questions?"

"I have not come yet to the end of them," answered Wogan. "There is one more."

"Ask it!" said his Eminence, crossing his legs.

"Will your Eminence oblige me with a history of the affection of Maria Vittoria, Mlle. de Caprara, for the King?"

The Cardinal uncrossed his legs and bounced in his chair.

"Here is a question indeed!" he stuttered.

"And a history of the King's response to it," continued Wogan, implacably, "with a particular account of why the King lingers in Spain after the Cadiz expedition has put out to sea."

Origo was now quite still. His face was pale, and he had lost in an instant that air of affectation which so contrasted with his broad features.

"This is very dangerous talk," said he, solemnly.

"Not so dangerous as silence."

"Some foolish slanderer has been busy at your ears."

"Not at my ears," returned Wogan.

The Cardinal took his meaning. "Is it so, indeed?" said he, thoughtfully, once or twice. Then he reached out his hand towards an escritoire. "But here's the King's letter come this morning."

A. E. W. Mason

"It is not enough," said Wogan, "for the King lingers in Spain, and the portrait of Maria Vittoria glows on the walls of the Caprara Palace, whither I was bidden to escort her Highness this morning."

The Cardinal walked thoughtfully to and fro about the room, but made up his mind in the end.

"I will tell you the truth of the matter, Mr. Wogan. The King saw Mlle. de Caprara for the first time while you were searching Europe for a wife for him. He saw her here one morning at Mass in the Church of the Crucifixion, and came away most silent. Of their acquaintance I need not speak. The King just for one month became an ardent youth. He appealed to the Pope for his consent to marry Mlle. de Caprara, and the Pope consented. The King was just sending off a message to bid you cease your search when you came back with the news that her Highness the Princess Clementina had accepted the King's hand and would shortly set out for Bologna. Sir, the King was in despair, though he showed to you a smiling, grateful face. Mlle. de Caprara went to Rome; the King stayed here awaiting his betrothed. There came the news of her imprisonment. The King, after all, is a man. If his heart leaped a little at the news, who shall blame him? Do you remember how you came privately one night to the King's cabinet and found me there in the King's company?"

"But," stammered Wogan, "I do remember that evening. I remember that the King was pale, discouraged—"

"And why?" said Origo. "Because her Highness's journey had been interrupted, because the marriage now seemed impossible? No, but because Mr. Charles Wogan was back in Bologna, because Mr. Charles Wogan had sought for a private interview, because the King had no more doubt than I as to what Mr. Charles Wogan intended to propose, and because the King knew that what Mr. Wogan set his hand to was as good as done. You remember I threw such hindrances as I could in your way, and made much of the risks you must run, and the impossibility of your task. Now you know why."

Never was a man more confused than Wogan at this story of the Cardinal's. "It makes me out a mere meddlesome fool," he cried, and sat stunned.

"It is an unprofitable question at this time of day," said the Cardinal, with a smile. "Matters have gone so far that they can no longer be remedied. This marriage must take place."

"True," said Wogan.

"The King, indeed, is firmly inclined to it."

"Yet he lingers in Spain."

"That I cannot explain to you, but he has been most loyal. That you must take my word for, so must your Princess."

"Yet this winter when I was at Schlestadt preparing the expedition to Innspruck," Wogan said with a certain timidity, for he no longer felt that it was within his right to make reproaches, "the King was in Rome visiting Mlle. de Caprara."

The Cardinal flushed with some anger at Wogan's persistence.

"Come, sir," said he, "what has soured you with suspicions? Upon my word, here is a man sitting with me who bears your name, but few of those good qualities the name is linked with in my memories. Your King saw Mlle. de Caprara once in Rome, once only. Major Gaydon had come at your request to Rome to fetch a letter in the King's hand, bidding her Highness entrust herself to you. Up to that moment the issue of your exploit was in the balance. But your request was to the King a very certain sign that you would indeed succeed. So the night before he wrote the letter he went to the Caprara Palace and took his farewell of the woman he loved. So much may be pardoned to any man, even by you, who, it seems, stand pinnacled above these earthly affections."

The blood rushed into Wogan's face at the sneer, but he bowed his head to it, being much humbled by Origo's disclosures.

"This story I have told you," continued the Cardinal, "I will make bold to tell to-morrow to her Highness."

"But you must also explain why the King lingers in Spain," Wogan objected. "I am very certain of it. The Princess has her pride; she will not marry a reluctant man."

"Well, that I cannot do," cried the Cardinal, now fairly exasperated. "Pride! She has her pride! Is it to ruin a cause, this pride of hers? Is it to wreck a policy?"

"No," cried Wogan, starting up. "I have a fortnight. I beg your Eminence not to speak one word to her Highness until this fortnight is gone, until the eve of the marriage in Bologna. Give me till then. I have a hope there will be no need for us to speak at all."

The Cardinal shrugged his shoulders.

"You must do more than hope. Will you pledge your word to it?"

Here it seemed to Wogan was an occasion when a man must dare.

"Yes," he said, and so went out of the house. He had spoken under a sudden inspiration; the Cardinal's words had shown him a way which with careful treading might lead to his desired result. He went first to his lodging, and ordered his servant Marnier to saddle his black horse. Then he hurried again to O'Toole's lodging, and found his friend back from the bookseller's indeed, but breathing very hard of a book which he slid behind his back.

"I am to go on a journey," said Wogan, "and there's a delicate sort of work I would trust to you."

O'Toole looked distantly at Wogan.

"*Opus*," said he, in a far-away voice.

"I want you to keep an eye on the little house in the garden—"

O'Toole nodded. "*Hortus, hortus, hortum*," said he, "*horti—hortus*," and he fingered the book at his back, "no, *horti, horto, horto*. Do you know, my friend, that the difference between the second and fourth declensions was solely invented by the grammarians for their own profit. It is of no manner of use, and the most plaguy business that ever I heard of."

"O'Toole," cried Wogan, with a bang of his fist, "you are no more listening to me than this table."

At once O'Toole's face brightened, and with a shout of pride he reeled out, "*Mensa, mensa, mensam, mensae, mensae, mensa*." Wogan sprang up in a rage.

A. E. W. Mason

"Don't *mensa, mensam* me when I am talking most seriously to you! What is it you are after? What's that book you are hiding? Let me look at it!" O'Toole blushed on every visible inch of him and handed the book to Wogan.

"It's a Latin grammar, my friend," said he, meekly.

"And what in the world do you want to be addling your brains with a Latin grammar for, when there's other need for your eyes?"

"Aren't we to be enrolled at the Capitol in June as Roman Senators with all the ancient honours, *cum titubis*—it is so— *cum titubis*, which are psalters or pshawms?"

"Well, what then?"

"You don't understand, Charles, the difficulty of my position. You have Latin at your finger-ends. Sure, I have often admired you for your extraordinary comprehension of Latin, but never more than I do now. It will be no trouble in the world for you to trip off a neat little speech, thanking the Senators kindly for the great honour they are doing themselves in electing us into their noble body. But it will not be easy for me," said O'Toole, with a sigh. "How can I get enough Latin through my skull by June not to disgrace myself?" He looked so utterly miserable and distressed that Wogan never felt less inclined to laugh. "I sit up at nights with a lamp, but the most unaccountable thing happens. I may come in here as lively as any cricket, but the moment I take this book in my hands I am overpowered with sleep—"

"Oh, listen to me," cried Wogan. "I have only a fortnight—"

"And I have only till June," sighed O'Toole. "But there! I am listening. I have no doubt, my friend, your business is more important than mine," he said with the simplicity of which not one of his friends could resist the appeal. Wogan could not now.

"My business," he said, "is only more important because you have no need of your Latin grammar at all. There's a special deputy, a learned professor, appointed on these occasions to make a speech for us, and all we have to do is to sit still and nod our heads wisely when he looks towards us."

"Is that all?" cried O'Toole, jumping up. "Swear it!"

"I do," said Wogan; and "Here's to the devil with the Latin grammar!" exclaimed O'Toole. He flung open his window and hurled the book out across the street with the full force of his prodigious arm. There followed a crash and then the tinkle of falling glass. O'Toole beamed contentedly and shut the window.

"Now what will I do for you in return for this?" he asked.

"Keep a watch on the little house and the garden. I will tell you why when I return. Observe who goes in to visit the Princess, but hinder no one. Only remember who they are and let me know." And Wogan got back to his lodging and mounted his black horse. He could trust O'Toole to play watchdog in his absence. If the mysterious visitor who had bestowed upon Clementina with so liberal a hand so much innuendo and such an artful combination of truth and falsity, were to come again to the little house to confirm the slanders, Wogan in the end would not fail to discover the visitor's identity.

He dismissed the matter from his mind and rode out from Bologna. Four days afterwards he presented himself at the door of the Caprara Palace.

A. E. W. Mason

## CHAPTER XXIV

## MARIA VITTORIA REAPPEARS

Maria Vittoria received the name of her visitor with a profound astonishment. Then she stamped her foot and said violently, "Send him away! I hate him." But curiosity got the better of her hate. She felt a strong desire to see the meddlesome man who had thrust himself between her and her lover; and before her woman had got so far as the door, she said, "Let him up to me!" She was again surprised when Wogan was admitted, for she expected a stout and burly soldier, stupid and confident, of the type which blunders into success through sheer ignorance of the probabilities of defeat. Mr. Wogan, for his part, saw the glowing original of the picture at Bologna, but armed at all points with hostility.

"Your business," said she, curtly. Wogan no less curtly replied that he had a wish to escort Mlle. de Caprara to Bologna. He spoke as though he was suggesting a walk on the Campagna.

"And why should I travel to Bologna?" she asked. Wogan explained. The explanation required delicacy, but he put it in as few words as might be. There were slanderers at work. Her Highness the Princess Clementina was in great distress; a word from Mlle. de Caprara would make all clear.

"Why should I trouble because the Princess Clementina has a crumpled rose-leaf in her bed? I will not go," said Mlle. de Caprara.

"Yet her Highness may justly ask why the King lingers in Spain." Wogan saw a look, a smile of triumph, brighten for an instant on the angry face.

"It is no doubt a humiliation to the Princess Clementina," said Maria Vittoria, with a great deal of satisfaction. "But she must learn to bear humiliation like other women."

"But she will reject the marriage," urged Wogan.

"The fool!" cried Maria Vittoria, and she laughed almost gaily. "I will not budge an inch to persuade her to it. Let her fancy what she will and weep over it! I hate her; therefore she is out of my thought."

Wogan was not blind to the inspiriting effect of his argument upon Maria Vittoria. He had, however, foreseen it, and he continued imperturbably,—

"No doubt you think me something of a fool, too, to advance so unlikely a plea. But if her Highness rejects the marriage, who suffers? Her Highness's name is already widely praised for her endurance, her constancy. If, after all, at the last moment she scornfully rejects that for which she has so stoutly ventured, whose name, whose cause, will suffer most? It will be one more misfortune, one more disaster, to add to the crushing weight under which the King labours. There will be ignominy; who will be dwarfed by it? There will be laughter; whom will it souse? There will be scandal; who will be splashed by it? The Princess or the King?"

Maria Vittoria stood with her brows drawn together in a

frown. "I will not go," she said after a pause. "Never was there so presumptuous a request. No, I will not."

Wogan made his bow and retired. But he was at the Caprara Palace again in the morning, and again he was admitted. He noticed without regret that Maria Vittoria bore the traces of a restless night.

"What should I say if I went with you?" she asked.

"You would say why the King lingers in Spain."

Maria Vittoria gave a startled look at Wogan.

"Do you know why?"

"You told me yesterday."

"Not in words."

"There are other ways of speech."

That one smile of triumph had assured Wogan that the King's delay was her doing and a condition of their parting.

"How will my story, though I told it, help?" asked Mlle. de Caprara. Wogan had no doubts upon that score. The story of the Chevalier and Maria Vittoria had a strong parallel in Clementina's own history. Circumstance and duty held them apart, as it held apart Clementina and Wogan himself. In hearing Maria Vittoria's story, Clementina would hear her own; she must be moved to sympathy with it; she would regard with her own generous eyes those who played unhappy parts in its development; she could have no word of censure, no opportunity for scorn.

"Tell the story," said Wogan. "I will warrant the result."

"No, I will not go," said she; and again Wogan left the house. And again he came the next morning.

"Why should I go?" said Maria Vittoria, rebelliously. "Say what you have said to me to her! Speak to her of the ignominy which will befall the King! Tell her how his cause will totter! Why talk of this to me? If she loves the King, your words will persuade her. For on my life they have nearly persuaded me."

"If she loves the King!" said Wogan, quietly, and Maria Vittoria stared at him. There was something she had not conjectured before.

"Oh, she does not love him!" she said in wonderment. Her wonderment swiftly changed to contempt. "The fool! Let her go on her knees and pray for a modest heart. There's my message to her. Who is she that she should not love him?" But it nevertheless altered a trifle pleasurably Maria Vittoria's view of the position. It was pain to her to contemplate the Chevalier's marriage, a deep, gnawing, rancorous pain, but the pain was less, once she could believe he was to marry a woman who did not love him. She despised the woman for her stupidity; none the less, that was the wife she would choose, if she must needs choose another than herself. "I have a mind to see this fool-woman of yours," she said doubtfully. "Why does she not love the King?"

Wogan could have answered that she had never seen him. He thought silence, however, was the more expressive. The silence led Maria Vittoria to conjecture.

"Is there another picture at her heart?" she asked, and again Wogan was silent. "Whose, then? You will not tell me."

A. E. W. Mason

It might have been something in Wogan's attitude or face which revealed the truth to her; it might have been her recollection of what the King had said concerning Wogan's enthusiasm; it might have been merely her woman's instinct. But she started and took a step towards Wogan. Her eyes certainly softened. "I will go with you to Bologna," she said; and that afternoon with the smallest equipment she started from Rome. Wogan had ridden alone from Bologna to Rome in four days; he had spent three days in Rome; he now took six days to return in company with Mlle. de Caprara and her few servants. He thus arrived in Bologna on the eve of that day when he was to act as the King's proxy in the marriage.

It was about four o'clock in the afternoon when the tiny cavalcade clattered through the Porta Castiglione. Wogan led the way to the Pilgrim Inn, where he left Maria Vittoria, saying that he would return at nightfall. He then went on foot to O'Toole's lodging. O'Toole, however, had no news for him.

"There has been no mysterious visitor," said he.

"There will be one to-night," answered Wogan. "I shall need you."

"I am ready," said O'Toole.

The two friends walked back to the Pilgrim Inn. They were joined by Maria Vittoria, and they then proceeded to the little house among the trees. Outside the door in the garden wall Wogan posted O'Toole.

"Let no one pass," said he, "till we return."

He knocked on the door, and after a little delay—for the night had fallen, and there was no longer a porter at the gate—a little hatch was opened, and a servant inquired his business.

"I come with a message of the utmost importance," said Wogan. "I beg you to inform her Highness that the Chevalier Wogan prays for two words with her."

The hatch was closed, and the servant's footsteps were heard to retreat. Wogan's anxieties had been increasing with every mile of that homeward journey. On his ride to Rome he had been sensible of but one obstacle,—the difficulty of persuading the real Vittoria to return with him. But once that had been removed, others sprang to view, and each hour enlarged them. There was but this one night, this one interview! Upon the upshot of it depended whether a woman, destined by nature for a queen, should set her foot upon the throne-steps, whether a cause should suffer its worst of many eclipses, whether Europe should laugh or applaud. These five minutes while he waited outside the door threw him into a fever. "You will be friendly," he implored Mlle. de Caprara. "Oh, you cannot but be! She must marry the King. I plead for him, not the least bit in the world for her. For his sake she must complete the work she has begun. She is not obstinate; she has her pride as a woman should. You will tell her just the truth,—of the King's loyalty and yours. Hearts cannot be commanded. Alas, mademoiselle, it is a hard world at the end of it. It is mortised with the blood of broken hearts. But duty, mademoiselle, duty, a consciousness of rectitude,—these are very noble qualities. It will be a high consolation, mademoiselle, one of these days, when the King sits upon his throne in England, to think that your self-sacrifice had set him there." And Mr. Wogan hopped like a bear on hot bricks, twittering irreproachable sentiments until the garden door was opened.

Beyond the door stretched a level space of grass intersected by a gravel path. Along this path the servant led Wogan and

A. E. W. Mason

his companion into the house. There were lights in the windows on the upper floor, and a small lamp illuminated the hall. But the lower rooms were dark. The servant mounted the stairs, and opening the door of a little library, announced the Chevalier Wogan. Wogan led his companion in by the hand.

"Your Highness," said he, "I have the honour to present to you the Princess Maria Vittoria Caprara." He left the two women standing opposite to and measuring each other silently; he closed the door and went down stairs into the hall. A door in the hall opened on to a small parlour, with windows giving on to the garden. There once before Lady Featherstone and Harry Whittington had spoken of Wogan's love for the Princess Clementina and speculated upon its consequences. Now Wogan sat there alone in the dark, listening to the women's voices overhead. He had come to the end of his efforts and could only wait. At all events, the women were talking, that was something; if he could only hear them weeping! The sound of tears would have been very comforting to Wogan at that moment, but he only heard the low voices talking, talking. He assured himself over and over again that this meeting could not fail of its due result. That Maria Vittoria had exacted some promise which held his King in Spain he was now aware. She would say what that promise was, the condition of their parting. She had come prepared to say it—and the thread of Wogan's reasonings was abruptly cut. It seemed to him that he heard something more than the night breeze through the trees,—a sound of feet upon the gravel path, a whispering of voices.

The windows were closed, but not shuttered. Wogan pressed his eyes to the pane and looked out. The night was dark, and the sky overclouded. But he had been sitting for some minutes in the darkness, and his eyes were able to prove that his ears had not deceived him. For he saw the dim figures of two men standing on the lawn before the window. They appeared to be looking at the lighted windows on the upper floor, then one of them waved to his companion to stand still, and himself walked towards the door. Wogan noticed that he made no attempt at secrecy; he walked with a firm tread, careless whether he set his foot on gravel or on grass. As this man approached the door, Wogan slipped into the hall and opened it. But he blocked the doorway, wondering whether these men had climbed the wall or whether O'Toole had deserted his post.

O'Toole had not deserted his post, but he had none the less admitted these two men. For Wogan and Maria Vittoria had barely been ten minutes within the house when O'Toole heard the sound of horses' hoofs in the entrance of the alley. They stopped just within the entrance. O'Toole distinguished three horses, he saw the three riders dismount; and while one of the three held the horses, the other two walked on foot towards the postern-door.

O'Toole eased his sword in its scabbard.

"The little fellows thought to catch Charles Wogan napping," he said to himself with a smile, and he let them come quite close to him. He was standing motionless in the embrasure of the door, nor did he move when the two men stopped and whispered together, nor when they advanced again, one behind the other. But he remarked that they held their cloaks to their faces. At last they came to a halt just in front of O'Toole. The leader produced a key.

"You stand in my way, my friend," said he, pleasantly, and he pushed by O'Toole to the lock of the door. O'Toole put out a hand, caught him by the shoulder, and sent him spinning into the road. The man came back, however, and though out of breath, spoke no less pleasantly than before.

A. E. W. Mason

"I wish to enter," said he. "I have important business."

O'Toole bowed with the utmost dignity.

"*Romanus civis sum*," said he. "*Sum* senator too. *Dic Latinam linguam, amicus meus.*"

O'Toole drew a breath; he could not but feel that he had acquitted himself with credit. He half began to regret that there was to be a learned professor to act as proxy on that famous day at the Capitol. His antagonist drew back a little and spoke no longer pleasantly.

"Here's tomfoolery that would be as seasonable at a funeral," said he, and he advanced again, still hiding his face. "Sir, you are blocking my way. I have authority to pass through that door in the wall."

"*Murus?*" asked O'Toole. He shook his head in refusal.

"And by what right do you refuse me?"

O'Toole had an inspiration. He swept his arm proudly round and gave the reason of his refusal.

"*Balbus aedificabat murum*," said he; and a voice that made O'Toole start cried, "Enough of this! Stand aside, whoever you may be."

It was the second of the two men who spoke, and he dropped the cloak from his face. "The King!" exclaimed O'Toole, and he stood aside. The two men passed into the garden, and Wogan saw them from the window.

Just as O'Toole had blocked the King's entrance into the garden, so did Wogan bar his way into the house.

"Who, in Heaven's name, are you?" cried the Chevalier.

"Nay, there's a question for me to ask," said Wogan.

"Wogan!" cried the Chevalier, and "The King!" cried Wogan in one breath.

Wogan fell back; the Chevalier pushed into the hall and turned.

"So it is true. I could not, did not, believe it. I came from Spain to prove it false. I find it true," he said in a low voice. "You whom I so trusted! God help me, where shall I look for honour?"

"Here, your Majesty," answered Wogan, without an instant's hesitation,—"here, in this hall. There, in the rooms above."

He had seized the truth in the same second when he recognised his King, and the King's first words had left him in no doubt. He knew now why he had never found Harry Whittington in any corner of Bologna. Harry Whittington had been riding to Spain.

The Chevalier laughed harshly.

"Sir, I suspect honour which needs such barriers to protect it. You are here, in this house, at this hour, with a sentinel to forbid intrusion at the garden door. Explain me this honourably."

"I had the honour to escort a visitor to her Highness, and I wait until the visit is at an end."

"What? Can you not better that excuse?" said the Chevalier. "A visitor! We will make acquaintance, Mr. Wogan, with

A. E. W. Mason

your visitor, unless you have another sentinel to bar my way;" and he put his foot upon the step of the stairs.

"I beg your Majesty to pause," said Wogan, firmly. "Your thoughts wrong me, and not only me."

"Prove me that!"

"I say boldly, 'Here is a servant who loves his Queen!' What then?"

"This! That you should say, 'Here is a man who loves a woman,—loves her so well he gives his friends the slip, and with the woman comes alone to Peri.'"

"Ah. To Peri! So I thought," began Wogan, and the Chevalier whispered,—

"Silence! You raise your voice too high. You no doubt are anxious in your great respect that there should be some intimation of my coming. But I dispense with ceremony. I will meet this fine visitor of yours at once;" and he ran lightly up the stairs.

Then Wogan did a bold thing. He followed, he sprang past the King, he turned at the stair-top and barred the way.

"Sir, I beg you to listen to me," he said quietly.

"Beg!" said the Chevalier, leaning back against the wall with his dark eyes blazing from a white face; "you insist."

"Your Majesty will yet thank me for my insistence." He drew a pocket-book out of his coat. "At Peri in Italy we were attacked by five soldiers sent over the border by the Governor of Trent. Who guided those five soldiers? Your

Majesty's confidant and friend, who is now, I thank God, waiting in the garden. Here is the written confession of the leader of the five. I pray your Majesty to read it."

Wogan held out the paper. The Chevalier hesitated and took it. Then he read it once and glanced at it again. He passed his hand over his forehead.

"Whom shall I trust?" said he, in a voice of weariness.

"What honest errand was taking Whittington to Peri?" asked Wogan, and again the Chevalier read a piece here and there of the confession. Wogan pressed his advantage. "Whittington is not the only one of Walpole's men who has hoodwinked us the while he filled his pockets. There are others, one, at all events, who did not need to travel to Spain for an ear to poison;" and he leaned forward towards the Chevalier.

"What do you mean?" asked the Chevalier, in a startled voice.

"Why, sir, that the same sort of venomous story breathed to you in Spain has been spoken here in Bologna, only with altered names. I told your Majesty I brought a visitor to this house to-night. I did; there was no need I should, since the marriage is fixed for to-morrow. I brought her all the way from Rome."

"From Rome?" exclaimed the Chevalier.

"Yes;" and Wogan flung open the door of the library, and drawing himself up announced in his loudest voice, "The King!"

A loud cry came through the opening. It was not Clementina's

A. E. W. Mason

voice which uttered it. The Chevalier recognised the cry. He stood for a moment or two looking at Wogan. Then he stepped over the threshold, and Wogan closed the door behind him. But as he closed it he heard Maria Vittoria speak. She said,—

"Your Majesty, a long while ago, when you bade me farewell, I demanded of you a promise, which I have but this moment explained to the Princess, who now deigns to call me friend. Your Majesty has broken the promise. I had no right to demand it. I am very glad."

Wogan went downstairs. He could leave the three of them shut up in that room to come by a fitting understanding. Besides, there was other work for him below,—work of a simple kind, to which he had now for some weeks looked forward. He crept down the stairs very stealthily. The hall door was still open. He could see dimly the figure of a man standing on the grass.

\*　\*　\*　\*　\*

When the Chevalier came down into the garden an hour afterwards, a man was still standing on the grass. The man advanced to him. "Who is it?" asked the Chevalier, drawing back. The voice which answered him was Wogan's.

"And Whittington?"

"He has gone," replied Wogan.

"You have sent him away?"

"I took so much upon myself."

The Chevalier held out his hand to Wogan. "I have good

reason to thank you," said he, and before he could say another word, a door shut above, and Maria Vittoria came down the stairs towards them. O'Toole was still standing sentry at the postern-door, and the three men escorted the Princess Caprara to the Pilgrim Inn. She had spoken no word during the walk, but as she turned in the doorway of the inn, the light struck upon her face and showed that her eyes glistened. To the Chevalier she said, "I wish you, my lord, all happiness, and the boon of a great love. With all my heart I wish it;" and as he bowed over her hand, she looked across his shoulder to Wogan.

"I will bid you farewell to-morrow," she said with a smile, and the Chevalier explained her saying afterwards as they accompanied him to his lodging.

"Mlle. de Caprara will honour us with her presence to-morrow. You will still act as my proxy, Wogan. I am not yet returned from Spain. I wish no questions or talk about this evening's doings. Your friend will remember that?"

"My friend, sir," said Wogan, "who was with me at Innspruck, is Captain Lucius O'Toole of Dillon's regiment."

"*Et* senator too," said the Chevalier, with a laugh; and he added a friendly word or two which sent O'Toole back to his lodging in a high pleasure. Wogan walked thither with him and held out his hand at the door.

"But you will come up with me," said O'Toole. "We will drink a glass together, for God knows when we speak together again. I go back to Schlestadt to-morrow."

"Ah, you go back," said Wogan; and he came in at the door and mounted the stairs. At the first landing he stopped.

A. E. W. Mason

"Let me rouse Gaydon."

"Gaydon went three days ago."

"Ah! And Misset is with his wife. Here are we all once more scattered, and, as you say, God knows when we shall speak together again;" and he went on to the upper storey.

O'Toole remarked that he dragged in his walk and that his voice had a strange, sad note of melancholy.

"My friend," said he, "you have the black fit upon you; you are plainly discouraged. Yet to-night sees the labour of many months brought to its due close;" and as he lit the candles on his chimney, he was quite amazed by the white, tired face which the light showed to him. Wogan, indeed, harassed by misgivings, and worn with many vigils, presented a sufficiently woe-begone picture. The effect was heightened by the disorder of his clothes, which were all daubed with clay in a manner quite surprising to O'Toole, who knew the ground to be dry underfoot.

"True," answered Wogan, "the work ends to-night. Months ago I rode down this street in the early morning, and with what high hopes! The work ends to-night, and may God forgive me for a meddlesome fellow. Cup and ball's a fine game, but it is ill playing it with women's hearts;" and he broke off suddenly. "I'll give you a toast, Lucius! Here's to the Princess Clementina!" and draining his glass he stood for a while, lost in the recollecting of that flight from Innspruck; he was far away from Bologna thundering down the Brenner through the night, with the sparks striking from the wheels of the berlin, and all about him a glimmering, shapeless waste of snow.

"To the Princess—no, to the Queen she was born to be,"

cried O'Toole, and Wogan sprang at him.

"You saw that," he exclaimed, his eyes lighting, his face transfigured in the intensity of this moment's relief. "Aye,— to love a nation,—that is her high destiny. For others, a husband, a man; for her, a nation. And you saw it! It is evident, to be sure. Yet this or that thing she did, this or that word she spoke, assured you, eh? Tell me what proved to you here was no mere woman, but a queen!"

The morning had dawned before Wogan had had his fill. O'Toole was very well content to see his friend's face once more quivering like a boy's with pleasure, to hear him laugh, to watch the despondency vanish from his aspect. "There's another piece of good news," he said at the end, "which I had almost forgotten to tell you. Jenny and the Princess's mother are happily set free. It seems Jenny swore from daybreak to daybreak, and the Pope used his kindliest offices, and for those two reasons the Emperor was glad to let them go. But there's a question I would like to ask you. One little matter puzzles me."

"Ask your question," said Wogan.

"To-night through that door in the garden wall which I guarded, there went in yourself and a lady,—the King and a companion he had with him,—four people. Out of that door there came yourself, the lady, and the King,—three people."

"Ah," said Wogan, as he stood up with a strange smile upon his lips, "I have a deal of clay upon my clothes."

O'Toole nodded his head wisely once or twice. "I am answered," he said. "Is it indeed so?" He understood, however, nothing except that the room had suddenly grown cold.

# CHAPTER XXV

## THE LAST

An account remains of the marriage ceremony, which took place the next morning in Cardinal Origo's house. It was of the simplest kind and was witnessed by few. Murray, Misset and his wife, and Maria Vittoria de Caprara made the public part of the company; Wogan stood for the King; and the Marquis of Monti Boulorois for James Sobieski, the bride's father. Bride and bridegroom played their parts bravely and well, one must believe, for the chronicler speaks of their grace and modesty of bearing. Clementina rose at five in the morning, dressed in a robe of white, tied a white ribbon about her hair, and for her only ornament fixed a white collar of pearls about her neck. In this garb she went at once to the church of San Domenico, where she made her confession, and from the church to the Cardinal's Palace. There the Cardinal, with one Maas, an English priest from Rome, at his elbow, was already waiting for her. Mr. Wogan thereupon read the procuration, for which he had ridden to Rome in haste so many months before, and pronounced the consent of the King his master to its terms. Origo asked the Princess whether she likewise consented, and the manner in which she spoke her one word, "Yes," seems to have stirred the historian to paeans. It seems that all the virtues launched that one little word, and were clearly expressed in it. The graces, too, for once in a way went hand in hand with the virtues. Never was a "Yes" so sweetly spoken since the earth rose out of the sea. In a word, there was no ruffle of the great passion which these two, man and woman, had trodden beneath their feet. She did not hint of Iphigenia; he borrowed no plumes from Don Quixote. Nor need one fancy that their contentment was all counterfeit. They were neither of them grumblers, and "fate" and "destiny" were words seldom upon their lips.

One incident, indeed, is related which the chronicler thought to be curious, though he did not comprehend it. The Princess Clementina brought from her confessional box a wisp of straw which clung to her dress at the knee. Until Wogan had placed the King's ring upon her finger, she did not apparently remark it; but no sooner had that office been performed than she stooped, and with a friendly smile at her makeshift bridegroom, she plucked it from her skirt and let it fall beneath her foot.

And that was all. No words passed between them after the ceremony, for her Royal Highness went straight back to the little house in the garden, and that same forenoon set out for Rome.

She was not the only witness of the ceremony to take that road that day. For some three hours later, to be precise, at half-past two, Maria Vittoria stepped into her coach before the Pilgrim Inn. Wogan held the carriage door open for her. He was still in the bravery of his wedding clothes, and Maria Vittoria looked him over whimsically from the top of his peruke to his shoe-buckles.

"I came to see a fool-woman," said she, "and I saw a fool-man. Well, well!" and she suddenly lowered her voice to a passionate whisper. "Why, oh, why did you not take your

A. E. W. Mason

fortunes in your hands at Peri?"

Wogan leaned forward to her. "Do you know so much?"

She answered him quickly. "I will never forgive you. Yes, I
know." She forced her lips into a smile. "I suppose you are
content. You have your black horse."

"You know of the horse, too," said Wogan, colouring to the
edge of his peruke. "You know I have no further use for it."

"Say that again, and I will beg it of you."

"Nay, it is yours, then. I will send him after you to Rome."

"Will you?" said Maria Vittoria. "Why, then, I accept.
There's my hand;" and she thrust it through the window to
him. "If ever you come to Rome, the Caprara Palace stands
where it did at your last visit. I do not say you will be
welcome. No, I do not forgive you, but you may come.
Having your horse, I could hardly bar the door against you.
So you may come."

Wogan raised her hand to his lips.

"Aye," said she, with a touch of bitterness, "kiss my hand.
You have had your way. Here are two people crossmated,
and two others not mated at all. You have made four people
entirely unhappy, and a kiss on the glove sets all right."

"Nay, not four," protested Wogan.

"Your manners," she continued remorselessly, ticking off the
names upon her fingers, "will hinder you from telling me to
my face the King is happy. And the Princess?"

"She was born to be a queen," replied Wogan, stubbornly. "Happiness, mademoiselle! It does not come by the striving after it. That's the royal road to miss it. You may build up your house of happiness with all your care through years, and you will find you have only built it up to draw down the blinds and hang out the hatchment above the door, for the tenant to inhabit it is dead."

Maria Vittoria listened very seriously till he came to the end. Then she made a pouting grimace. "That is very fine, moral, and poetical. Your Princess was born to be a queen. But what if her throne is set up only in your city of dreams? Well, it is some consolation to know that you are one of the four."

"Nay, I will make a shift not to plague myself upon the way the world treats you."

"Ah, but because it treats you well," cried she. "There will be work for you, hurryings to and fro, the opportunities of excelling, nights in the saddle, and perhaps again the quick red life of battlefields. It is well with you, but what of me, Mr. Wogan? What of me?" and she leaned back in her carriage and drove away. Wogan had no answer to that despairing question. He stood with his head bared till the carriage passed round a corner and disappeared, but the voice rang for a long while in his ears. And for a long while the dark eyes abrim with tears, and the tortured face, kept him company at nights. He walked slowly back to his lodging, and mounting a horse rode out of Bologna, and towards the Apennines.

On one of the lower slopes he came upon a villa just beyond a curve of the road, and reined in his horse. The villa nestled on the hillside below him in a terraced garden of oleander and magnolias, very pretty to the eye. Cypress hedges enclosed it; the spring had made it a bower of rose blossoms, and depths of shade out of whose green darkness glowed here and there a red statue like a tutelary god. Wogan dismounted and led his horse down the path to the door. He inquired for Lady Featherstone, and was shown into a room from the windows of which he looked down on Bologna, that city of colonnades. Lady Featherstone, however, had heard the tramp of his horse; she came running up from the garden, and without waiting to hear any particulars of her visitor, burst eagerly into the room.

"Well?" she said, and stopped and swayed upon the threshold. Wogan turned from the window towards her.

"Your Ladyship was wise, I think, to leave Bologna. The little house in the trees there had no such wide prospect as this."

He spoke rather to give her time than out of any sarcasm. She set a hand against the jamb of the door, and even so barely sustained her trifling weight. Her knees shook, her childlike face grew white as paper, a great terror glittered in her eyes.

"I am not the visitor whom you expect," continued Wogan, "nor do I bring the news which you would wish to hear;" and at that she raised a trembling hand. "I beg you—a moment's silence. Then I will hear you, Mr. Warner." She made a sort of stumbling run and reached a couch. Wogan shut the door and waited. He was glad that she had used the name of Warner. It recalled to him that evening at Ohlau when she had stood behind the curtain with a stiletto in her hand, and the three last days of his perilous ride to Schlestadt. He needed his most vivid recollections to steel his heart against her; for he was beginning to think it was his weary lot to go up and down the world causing pain to women. After a while she said, "Now your news;" and she held her hand lightly to her heart to await the blow.

"The King married this morning the Princess Clementina," said Wogan. Lady Featherstone did not move her hand; she still waited. It was just to hinder this marriage that she had come to Italy, but her failure was at this moment of no account. She heard of it with indifference; it had no meaning to her. She waited. Wogan's mere presence at the villa told her there was more to come. He continued:—

"Last night Mr. Whittington came with the King to Bologna—you understand, no doubt, why;" and she nodded without moving her eyes from his face. She made no pretence as to the part she had played in the affair. All the world might know it. That was a matter at this moment of complete indifference. She waited.

"The King and Mr. Whittington came at nine of the night to the little house which you once occupied. I was there, but I was not there alone. Can your Ladyship conjecture whom I brought there? Your Ladyship, as I learned last night from Mr. Whittington's own lips, had paid a visit secretly, using a key which you had retained to the house on an excuse that you had left behind jewels of some value. You saw her Highness the Princess. You told her a story of the King and Mlle. de Caprara. I rode to Rome, and when the King came last night Mlle. de Caprara was with the Princess. I had evidence against Mr. Whittington, a confession of one of the soldiers of the Governor of Trent, the leader of a party of five who attacked me at Peri. No doubt you know of that little matter too;" and again Lady Featherstone nodded.

"Thus your double plot—to set the King against the Princess, and the Princess against the King—doubly failed."

"Go on," said Lady Featherstone, moistening her dry lips.

Wogan told her how from the little sitting-room on the ground-floor he had seen the King and Whittington cross the lawn; he described his interview with the King, and how he had come quietly down the stairs.

"I went into the garden," he went on, "and touched Whittington on the elbow. I told him just what I have explained to you. I said, 'You are a coward, a liar, a slanderer of women,' and I beat him on the mouth."

Lady Featherstone uttered a cry and drew herself into an extraordinary crouching attitude, with her eyes blazing steadily at him. He thought she meant to spring at him; he looked at that hand upon her heart to see whether it held a weapon hidden in the fold of her bosom.

"Go on," she said; "and he?"

"He answered me in the strangest quiet way imaginable. 'You insulted Lady Featherstone at Ohlau, Mr. Wogan,' said he, 'one evening when she hid behind your curtain. It was a very delicate piece of drollery, no doubt. But I shall be glad to show you another, view of it.' It is strange how that had rankled in his thoughts. I liked him for it,—upon my soul, I did,—though it was the only thing I liked in him."

"Go on," said Lady Featherstone. Mr. Wogan's likes or dislikes were of no more interest to her than the failure of her effort to hinder the marriage.

"We went to the bottom of the garden where there is a little square of lawn hedged in with myrtle-trees. The night was very dark, so we stripped to our shirts. From the waist upwards we were visible to each other as a vague glimmer of white, and thus we fought, foot to foot, among the myrtle-trees. We could not see so much as our swords unless they clashed more than usually hard, and a spark struck from them. We fought by guesswork and feel, and in the end luck served me. I drove my sword through his chest until the hilt rang upon his breast-bone."

Then just a movement from Lady Featherstone as though she drew up her feet beneath her.

"He lived for perhaps five minutes. He was in great distress lest harm should come to you; and since there was no one but his enemy to whom he could speak, why, he spoke to his enemy. I promised him, madam, that with his death the story should be closed, if you left Italy within the week."

"And he?" she interrupted,—"he died there. Well?"

"You know the laurel hedge by the sun-dial? There is an out-house where the gardener keeps his tools. I found a spade there, and beneath that laurel hedge I buried him."

Lady Featherstone rose to her feet. She spoke no word; she uttered no cry; her face was white and terrible. She stood rigid like one paralysed; then she swayed round and fell in a swoon upon the floor. And as she fell, something bright slipped from her hand and dropped at Wogan's feet. He picked it up. It was a stiletto. He stood looking down at the childish figure with a queer compassionate smile upon his face. "She could love," said he; "yes, she could love."

He walked out of the house, led his horse back onto the road and mounted it. The night was gathering; there were purple shadows upon the Apennines. Wogan rode away alone.

# EPILOGUE

Sir Charles Wogan had opportunities enough to appreciate in later years the accuracy of Maria Vittoria's prophecy. "Here are two people cross-mated," said she, and events bore her out. The jealousies of courtiers no doubt had their share in the estrangement of that unhappy couple, but that was no consolation to Wogan, who saw, within so short a time of that journey into Italy, James separated from the chosen woman, and the chosen woman herself seeking the seclusion of a convent. As his reward he was made Governor of La Mancha in Spain, and no place could have been found with associations more suitable to this Irishman who turned his back upon his fortunes at Peri. At La Mancha he lived for many years, writing a deal of Latin verse, and corresponding with many distinguished men in England upon matters of the intellect. Matters of the heart he left alone, and meddled with no more. Nor did any woman ever ride on his black horse into his city of dreams. He lived and died a bachelor. The memory of that week when he had rescued his Princess and carried her through the snows was to the last too vivid in his thoughts. The thunderous roll of the carriage down the slopes, the sparks striking from the wheels, the sound of Clementina's voice singing softly in the darkness of the carriage, the walk under the stars to Ala, the coming of the dawn about that lonely hut, high-placed amongst the pines. These recollections bore him company through many a solitary evening. Somehow the world had gone awry. Clementina, withdrawn into her convent, was, after all, "wasted," as he had sworn she should not be. James was fallen upon a deeper melancholy, and diminished hopes. He himself was an exile alone in his white *patio* in Spain. In only one point was Maria Vittoria's prophecy at fault. She had spoken of two who were to find no mates, and one of the two was herself. She married five years later.

THE END

# ABOUT THE AUTHOR

**Alfred Edward Woodley Mason** (7 May 1865 Dulwich, London - 22 November 1948 London) was a British author.

He studied at Dulwich College and graduated from Trinity College, Oxford in 1888.

His first novel, A Romance of Wastdale, was published in 1895. He is the author of more than twenty books, among them The Four Feathers, originally published in London in 1902. His next successful work was At The Villa Rose (1910), where he introduced his French detective, Hanaud.

Mason was elected as a Liberal Member of Parliament for Coventry in the 1906 general election. He served only a single term in Parliament, retiring at the next general election in January 1910.

Mason rose to the rank of major during the First World War serving with The Manchester Regiment and the Royal Marine Light Infantry. His military career included work in naval intelligence, serving in Spain and Mexico, where he set up counter-espionage networks on behalf of the British government.

He died in 1948 while working on a non-fiction book about Admiral Robert Blake.

# Choose from Thousands of 1stWorldLibrary Classics By

A. M. Barnard
Ada Leverson
Adolphus William Ward
Aesop
Agatha Christie
Alexander Aaronsohn
Alexander Kielland
Alexandre Dumas
Alfred Gatty
Alfred Ollivant
Alice Duer Miller
Alice Turner Curtis
Alice Dunbar
Allen Chapman
Alleyne Ireland
Ambrose Bierce
Amelia E. Barr
Amory H. Bradford
Andrew Lang
Andrew McFarland Davis
Andy Adams
Angela Brazil
Anna Alice Chapin
Anna Sewell
Annie Besant
Annie Hamilton Donnell
Annie Payson Call
Annie Roe Carr
Annonaymous
Anton Chekhov
Archibald Lee Fletcher
Arnold Bennett
Arthur C. Benson
Arthur Conan Doyle
Arthur M. Winfield
Arthur Ransome
Arthur Schnitzler
Arthur Train
Atticus
B. H. Baden-Powell
B. M. Bower
B. C. Chatterjee
Baroness Emmuska Orczy
Baroness Orczy
Basil King
Bayard Taylor
Ben Macomber
Bertha Muzzy Bower
Bjornstjerne Bjornson

Booth Tarkington
Boyd Cable
Bram Stoker
C. Collodi
C. E. Orr
C. M. Ingleby
Carolyn Wells
Catherine Parr Traill
Charles A. Eastman
Charles Amory Beach
Charles Dickens
Charles Dudley Warner
Charles Farrar Browne
Charles Ives
Charles Kingsley
Charles Klein
Charles Hanson Towne
Charles Lathrop Pack
Charles Romyn Dake
Charles Whibley
Charles Willing Beale
Charlotte M. Braeme
Charlotte M. Yonge
Charlotte Perkins Stetson
Clair W. Hayes
Clarence Day Jr.
Clarence E. Mulford
Clemence Housman
Confucius
Coningsby Dawson
Cornelis DeWitt Wilcox
Cyril Burleigh
D. H. Lawrence
Daniel Defoe
David Garnett
Dinah Craik
Don Carlos Janes
Donald Keyhoe
Dorothy Kilner
Dougan Clark
Douglas Fairbanks
E. Nesbit
E. P. Roe
E. Phillips Oppenheim
E. S. Brooks
Earl Barnes
Edgar Rice Burroughs
Edith Van Dyne
Edith Wharton

Edward Everett Hale
Edward J. O'Biren
Edward S. Ellis
Edwin L. Arnold
Eleanor Atkins
Eleanor Hallowell Abbott
Eliot Gregory
Elizabeth Gaskell
Elizabeth McCracken
Elizabeth Von Arnim
Ellem Key
Emerson Hough
Emilie F. Carlen
Emily Bronte
Emily Dickinson
Enid Bagnold
Enilor Macartney Lane
Erasmus W. Jones
Ernie Howard Pie
Ethel May Dell
Ethel Turner
Ethel Watts Mumford
Eugene Sue
Eugenie Foa
Eugene Wood
Eustace Hale Ball
Evelyn Everett-green
Everard Cotes
F. H. Cheley
F. J. Cross
F. Marion Crawford
Fannie E. Newberry
Federick Austin Ogg
Ferdinand Ossendowski
Fergus Hume
Florence A. Kilpatrick
Fremont B. Deering
Francis Bacon
Francis Darwin
Frances Hodgson Burnett
Frances Parkinson Keyes
Frank Gee Patchin
Frank Harris
Frank Jewett Mather
Frank L. Packard
Frank V. Webster
Frederic Stewart Isham
Frederick Trevor Hill
Frederick Winslow Taylor

Friedrich Kerst
Friedrich Nietzsche
Fyodor Dostoyevsky
G.A. Henty
G.K. Chesterton
Gabrielle E. Jackson
Garrett P. Serviss
Gaston Leroux
George A. Warren
George Ade
Geroge Bernard Shaw
George Cary Eggleston
George Durston
George Ebers
George Eliot
George Gissing
George MacDonald
George Meredith
George Orwell
George Sylvester Viereck
George Tucker
George W. Cable
George Wharton James
Gertrude Atherton
Gordon Casserly
Grace E. King
Grace Gallatin
Grace Greenwood
Grant Allen
Guillermo A. Sherwell
Gulielma Zollinger
Gustav Flaubert
H. A. Cody
H. B. Irving
H.C. Bailey
H. G. Wells
H. H. Munro
H. Irving Hancock
H. R. Naylor
H. Rider Haggard
H. W. C. Davis
Haldeman Julius
Hall Caine
Hamilton Wright Mabie
Hans Christian Andersen
Harold Avery
Harold McGrath
Harriet Beecher Stowe
Harry Castlemon
Harry Coghill
Harry Houidini

Hayden Carruth
Helent Hunt Jackson
Helen Nicolay
Hendrik Conscience
Hendy David Thoreau
Henri Barbusse
Henrik Ibsen
Henry Adams
Henry Ford
Henry Frost
Henry James
Henry Jones Ford
Henry Seton Merriman
Henry W Longfellow
Herbert A. Giles
Herbert Carter
Herbert N. Casson
Herman Hesse
Hildegard G. Frey
Homer
Honore De Balzac
Horace B. Day
Horace Walpole
Horatio Alger Jr.
Howard Pyle
Howard R. Garis
Hugh Lofting
Hugh Walpole
Humphry Ward
Ian Maclaren
Inez Haynes Gillmore
Irving Bacheller
Isabel Cecilia Williams
Isabel Hornibrook
Israel Abrahams
Ivan Turgenev
J.G.Austin
J. Henri Fabre
J. M. Barrie
J. M. Walsh
J. Macdonald Oxley
J. R. Miller
J. S. Fletcher
J. S. Knowles
J. Storer Clouston
J. W. Duffield
Jack London
Jacob Abbott
James Allen
James Andrews
James Baldwin

James Branch Cabell
James DeMille
James Joyce
James Lane Allen
James Lane Allen
James Oliver Curwood
James Oppenheim
James Otis
James R. Driscoll
Jane Abbott
Jane Austen
Jane L. Stewart
Janet Aldridge
Jens Peter Jacobsen
Jerome K. Jerome
Jessie Graham Flower
John Buchan
John Burroughs
John Cournos
John F. Kennedy
John Gay
John Glasworthy
John Habberton
John Joy Bell
John Kendrick Bangs
John Milton
John Philip Sousa
John Taintor Foote
Jonas Lauritz Idemil Lie
Jonathan Swift
Joseph A. Altsheler
Joseph Carey
Joseph Conrad
Joseph E. Badger Jr
Joseph Hergesheimer
Joseph Jacobs
Jules Vernes
Julian Hawthrone
Julie A Lippmann
Justin Huntly McCarthy
Kakuzo Okakura
Karle Wilson Baker
Kate Chopin
Kenneth Grahame
Kenneth McGaffey
Kate Langley Bosher
Kate Langley Bosher
Katherine Cecil Thurston
Katherine Stokes
L. A. Abbot
L. T. Meade

L. Frank Baum
Latta Griswold
Laura Dent Crane
Laura Lee Hope
Laurence Housman
Lawrence Beasley
Leo Tolstoy
Leonid Andreyev
Lewis Carroll
Lewis Sperry Chafer
Lilian Bell
Lloyd Osbourne
Louis Hughes
Louis Joseph Vance
Louis Tracy
Louisa May Alcott
Lucy Fitch Perkins
Lucy Maud Montgomery
Luther Benson
Lydia Miller Middleton
Lyndon Orr
M. Corvus
M. H. Adams
Margaret E. Sangster
Margret Howth
Margaret Vandercook
Margaret W. Hungerford
Margret Penrose
Maria Edgeworth
Maria Thompson Daviess
Mariano Azuela
Marion Polk Angellotti
Mark Overton
Mark Twain
Mary Austin
Mary Catherine Crowley
Mary Cole
Mary Hastings Bradley
Mary Roberts Rinehart
Mary Rowlandson
M. Wollstonecraft Shelley
Maud Lindsay
Max Beerbohm
Myra Kelly
Nathaniel Hawthrone
Nicolo Machiavelli
O. F. Walton
Oscar Wilde

Owen Johnson
P.G. Wodehouse
Paul and Mabel Thorne
Paul G. Tomlinson
Paul Severing
Percy Brebner
Percy Keese Fitzhugh
Peter B. Kyne
Plato
Quincy Allen
R. Derby Holmes
R. L. Stevenson
R. S. Ball
Rabindranath Tagore
Rahul Alvares
Ralph Bonehill
Ralph Henry Barbour
Ralph Victor
Ralph Waldo Emmerson
Rene Descartes
Ray Cummings
Rex Beach
Rex E. Beach
Richard Harding Davis
Richard Jefferies
Richard Le Gallienne
Robert Barr
Robert Frost
Robert Gordon Anderson
Robert L. Drake
Robert Lansing
Robert Lynd
Robert Michael Ballantyne
Robert W. Chambers
Rosa Nouchette Carey
Rudyard Kipling
Saint Augustine
Samuel B. Allison
Samuel Hopkins Adams
Sarah Bernhardt
Sarah C. Hallowell
Selma Lagerlof
Sherwood Anderson
Sigmund Freud
Standish O'Grady
Stanley Weyman
Stella Benson
Stella M. Francis

Stephen Crane
Stewart Edward White
Stijn Streuvels
Swami Abhedananda
Swami Parmananda
T. S. Ackland
T. S. Arthur
The Princess Der Ling
Thomas A. Janvier
Thomas A Kempis
Thomas Anderton
Thomas Bailey Aldrich
Thomas Bulfinch
Thomas De Quincey
Thomas Dixon
Thomas H. Huxley
Thomas Hardy
Thomas More
Thornton W. Burgess
U. S. Grant
Upton Sinclair
Valentine Williams
Various Authors
Vaughan Kester
Victor Appleton
Victor G. Durham
Victoria Cross
Virginia Woolf
Wadsworth Camp
Walter Camp
Walter Scott
Washington Irving
Wilbur Lawton
Wilkie Collins
Willa Cather
Willard F. Baker
William Dean Howells
William le Queux
W. Makepeace Thackeray
William W. Walter
William Shakespeare
Winston Churchill
Yei Theodora Ozaki
Yogi Ramacharaka
Young E. Allison
Zane Grey